# Utilitarianism

This is the first general overview in many years of the history and the present condition of utilitarian ethics. Unlike other introductions to the subject, which narrowly focus on the Enlightenment and Victorian eras, *Utilitarianism* takes a wider view. Geoffrey Scarre introduces the major utilitarian philosophers from the Chinese sage Mo Tzŭ in the fifth century BC through to Richard Hare in the twentieth.

But Scarre not only surveys the history of the 'doctrine of utility'; in later chapters he also enters the current debates on the viability of the theory.

Utilitarianism today faces challenges on several fronts: its opponents argue that it lacks a credible theory of value, that it fails to protect the essential interests of individuals and that it denies them the space to pursue the personal concerns that give meaning to their lives. Geoffrey Scarre examines and discusses these charges, but he concludes that, despite the flaws of utilitarian theory, its positions are still relevant and significant today.

Written especially with undergraduates in mind, this is an ideal course book for those studying and teaching moral philosophy.

**Geoffrey Scarre** is Lecturer in Philosophy at the University of Durham. He is the author of *Logic and Reality in the Philosophy of John Stuart Mill* and the editor of *Children, Parents and Politics*.

## The Problems of Philosophy

Founding editor: Ted Honderich
Editors: Tim Crane and Jonathan Wolff, *University College London*

This series addresses the central problems of philosophy. Each book gives a fresh account of a particular philosophical theme by offering two perspectives on the subject: the historical context and the author's own distinctive and original contribution.

The books are written to be accessible to students of philosophy and related disciplines, while taking the debate to a new level.

DEMOCRACY*
Ross Harrison

THE EXISTENCE OF THE
WORLD*
Reinhardt Grossman

NAMING AND REFERENCE
R. J. Nelson

EXPLAINING EXPLANATION*
David-Hillel Ruben

IF P, THEN Q*
David H. Sanford

SCEPTICISM
Christopher Hookway

HUMAN CONSCIOUSNESS
Alastair Hannay

THE IMPLICATIONS OF
DETERMINISM
Roy Weatherford

THE INFINITE*
A. W. Moore

KNOWLEDGE AND BELIEF
Frederic F. Schmitt

KNOWLEDGE OF THE
EXTERNAL WORLD
Bruce Aune

MORAL KNOWLEDGE*
Alan Goldman

MIND–BODY IDENTITY
THEORIES*
Cynthia Macdonald

THE NATURE OF ART*
A. L. Cothey

PERSONAL IDENTITY*
Harold W. Noonan

POLITICAL FREEDOM
George G. Brenkert

THE RATIONAL FOUNDATIONS
OF ETHICS*
T. L. S. Sprigge

PRACTICAL REASONING*
Robert Audi

RATIONALITY*
Harold I. Brown

THOUGHT AND LANGUAGE*
J. M. Moravcsik

THE WEAKNESS OF THE WILL
Justine Gosling

VAGUENESS
Timothy Williamson

PERCEPTION
Howard Robinson

THE NATURE OF GOD
Gerard Hughes

* Also available in paperback

# Utilitarianism

## Geoffrey Scarre

London and New York

First published 1996
by Routledge
11 New Fetter Lane, London EC4P 4EE

Simultaneously published in the USA and Canada
by Routledge
29 West 35th Street, New York, NY 10001

Routledge is an International Thomson Publishing company.

© 1996 Geoffrey Scarre

Typeset in Times by
Ponting–Green Publishing Services, Chesham, Bucks
Printed and bound in Great Britain by
Mackays of Chatham PLC, Chatham, Kent

*British Library Cataloguing in Publication Data*
A catalogue record for this book is available from the British Library.

*Library of Congress Cataloging in Publication Data*
Scarre, Geoffrey.
Utilitarianism/Geoffrey Scarre.
1. Includes bibliographical references and index. 2. Ethics.
3. Utilitarianism. I. Title.
BJ1012.S336     1995
171'.5–dc20                 95–38889
CIP

ISBN 0–415–09527–1 (hbk)
ISBN 0–415–12197–3 (pbk)

# Contents

# Contents

# Preface

Utilitarianism is a large subject with a long history. To borrow the words of St John, if all were written down about it, the world itself would not hold all the books that would have to be written. Any attempt to survey the past and present states of the doctrine within a single set of covers must necessarily be highly selective, and no doubt controversial in its selections. The present book is more concerned with utilitarianism as a theory of individual morality than as a theory of collective choice; its province is therefore moral philosophy rather than political science or welfare economics. For some time there has been a need for a new overview to relate the lively contemporary debate about utilitarian ethics to the historical development of the theory, some aspects of which are not well known. How far the present book is from adequately satisfying that need, it is the reader's prerogative to decide.

A few words about structure are in order. Following an introductory chapter setting out the basic features of modern utilitarianism, four historical chapters provide a critical survey of some of the most important utilitarian thinkers from the fifth century BC to the present. There is no sharp transition from the historical to the non-historical parts of the book; the final section of Chapter V, on rule-utilitarianism, appraises a debate within utilitarianism which began over half a century ago and is still going strong. The last three chapters are purely analytical and focus on what I believe to be the three most important areas of concern for contemporary utilitarian moral theorists: the definition of a philosophically viable concept of utility; the justification of utilitarian ideas about justice and fair treatment; and the defence of utilitarianism against the charge that it is too demanding a moral doctrine, requiring of individual agents a readiness for self-sacrifice that is possible only for moral saints. Special emphasis has been laid, in the historical sections, on the contributions made by older writers to clear thinking in these problem areas.

*Preface*

I am very grateful to Jonathan Wolff and to an anonymous reader for the publisher for extremely helpful comments on an earlier draft of this work. I have learned much also from spirited discussion of many of its themes with colleagues and students in the University of Durham. All have forced me to clarify the exposition and sharpen the argument at many points. It is hoped that the errors it contains will be fewer and less egregious for their assistance. I should also like to express my gratitude to my copy-editor, Marguerite Nesling, for exemplary editing of the text.

After some hesitation, I have decided to follow the traditional practice of using masculine word-forms throughout in gender-neutral contexts. It is difficult to incorporate 'she or he' and 'his or her' into a text while retaining tolerable prose, and the switch to feminine forms constitutes merely a kind of stylistic 'out of the frying pan into the fire'. The only really satisfactory solution would be to introduce some new gender-neutral terms into the language: a task to be attempted by some bolder writer of the future.

Ancestors of two sections of the text have appeared in the pages of *Utilitas*: 'Epicurus as a forerunner of utilitarianism' was a longer version of Chapter II, section (4), while 'Utilitarianism and self-respect' corresponds to the first half of Chapter VII; fuller references are given in the Bibliography.

*Geoffrey Scarre*
Durham, June 1995

# CHAPTER I

# Introduction:
# The Character of the Theory

Utilitarianism is not, strictly speaking, a problem of philosophy, but it is a problematic approach to moral philosophy which has always attracted both ardent defenders and ardent opponents. Seen by its enthusiasts as a down-to-earth and liberating theory which enjoins an empirical attitude to practical decision-making and refuses to accept the tyranny of questionable moral conventions, utilitarianism has been condemned by the more severe of its critics as a pernicious doctrine which treats our most precious values with scorn and prescribes the universal sacrifice of principle to expediency. Between the extremes, of course, there are more muted shades of opinion. Many philosophers have granted the intuitive appeal of core utilitarian ideas while remaining dubious about the theory's ultimate adequacy. There is something undeniably appealing in the classical utilitarian notion that actions are ethically justified when they lead to happiness, or diminish misery: 'You count the consequences for human happiness of one or another course, and you go with the one with the highest favourable total' (Taylor 1982: 129). Yet some people suspect that utilitarianism lacks sufficient conceptual resources to make complete sense of morality – that, in Bernard Williams's words, it has 'too few thoughts and feelings to match the world as it really is' (Williams 1973: 149). Utilitarianism deals with something that is undoubtedly important in human life, the promotion of happiness (or, as many modern theorists would have it, the satisfaction of human prefer- ences); but it is less clear that it deals with *everything* of importance.

This book is concerned both with the history of utilitarianism as an ethical theory and with the lively contemporary debate over its forms, problems and prospects. It will become clear as I proceed, but it is only fair to declare at the outset, that my own sympathies run broadly in favour of the utilitarian point of view, though I am not convinced that a wholly satisfactory form of the theory is yet available. Perhaps the best that can

1

currently be said about utilitarianism is that it is a very bad form of moral philosophy, but that all the others are so much worse. At any rate, I am far from believing, as some philosophers profess to do, that the days of utilitarianism are numbered. Reports of the death, or imminent demise, of utilitarianism have been greatly exaggerated. 'Utilitarianism is destroyed,' claimed John Plamenatz in 1949, 'and no part of it left standing' (Plamenatz 1966: 145). Yet there was still enough life left in the corpse a quarter of a century later for Bernard Williams to hope that 'The day cannot be too far off in which we hear no more of it' (Williams 1973: 150). Twenty years further on we hear as much about utilitarianism as we ever did, and the flow of new writings on the subject is unceasing. For a viewpoint often accused of simple-mindedness, utilitarianism has demonstrated a striking ability to go on stimulating forceful and subtle argument on both sides of the case. If the utilitarian theory is *wrong*, proving it to be so is taking a remarkable amount of intellectual effort.

John Stuart Mill believed that the appeal of utilitarianism, to a certain cast of mind, was perennial. In every age of philosophy, he thought, one of its schools had been utilitarian (J.S. Mill 1838: 87). But in every era too, the doctrine had provoked virulent opposition: from a very early period, the theory of utility had by some been designated as 'utterly mean and grovelling' and 'worthy only of swine' (J.S. Mill 1861: 210). Utilitarianism is to the present day the moral philosophy *par excellence* which people love to hate, though recent debate has mostly been couched in more temperate language than in the days of Mill. It should be noted, however, that utilitarianism is not so much a single theory of morals as a family of theories, of markedly differing sophistication and plausibility. Few contemporary utilitarians would now defend without large qualifications the views of a Godwin or a Bentham, and the failure of the more primitive versions of the doctrine does not entail that all varieties of it must fail. But the existence of several forms of utilitarianism gives rise to a problem of definition: it is not easy to say in few words exactly what the essence of utilitarianism *is*.

Consider, for instance, Mill's thumb-nail characterisation of it at the beginning of *Utilitarianism*:

> The creed which accepts as the foundation of morals, Utility, or the Greatest Happiness Principle, holds that actions are right in proportion as they tend to promote happiness, wrong as they tend to produce the reverse of happiness. By happiness is intended pleasure, and the absence of pain; by unhappiness, pain, and the privation of pleasure (210).

2

This is inadequate even as a statement of Mill's own theory, though it is a fair representation of Bentham's. Mill, as we shall see later, thought that intellectual and moral activities like reading poetry or being kind to one's neighbour contribute much more fully to our happiness than the merely physical pleasures of sex or eating caviare. Moreover in some of his writings he moved away from a pleasure–pain definition of happiness towards a more Aristotelian conception of the happy subject as one who concentrates on developing the excellence of his character. Later utilitarians have also devoted careful attention to the analysis of happiness, and while many believe that it involves more than the attainment of pleasant experiences and the avoidance of painful ones, specific accounts of it vary. Some, particularly those influenced by developments in economics and decision theory, have jettisoned altogether the idea of *happiness* as the proper goal of moral action. In the tradition of utilitarian welfare economics, utility has generally been explained, as Alfred Marshall expressed it, as 'correlative to Desire or Want' (Marshall 1920: 92). On this approach, the maximal satisfaction of human preferences (alternatively, of interests or desires) is considered to be the central concern of a utilitarian theory. A few writers again have opted for a broader construal of utility, to embrace not merely human satisfactions but also intrinsic goods like knowledge and beauty – a position sometimes referred to as 'Ideal Utilitarianism' (though it is arguable that the term 'utility' is being stretched here beyond tolerable limits). Attempts to sum up the doctrine of utility in a few sentences, then, are likely to fail; 'utilitarianism' names a large, and loosely connected, group of theories.

For Mill, the label 'utilitarian' 'supplies a want in the language, and offers, in many cases, a convenient mode of avoiding tiresome circumlocution' (J.S. Mill 1861: 210n.). But he acknowledged, as subsequent writers have done, that the name adds little to the theory's attractions. The word 'utilitarian' presents to many people an uninviting picture of an earth-bound and limited philosophy which cheerfully sacrifices more inspiring ideals on the altar of the useful. Bentham, who coined the term, took his cue from Hume's advocacy of 'utility' in the *Enquiry Concerning the Principles of Morals* as the justifying ground of both the social virtues and the rules of equity and justice.[1] Hume had claimed that no principles of action or habits of mind were praiseworthy unless they conduced to the 'happiness and welfare', either of the individual or society:

> In common life, we may observe, that the circumstance of utility
> is always appealed to; nor is it supposed, that a greater eulogy can

be given to any man, than to display his usefulness to the public, and enumerate the services, which he has performed to mankind and society (Hume 1751: 212).

Bentham adopted the term 'utility', in the *Fragment on Government* of 1776, to denominate the 'tendency' of actions to promote 'the common *end* of all of them', namely 'Happiness' (Bentham 1776: 237). According to the *Oxford English Dictionary*, the neologism 'utilitarian' occurs for the first time in a letter of Bentham's of 1781, where a certain clergyman is described as 'a very worthy creature . . . a naturalist, a chemist, a physician' – and 'a utilitarian'. Despite his invention of the name 'utilitarianism', however, Bentham was not the inventor of the doctrine, and did not claim to be. But the almost casual way in which the name entered the philosophical (and later, the popular) vocabulary suggests that he gave little thought to its suitability for the position he championed. By the early nineteenth century the label was too well established to be dropped, though Mill was not the only writer to regret the mis-understandings it so frequently caused: utility, he noted, was often thought to be opposed not merely to the 'agreeable and ornamental' but, ironically, even to the pleasant (J.S. Mill 1861: 209). A major purpose of Mill's 1861 manifesto for *Fraser's Magazine* was thus to counter the prevalent impression (recently reinfored by Dickens's satirical novel *Hard Times* (1854)) that the utilitarian theory was dour, dry and informed by the lowest estimate of human possibilities.[2]

Although resistant to any simple definition, utilitarianism is not quite beyond characterisation in general terms. The theories which compose the family are linked by some common ideas and structural features which roughly set utilitarian positions off from others. There are five points of 'family resemblance' of particular importance, though not every version of the doctrine exhibits them all. For the most part (exceptions will be pointed out as we proceed), utilitarian theories have been *welfarist, consequentialist, aggregative* and *maximising*; historically, too, many have been *universalist*. Each of these notions requires some careful explanation.

**1 Welfarist** The 'utility' of which utilitarians speak is most commonly identified with the welfare (the *faring well*) of human beings, though some utilitarians (following Bentham) extend their concern to the well-being of animals too. (Roughly, any subjects capable of having a better or a worse quality of life – which includes even the lowliest creatures capable of sentience – may be thought of as fit objects of utilitarian

4

consideration.) Views of utility, or welfare, however, vary widely. The eighteenth-century utilitarians tended to construe welfare, as Bentham did, in terms of pleasure and pain: a life was held to be going well to the extent that it contained a balance of pleasurable sensations over painful ones. On the whole, these early writers disregarded a long tradition going back to Aristotle whereby pleasure was to be distinguished from *happiness*. For Aristotle, happiness (*eudaimonia*) consisted in worthwhile activity (specifically, activity in accordance with human excellences of mind and character), rather than in pleasant amusements; happiness, moreover, was more properly ascribed to a life as a whole – a life exhibiting a certain structured and successful directedness on suitable ends – than to individual phases of it. Pleasures were, rather, experiences of the moment, and while Aristotle did not, like the Cynic Antisthenes, consider that pleasure was a thing best avoided, he firmly rejected the identification of the happy existence with the life of pleasure; to prefer the latter to the former was to prefer a life more 'suitable to beasts' – and 'we call neither ox nor horse nor any of the other animals happy' (Aristotle, *Nicomachean Ethics*, 1095b, 1099b). Bentham, in contrast, notoriously declared that the words 'utility', 'benefit', 'advantage', 'pleasure', 'good', and 'happiness' all came to the same thing (Bentham 1789: 1–2).

Mill's subtler position, which we shall investigate more fully in later chapters, owes more to Aristotle in its definition of happiness than it does to Bentham; but Mill was in verbal agreement with Bentham that morally right actions were those which promoted happiness. Yet Mill's theory raises a difficulty which does not affect the less sophisticated utilitarianism of his predecessor. Mill believed that the happy person is someone who pays close attention to his self-development, who works hard to hone his talents, refine his tastes and increase his sympathies – in short, a person who desires 'for its own sake, the conformity of his own character to his standard of excellence' (J.S. Mill 1838: 95). But this reference to a 'standard of excellence' raises the question whether happiness is still being treated as the sole ultimate criterion of right action. Mill plausibly says that the development of personal excellence is a major source of happiness; but it is hard to see how achieving excellence could have this effect unless it were seen as something valuable in its own right; and if it *were* valuable for its own sake, it would presumably be worth pursuing independently of its propensity to create happiness. Mill usually denied a causal model of the relations between happiness and whatever makes us happy, holding that happiness is not

5

so much the *effect* of happiness-making activities as a condition *constituted* by them. But even if improving one's character is (in Mill's terminology) a 'part of happiness' (J.S. Mill 1861: ch. 4), it seems not to be a part of it in the way that (say) listening to jazz or eating cream buns may be parts. These activities are valued just because they help us to be happy; whereas the pursuit of personal excellence would seem capable of making us happy only because it is valued. We can postpone until later a fuller scrutiny of these issues, but it is worth noting now that there is a question how purely utilitarian a theory is, once it allows that other things besides welfare have basic value.

Some contemporary utilitarians, in a tradition which might reasonably be described as Millian, affirm that the holding of certain objective facts about a person's condition is more salient than the history of his subjective states to judgements about the satisfactoriness of his life. David Brink, for instance, has proposed that utilitarians should adopt an 'objective' theory of well-being whereby

> a valuable life consists in the possession of certain character traits, the exercise of certain capacities, and the development of certain relations with others and to the world, and . . . the value of such a life is independent of the pleasure it contains and whether or not this sort of life is desired or would be desired in some preferred epistemic state (Brink 1989: 221).

Brink thinks such a theory called for because he disbelieves that any amount of purely pleasing experience could be sufficient to make a life worth living. A brain in a vat might be fed an unbroken sequence of pleasures, without having an existence which anyone would envy. We want to *be* certain sorts of people, and to *do* certain kinds of thing, rather than merely have illusory subjective experiences (however pleasant) of being those persons and of doing those things (223–4; cf. Nozick 1974: 42). Brink concludes that a plausible theory of well-being 'counts reflective pursuit and realization of agents' reasonable projects and certain personal and social relationships as the primary components of valuable lives' (231). (This idea of the good life corresponds quite closely to what Elizabeth Telfer has called 'eudaimonistic happiness', defined as the state of someone who is 'truly fortunate' or 'truly well-off' according to some objective standard of worthwhile life (Telfer 1980: 37).)

Objectivist views of welfare are controversial. They imply that even a rational, well-informed person's evaluation of the satisfactoriness of his life could in principle be wrong. (Even rational, well-informed people can make mistakes about objective facts.) John Harsanyi has argued in favour of a more subjectivist account of individual utility on the ground that an impartial sympathetic observer 'cannot determine what is "good" for different persons with reference to any pre-existing moral standard, but only with reference to the preferences of these persons themselves'. To the question *how* do we want to be treated by other people, the 'only answer necessarily true, because tautologically true, ... is: "I want to be treated in accordance with my own wants"' (Harsanyi 1976: 31; cf. Harsanyi 1977: 27). Yet not all a person's wants are sensible ones, and Harsanyi recognises that 'benevolence cannot require us to satisfy people's foolish wants and preferences in the same way as their sensible wants and preferences'. Rejecting any objectivist criterion of the distinction between rational and foolish wants, he proposes to represent the difference 'without reference to any standard outside of the own attitudes of the persons concerned', by identifying the 'true preferences' which a person would manifest 'on due reflection and in possession of all relevant information (including information on the pleasures and pains resulting from alternative courses of action)' (1976: 31–2).

Objectivists may complain, however, that the identification of a person's 'true' preferences will often call for some very difficult counterfactual reflection. (How do we determine what Jim, who is feckless and silly, would have chosen had he been sensible? And in what sense anyway would any inferred preference be a 'true' one if it were one which Jim would never actually have had?) Moreover, even the preferences which were, for a given person, the most rational which could realistically be expected *from him* may not seem to wiser judges to be for things which were truly in his interests (he may, for instance, be a child, or a mentally defective person). T.M. Scanlon has consequently suggested that in practice 'the criteria of well being that we actually employ in making moral judgements are objective', and that our appraisals of a person's well-being could be reasonable even where they 'conflicted with the preferences of the individual in question, not only as he believes they are but even as they would be if rendered consistent, corrected for factual errors, etc.' (Scanlon 1975: 658; cf. Scanlon 1993). Nevertheless objectivists need not deny the importance of subjective preferences to well-being; in Scanlon's view, 'A high objective value may be attached to providing those conditions which are necessary to allow individuals to develop their own preferences and interests and to make these felt in the determination of social policy' (1975: 658).

One reason why preference-satisfaction accounts of utility have been popular is that they appear nicely liberal in their refusal to make more than limited assumptions a priori about the character of reasonable goals:

utility is identified with the satisfaction of whatever goals people happen to have, provided that they attain some threshold degree of rationality (admittedly there is room for dispute as to where this threshold lies and, in regard to some preferences, on which side of the line they fall). Sen expresses such a conception when he explains utility 'to stand for a person's conception of his own well-being' (Sen 1979: 463). No question-begging claims are made about the nature of happiness or the good life; no attempt is made to lay down what human beings should want for themselves or for others; and one man's meat is conceded to be another man's poison. (This is related to the doctrine, popular with economists, of the 'supremacy of the consumer'.) While the preferences of different persons can conflict, and a calculation needs to be done to determine how to maximise preference-satisfaction overall, no (minimally rational) preferences are deemed to be intrinsically less suitable than any others to enter the calculation. Harsanyi explains why it is better to judge what is good or bad for persons in terms of their *preferences* rather than their *desires* or *wants*: a person can have conflicting wants and desires, and these can therefore guide his behaviour or those of other people who wish to benefit him only if he decides which wants or preferences represent his considered preferences (Harsanyi 1976: 32). To be measurable these preferences must of course be revealed by 'outward phenomena', such as, in the easiest case, the price which an individual is willing to pay for their satisfaction (cf. Marshall 1920: 92).

It is a standard assumption of the utilitarian doctrine that utility comes in greater and lesser amounts. The right action or policy is normally that one of the available alternatives which is likely to realise the largest quantity of utility. Many utilitarians, from Hutcheson and Bentham to Brandt, have accordingly been tantalised by the prospect of a 'calculus of utility' – a method of reducing moral decisions to mathematical calculation. For outcomes to be evaluated mathematically, it is necessary, first of all, to have a way of calibrating individual utility. (It is also necessary to define a consistent notion of social utility which takes account of the fact of conflicts among the preferences of individuals; but of this more later.) The trouble is that the philosophical sophistication of a concept of utility and its susceptibility to quantitative treatment are generally in inverse proportion to one another. It is not easy to see, for instance, how we could calibrate utility as represented in Brink's rich account of the 'valuable life', or even in Sen's more subjectivist sense of 'a person's conception of his own well-being' (cf. Mirlees 1982: 65).

Nevertheless, following the pioneering work in game theory of J. von Neumann and O. Morgenstern, progress has been made in providing a mathematical theory of utility capable at least of application in such a limited domain as welfare economics. While the idea of a calculus of utilities able to generate solutions to all moral problems is likely to remain a philosopher's pipe-dream, mathematical techniques have been used with some success in appraising the relative utility of economic outcomes. Von Neumann and Morgenstern explained how an individual can compare the utilities not only of single events, but of combinations of events with stated probabilities. Suppose that a person prefers, in regard to three events $A$, $B$ and $C$, event $A$ over event $B$, but also event $C$ over event $A$. Let $\alpha$ be a real number in the interval 0 to 1, such that the desirability of $A$ is exactly equal to that of the combined event consisting of a chance of probability $1-\alpha$ for $B$ and the chance of probability $\alpha$ for $C$. Von Neumann and Morgenstern's ingenious suggestion is that $\alpha$ can now be employed to provide a numerical estimate for the ratio of the preference of $A$ over $B$ to that of $C$ over $B$. This germ of theory is the starting point for an elaborate mathematical treatment of utility by axiomatic methods (Von Neumann and Morgenstern 1953: 17–19).

Economic utilitarians have laid much stress on the fact that measurability of utility is attainable provided that some standard of comparison can be determined. One way of doing this is as follows. An individual arbitrarily fixes two very similar outcomes, $A$ and $B$, as his standard of comparison, assigning zero utility to $A$ and unit utility to $B$. The utility difference between two different outcomes $C$ and $D$ can then be taken to be unity if he is indifferent between the combinations $(A, D)$ and $(B, C)$ (cf. Mirlees 1982: 65). Such methods presuppose, however, that a person is able to determine clear orders of preference among alternative outcomes, a condition which is not always fulfilled in practice. One source of difficulty here is that outcomes to be compared may differ in more than one parameter. A person would have little difficulty in deciding between a trip to London plus £100 spending money and a trip to London with only £95 spending money. But he might find it much harder to choose between a trip to Paris with £75 worth of spending money and a trip to London with £100 (this example simplified from Vickrey 1960: 520–1).

We shall return in Chapter VI to the question of the relative merits of 'happiness' versus 'preference-satisfaction' theories of utility. The case will be argued there that a satisfactory utilitarian ethics demands a richer, more expansive theory of human well-being – of what is required for a life to go well – than can readily be supplied on a preference-satisfaction account. For the moment, however, the differences between classical and welfare-economic-inspired approaches are less important than the common emphasis in their theories of value on the living of satisfying lives – in short, their shared concern with welfare, in a broad sense of that term.

**2 Consequentialist** Utilitarianism is a *consequentialist* (or, to use an older term, a 'teleological') doctrine in the sense that it maintains that the proper response to its values is to promote them (cf. Pettit 1993a: 231). Act consequentialism (the simplest form) maintains that an action is right if it can reasonably be expected to result in a state of affairs at least as good as the alternative states of affairs that would have resulted from alternative feasible acts (cf. Sen 1979: 464). Rule consequentialism is a little more complicated: it holds that actions are right if they conform to rules whose general observance could reasonably be expected to result in a set of states of affairs at least as good as the sets of states of affairs that would have resulted from the adoption of alternative feasible rules. (Rule-utilitarianism is open to a number of interpretations, as we shall see in Chapter V.) For all forms of consequentialism the good is logically prior to the right, as no criterion of right action can be laid down until a conception of the good is specified.

Utilitarian theories agree that the good is utility, though they differ in their accounts of what utility is; they also differ, as we shall see, as to whether it is the total utility, or the average utility of individuals, that we should be seeking to maximise. But non-utilitarian forms of consequentialism are conceivable as well. For instance, egoism is a species of consequentialism which evaluates outcomes according to their propensity to enhance the agent's own welfare. So too is counter-utilitarianism (or 'philosophical sadism'), which affirms that right actions are the ones which diminish human welfare. Other possible consequentialist views hold that actions are right if, and only if, they promote the advantage of a certain god or king or social grouping. But the only form of consequentialism other than utilitarianism which will be considered in this book is the ethical theory of Epicurus, which while strictly a variety of egoism is in important respects a precursor of utilitarian ideas.

It is easy to misrepresent the character of consequentialism. Thus a recent, and sympathetic, writer has described utilitarianism as 'a member of the family of moral doctrines which judge actions neither by their motives nor their intrinsic qualities, but by their consequences' (Brittan 1990: 76). This gives the misleading impression that utilitarians take no account of motives in the appraisal of actions. Consequentialists reject a view like Kant's, that only actions done from a sense of duty and respect for the Moral Law are morally praiseworthy, but they do not judge an action solely on the basis of its actual consequences without regard to the outcome which the agent *intended* to produce. It is a very common human experience to intend the best, yet produce the worst. Consider Mr Good-Heart, who in diving into his pocket to produce a coin for Mr Needy, startles Mr Needy into stepping back into the road where he is struck by a car. No sensible utilitarian would condemn Mr Good-Heart's well-meant action on the basis of its tragic outcome. Nor ought a utilitarian to commend an action done from bad motives (that is, an intention to produce a bad outcome) where it unexpectedly turns out to have good results. The world would have been spared a vile dictator if the infant Hitler had been smothered by his nurse, but the killing would still have been wrong, from a utilitarian perspective, unless the nurse had possessed remarkable powers of clairvoyance.

It would be a further crude mistake to suppose that for consequentialists it is not actions themselves but only their 'consequences', in the sense of their further effects, which are morally significant. It would be a highly eccentric doctrine which held that if a robber shoots a bank guard dead, he is culpable not for killing the guard, but only for the bad effects which ensue from the killing (for example, the grief of the guard's wife and family and the fear and insecurity generated among bank staff). A view of this kind would in any case be difficult to maintain in view of the fact that actions can usually be described in a variety of ways which draw the division between the 'action' and its 'consequences' in different places. (Should we describe the robber's action as 'shooting the guard', from which death resulted, or as 'killing the guard'?) No credible moral theory can allow questions of praise and blame to turn on which of a number of equally applicable descriptions of a train of action and its results is selected. As Brandt has observed, 'It normally makes no difference where we draw the line [between actions and their consequences] (as long any utility of the act itself is counted along with the utility of the consequences)' (Brandt 1979: 271).

This may seem to raise the question whether 'consequentialism' is really the best name for that group of theories of which utilitarianism is the most prominent member. But the original point of the term was not to signal the contrast between actions and their results, but a quite different one: the contrast between judging the moral qualities of actions on the basis of their accord, or lack of it, with some specified set of moral laws, rules or principles, and judging it according to their consequences for the promotion of a particular set of values. *Deontological* views (from the Greek word *deon*, roughly signifying the *right*) hold that some

11

things ought to be done or ought not to be done, without reference to the results to be expected from doing or omitting to do them. A deontologist might, for instance, insist that breaking a promise is an evil, or 'intrinsically wrong', deed which must be avoided even in cases where keeping the promise can be predicted to have disastrous effects. An act-utilitarian, by contrast, will consider that *not* breaking a promise in such circumstances would be wrong, because of the serious negative results of telling the truth.

Deontological theories, like consequentialist ones, come in several guises. Some, like Kant's, take a stand on the notion of moral law, and Kant himself firmly denied that the morally obligatory maxims (the precepts of duty) can be identified by evaluating the consequences likely to flow from following them (Kant 1785: section 1). God may be expected to make the law-abiding happy (in the next world if not in this), but in the Kantian system duty should always be done for its own sake, and not as a means to happiness (or to anything else). Modern deontological theories have tended to place less emphasis on concepts of duty than on concepts of natural *rights*, and the language of rights has become a well-established part of popular moral discourse. We hear a great deal nowadays (and not just from philosophers) about individual and collective human rights, and many people have extended the idiom of rights to animals too. When a subject has a 'right' to something, this imposes constraints on moral agents' freedom of action. Thus a person's right to life imposes an obligation on others not to kill him, even in those situations where his death might avert a greater evil. (Strict deontologists would never assent to Caiaphas' statement that 'It is better that one man should die for the good of the people' (John 18:14).) But rights theories raise some well-known problems of justification. The common recourse to moral intuition to determine what rights there are involves appeal to a mysterious faculty for which there are no satisfactory criteria of correctness, and which runs into serious theoretical and practical problems when people's intuitions clash. Accordingly some writers sympathetic to the idea of rights have attempted to defend them, instead, on a contractarian basis, maintaining that what rights there are should be settled by determining what arrangements for mutual assistance and forbearance a set of rational and self-interested persons or citizens could reasonably be expected to agree upon. Although theories of this kind have been developed with considerable ingenuity (e.g. in Rawls 1971), it is doubtful whether they can provide the foundation for a truly disinterested morality which accommodates the other-regarding values which most ordinary people possess.[3]

12

It is worth emphasising that consequentialist and deontological approaches generally lead, in practice, to similar moral conclusions. A deontologist may claim that breaking promises or stealing people's goods are wrong because they break the moral law, or because they infringe people's rights to be told the truth or to retain their private property. A utilitarian will agree that promise-breaking and theft are normally wrong, but his condemnation refers to the typical negative impact of these practices on human welfare, not their intrinsic wrongness. Judgements will diverge, however, in those exceptional cases where doing the normally wrong thing is likely to *increase* utility. Kant considers an example in which an evil man pursuing an innocent victim with violent intent asks you to tell him where his quarry is hiding. In Kant's view you would do wrong to lie to the man, even though your telling him the truth leads to his victim's death (Kant 1909a). Most utilitarians have seen this response as unreasonable, because the harm of being lied to is enormously less grievous than the harm of being killed. But for the Kantian, this value-comparison is beside the point: lying is something you should never do, *whatever* the consequences.

One further and somewhat complex question about the consequentialist aspect of utilitarianism will require some close attention later. It is clear that utilitarianism is a *theory of moral justification*, concerned to lay down conditions of right and wrong actions. But should it also be seen as a *theory of moral deliberation*, aiming to inform us how to decide which actions to perform and which to avoid? This distinction was little noted by the early utilitarians, but it was familiar to Mill and Sidgwick and has been significant in the work of some recent writers. It is sometimes claimed that utilitarianism should not be regarded as a guide to deliberation, on the ground that attempting to live as a utilitarian agent is not the most efficient way to promote utilitarian values. Engaging in long and complicated calculations of utility may make one ineffectual and over-hesitant as an agent (one reaches one's decision about what to do when the moment for action has passed); and human welfare is arguably better promoted by people who act habitually on simple moral rules like 'Keep your promises', 'Pay your debts', and 'Be charitable to the needy'. Yet there is room even within an act-utilitarian model of deliberation for the adoption of principles like these as convenient *rules of thumb*[4] to guide and speed up the deliberative process; and many utilitarians willingly concede that only agents of super-human intellect ('archangels', in R.M. Hare's terminology (Hare 1981: ch. 3)) could hope to resolve every fresh practical dilemma from first principles alone. Act-utilitarians insist, however, that moral rules should not be regarded as deontologists regard them, as principles about intrinsic rightness or wrongness, but only as rough pointers or *aides-mémoire*, which should be dropped in circumstances where conforming to them is plainly disutilitarian. Rule-utilitarians, by contrast, do not believe that rules which normally promote utility should be readily abandoned even in situations where they conspicuously fail to do so. This position is often justified by appeal to the beneficial social consequences (for example, increased predictability of others' actions and larger scope for cooperative behaviour) which maintenance of rigid rule systems should bring; yet there is some room for suspicion that some rule-utilitarians at least are really deontologists in consequentialists' clothing.

Some philosophers think that utility would be most effectively maximised by agents who neither calculate the consequences of individual actions nor seek to conform their behaviour to rules, but try instead to become more loving, more virtuous or more noble of soul. The merits of this view will concern us later, but it may be remarked for now that such a view of moral deliberation poses no threat to utilitarianism as a *theory of moral justification*: for the development of welfare-promoting traits of character would remain readily justifiable on utilitarian grounds. While utilitarians may feel qualms about accepting the extreme claim sometimes heard that utility is best promoted by agents who actually *disbelieve* utilitarianism's explanations of right and wrong, they need not deny that the most efficient utility-producers may not always be those whose sole preoccupation is to promote utility.

But there is another troubling issue lurking just below the surface here. Love and benevolence, the virtues and excellences of character, may seem to be valued by utilitarians rather for their instrumentality in enhancing utility than for their own intrinsic qualities. Many people feel that this attitude omits something of importance. They are uncomfortable, for instance, with the idea that a husband's and wife's love for each other are important *just* because they stimulate each partner to work for the other's welfare. John Kekes has remarked on the appeal of regarding some character traits 'as *constituents* of good lives, rather than as means to them' (Kekes 1993: 136). It remains to be seen whether any form of utilitarianism can give due weight to this outlook.

**3 Aggregative**  Utilitarianism assumes that it is possible to sum everyone's utility to give an overall utility total. Utility is viewed as a measurable good distributed among different individuals: we can assess the amount of Smith's utility and the amount of Jones's utility and calculate their net sum. The goodness of states of affairs can therefore be assessed according to the magnitude (or alternatively the per capita average) of this sum. Bentham's 'hedonic calculus' is a clear, if simple, example of this conception. Utility, identified with pleasure, is a commodity obtainable from different sources, in greater or lesser amounts. One person's pleasures are commensurable with another person's, and the pleasures of different subjects can be summed together. Where an agent faces a choice of actions, his proper course, in Bentham's view, is to estimate how much pleasure will flow, for all affected subjects, from the various available options, and to select the one likely to produce the greatest amount of it. (Pains are included in the same equations as negative quantities of pleasure.) Later utilitarians, though refining Bentham's theories of psychology and value, have generally followed his lead in treating utility as a theoretically aggregative good.

It is not difficult to see the attraction of this view. If utility has the formal features which utilitarians ascribe to it, then moral evaluation can be reduced to a (conceptually) simple matter of calculation. Even the most difficult moral dilemmas are in principle resoluble by a quasi-algorithmic method: we have only to work out the value of the consequences likely to flow from the different feasible courses of action (taking into account the probability of completing each of those courses successfully), and identify the most optimific one. But many philosophers have doubted the realism of this picture, which raises problems both procedural and moral.

The moral difficulty arises because the sum-ranking idea – that one set of individual utilities is at least as good as another if, and only if, it has at least as large a sum total – is quite insensitive to the question of *how* the utilities are distributed (cf. Sen 1979: 468). Leaving aside this problem for now, we may note that the notion of aggregating utility presupposes that the utilities of different individuals can be calibrated, measured, compared and totalled up. For utility to be amenable to precise quantitative analysis, we have seen that some fairly restrictive assumptions will need to be made about its nature. But utilitarians rightly point out that rough and ready probability judgements and orderings of our preferences, or states of satisfaction, are often sufficient to make utilitarian calculation possible. Most people are adept at resolving dilemmas like the following. John, who has set his heart on a career in sport, mildly prefers hockey to football but has insufficient time to practise both. If John also knows that there are far more team places available in professional football than in professional hockey, simple utilitarian reflection should persuade him to concentrate on developing his football skills.

Matters are more complicated when we turn from the one-person to the many-persons case. How feasible is it to compare the utilities of different subjects, taking into account the difficulty of knowing just what is going on in other minds and the great variety of personal tastes and aspirations? We need to estimate other people's needs and interests as sensitively as we can from *their* point of view, rather than our own. But even conceding the variation in human desires, there are certain goods which we can normally expect our neighbours to want. It is plausible to ascribe to everyone an interest in acquiring what John Rawls has called the 'primary goods' – 'things that every rational man is presumed to want' – such as health, vigour, intelligence, imagination, political freedoms and social opportunities, adequate income and a basis for self-respect (Rawls 1971: 62). In addition, certain 'secondary goods' (that is, goods which not all rational members of the human race require) may be wanted within particular social settings (in our own society, say, a voice in the democratic process of electing our leaders, and a certain minimal level of education; in some other societies the need to have a clearly defined position within a family or a tribe).[5] A person who lacks requisite primary or secondary goods can be assumed to have a life which is less than fully satisfactory; and for utilitarianism this establishes a prima-facie case for improving his lot in respect of those goods.

As for the many other goods which help to make lives go well but which are subject to more variation in tastes, it is often not so very hard to discover what people like or dislike. We can listen to their reports of their loves and hates, and note what they choose or avoid. Only an extreme sceptic about knowledge of other minds would doubt that we can often form fairly accurate estimates of the importance of a person's more individual objectives within the pattern of his life. In order to carry out interpersonal comparisons of utility it is necessary to employ what Harsanyi has called 'imaginative empathy': we must put ourselves in another person's shoes and ask how much satisfaction *we* would gain in his circumstances if we shared his particular position, education, values, tastes and psychological make-up (Harsanyi 1982: 50). Naturally we find it easiest to appraise the situations of people who are most similar to ourselves. But even when we need to evaluate the utilities of people who are fairly different from us, it is still sometimes possible, as Mirlees has noted, to discover rough isomorphisms between our conditions which make the comparisons easier: for example, I may consider myself to derive half as much satisfaction as a child does from consumption of a chocolate bar, but twice as much satisfaction as the child gets from five minutes' contemplation of the sunset (Mirlees 1982: 72–4).

The range of human goods, then, is not so great, or the variation in tastes so unfathomable, as to create insurmountable problems for the utilitarian position. We can assume that human beings are governed by the same psychological laws. And we can reasonably suppose that imaginative empathy is not so uncommon a quality as to make the demand to see things from others' point of view impractical. In any case, one does not always need extensive knowledge about a person to evaluate his utility: 'To decide how much someone enjoys life, one does not usually need to get inside his skin; one needs to know both what makes life enjoyable and how he, with his individual differences, is placed to exploit its possibilities' (Griffin 1986: 118). No doubt some of our judgements of other people's utility are wrong, but that is a fact of life we have to live with. That utilitarianism calls for interpersonal comparisons, and that such comparisons are often difficult, is not a good reason to reject the theory. (How else could we judge the morality not only of social policies but of any of the interactions of everyday life if we did not try to put ourselves in the shoes of the various parties concerned?) Harsanyi remarks that utilitarianism makes no assumption that people are good at making interpersonal comparisons, but only that such comparisons *have* to be made in order that moral decisions may be reached (1982: 50; 1976: 50–1). (For objectivist forms of utilitarianism like Brink's, the need for careful interpersonal comparisons is to some extent reduced, for it is not what people *want* so much as what they *should have* which settles how we should act towards them; but we now face the problem of finding a convincing criterion of objective well-being.)

Some utilitarians think that we can make our greatest impact for good if we aim rather to diminish misery than to increase happiness. At its most extreme, so-called 'negative utilitarianism' holds that the elimination of suffering should be the *only* concern of utility-minded agents. In Sir Karl Popper's words, 'Instead of the greatest happiness for the greatest number, one should demand, more modestly, the least amount of avoidable suffering for all' (Popper 1966: vol. 1, 284–5). This position is undoubtedly overstated, and Timothy Sprigge has noted its 'absurd consequence that the best thing to do would be to exterminate all life in which there is any distress at all' (Sprigge 1990b: 198). But it is not absurd to propose that utilitarians should place a special, though not exclusive, emphasis on the removal of suffering. In part, this is a point about efficiency – about making the most of our capacities for doing good. If, as Griffin suggests, 'a fairly small amount of misery will turn out to make life worse to a greater degree than a fairly large amount of happiness makes it better' (Griffin 1986: 84), the finite energies we possess for promoting the public weal may be better directed at righting wrongs than at multiplying goods. It is also easier to identify the general factors which spoil lives than to know which precise positive goods would make particular lives go better. Moreover, many of the positive things which do make lives go well, such as the forming of affections and relationships, the pursuit and attainment of goals, and the acquisition of self-respect and the respect of others, are things which an individual must largely secure for himself, others' capacity to assist him being mainly limited to the reduction of the obstacles (e.g. sickness, poverty, isolation, economic and social oppression) which stand in his way.

Admittedly, the division between positive and negative services is not a hard-and-fast one: we could, for example, classify the provision of schooling for children either negatively, as removing the evil of ignorance, or positively, as providing the benefit of knowledge. But to the degree that meaningful distinctions can be drawn between suffering and disadvantage on the one hand, and happiness and prosperity on the other, utilitarians with a sharper eye on diminishing the former than on increasing the latter have a simpler strategy than others for determining the relative merits of different policies. Faced with a choice between spending its surplus revenue on constructing a hospital for cancer victims or a concert hall, a government with leanings towards negative utilitarianism would unhesitatingly decide in favour of the hospital.

**4 Maximising**    The maximising element in utilitarianism draws its support from an apparently compelling principle of practical reason. If something is a good, it seems irrational to choose to produce a smaller amount of it where one could produce a larger.[6] If human welfare is a valuable end, then the more fully one promotes it the better. However, we need to explain exactly what we mean by 'maximising the general utility'. Utilitarians standardly believe that social welfare is some function of the utilities of individuals. But they have sometimes talked as if any increase in the utility of an individual must also increase the social utility, and this generalisation is clearly false. Not only does one person's gain often necessitate another person's loss, as when Poor benefits from the taxes paid by Rich, but interpersonal differences in values and tastes create conflicting preferences regarding such policy issues as the allocation of scarce resources, the educational, cultural and recreational priorities of the community, and the management of the shared environment. Public decisions which please some may make others miserable: thus motoring enthusiasts plead for more roads to be built while lovers of rural peace want the road-building programme curbed; Lewd wishes pornography to be more freely available but Prude would like to see its total ban. Social-policy makers must recognise the impossibility of pleasing all of the people all of the time.

A great deal of work, much of it highly technical, has been done on the problem of how to combine together the preferences of individuals to yield a reasonable collective choice. Individual utilities are assumed to be aggregative; the task is to determine how best to aggregate them. A significant result in this area is the Impossibility Theorem of Kenneth Arrow, which demonstrates that no social-welfare function is possible which satisfies a number of prima-facie highly reasonable assumptions that one might have antecedently made about such a function (see e.g. Arrow 1950; Vickrey 1960; Mackay 1980). This startling result implies that 'there can be no ideally rational aggregation device' (Mackay 1980: 1), and welfare economists have devoted a lot of energy to deciding which postulate of the inconsistent set should be abandoned or weakened. Although we cannot enter into the details of this debate, its moral is important: if Arrow is correct, then we cannot safely trust to our intuitions to show us how to construct a satisfactory social-welfare function.

In spite of these theoretical worries, we often have little difficulty in deciding which member of a set of alternative feasible actions is likely to yield the greatest utility. It is obvious that donating £10 to save the life of a starving peasant in a famine area will produce a larger increase in the general utility than spending the same sum on a fashionable T-shirt or a compact disc of one's favourite music. And anyone unlucky enough to find himself in the predicament envisaged by Bernard Williams, in which he can prevent the shooting of twenty innocent hostages only by shooting one of those hostages himself, will plainly see that he will maximise utility (more strictly, *mini*mise *dis*utility) by shooting the hostage (Williams 1973: 98–9). (Whether he would therefore do the *right* thing if he blows the man's brains out is another question.) The problem of defining an acceptable social-welfare function is an acute one chiefly in regard to the appraisal of public policy and action. Much of the morally significant behaviour of individuals affects fewer people, and affects them in more limited ways, than the actions of governments and institutions; and it is often not very hard in practice for individuals to rank the feasible options open to them in respect of their probable utility yields.

Classical utilitarian theories hold that it is the *total* utility that should be maximised; some twentieth-century theorists have suggested that the *average per capita* utility is a more defensible maximand.[7] Harsanyi has proposed to define social utility as 'the arithmetic mean of all *individual utilities*' on the decision-theoretical ground that a self-interested individual who was asked to choose between two social policies without knowing what his own position would be in the resulting social system, would rationally prefer the policy which yielded the higher *average* utility (1977: 28). Clearly, however, there will be no operational difference between maximising total utility and maximising average utility where the size of the population remains constant. But would it be right to increase the amount of utility in the world by increasing the size of the human population, even if this meant reducing the mean standard of living as more and more people were forced to share the planet's limited resources? Perhaps ten billion people with a low, but tolerable, standard of living would enjoy greater total utility than five billion with a better average standard. But is a crowded world with a higher total but lower average utility preferable to a less heavily peopled world with a lower total but higher mean utility?

There is not *within* utilitarianism a basis for choosing between total or average utility as the more eligible maximand. We simply have to make up our minds which form of the theory we prefer. Harsanyi's claim that average utilitarianism is a more rational choice for an individual concerned to maximise his own expected utility needs to be set against the thought that from the point of view of an impartial ideal observer who delights in every increase in the amount of human good, total utilitarianism would seem to be the more attractive. But even the keenest total utilitarian, who believes that those of us who are now relatively well off should be prepared to put up with a decline in our standard of living as the price of sustaining a larger number of (moderately) contented people, needs to consider the serious risks involved in pushing the planet's fragile eco-systems too close to the limit. (Pessimists would say that the world's present population of around five billion has already passed the point beyond which further increases precipitate a decline in net, as well as in average, utility.)

Utilitarianism, both classical and average, applies cost-benefit calculations at the social level similar to those which individuals apply in their own case. It is sometimes necessary to sacrifice smaller benefits in order to secure larger ones; occasionally even quite painful things may need to be endured as the price to be paid for really valuable goods. Such cost-benefit calculation is a standard component of any rational individual's prudential reasoning. 'For consider,' Rawls writes, that

> each man in realizing his own interests is certainly free to balance
> his own losses against his own gains. We may impose a sacrifice

20

on ourselves now for the sake of a greater advantage later. A person quite properly acts, at least when others are not affected, to achieve his own greatest good, to advance his interests as far as possible (Rawls 1971: 23).

Utilitarianism (wrongly, in Rawls's opinion) applies exactly the same principle on the social plane:

> Just as an individual balances present and future gains against present and future losses, so a society may balance satisfactions and dissatisfactions between different individuals. And so by these reflections one reaches the principle of utility in a natural way: a society is properly arranged when its institutions maximize the net [or average] balance of satisfaction (Rawls 1971: 24).

Although utilitarianism is scrupulously impartial between persons, in the sense that no one is allowed to count for more or for less than anyone else,[8] many critics, including Rawls, have charged it with permitting highly *unjust* things to be done to human beings when the utility sums require them. Where an individual freely chooses to purchase a substantial future benefit for the price of a small temporary discomfort, he both pays the cost and reaps the benefit himself. But if one person is made to suffer in order that *others* may reap the benefit, the deal, while rational by utilitarian logic, is much more doubtfully fair. Forcing some to be benefactors so that others may be beneficiaries strikes many people as blatantly unjust. Philosophers who talk the language of rights complain that utilitarianism not only condones but positively encourages the infringement of individuals' rights in the name of the general good.

It must be conceded that utilitarianism draws weaker protective boundaries around individual persons than most deontological theories do. Yet whether the boundaries which utilitarianism permits are quite as flimsy as critics charge is a question calling for careful discussion; it will receive this in Chapter VII. It is worth noting meanwhile that our pre-reflective moral intuitions do not invariably run counter to the maximising tendency of utilitarianism. Other things being equal, we prefer that individuals should make their own decisions on whether to sacrifice their personal interests for the public good: self-determination is rightly recognised as a good by many theories, whether or not it is regarded as a right. We admire heroism like that of Captain Oates, who lost himself in an Antarctic blizzard to relieve the Scott expedition of a lame member who was dangerously delaying their progress. It would be harder to admire a decision on the part of his companions to evict him from their tent. But we do not always believe it morally unreasonable to make some people suffer for the greater good of others. Wartime provides such situations in abundance. Thus it might be proposed, in order to end a terrible war, to bomb a crucial military installation in the centre of a heavily populated area of an enemy city. Although a large number of innocent civilians are likely to die in the raid, many people would judge the projected raid to be morally justified – a 'cruel necessity', in Cromwell's phrase. Assuming that people's lives are roughly equal in regard to the amount of their (expected) utility, the death of a few hundred innocent citizens, albeit tragic, appears a price worth paying to save the lives of thousands or millions of others. If human lives are valuable, then it seems better to save more rather than fewer of them.

Rigorous utilitarians would even say that *not* carrying out the raid would be deeply immoral, on the ground that agents are as responsible for the deaths they could prevent but allow to happen, as they are for the deaths they deliberately cause. This doctrine is problematic, however, if it implies that (say) failing to save a starving peasant in sub-Saharan Africa is just as bad as taking a gun and shooting him, and not all utilitarians believe that a maximising policy entails it. Many believe that limits must be placed on our 'negative responsibility' for ills we could remedy if we went out of our way to do so, otherwise utilitarianism becomes too demanding a doctrine, requiring every agent to be a moral saint. Normal lives are filled with a range of concerns and commitments which make an essential contribution to the satisfaction of their subjects, yet it is a difficult question how far utilitarianism, consistently with its maximising aspect, can justify the pursuit by individuals of such private goods and goals. The view that it cannot justify them at all – that utilitarianism threatens to destroy the 'integrity' of individuals by compelling them to consider themselves as no more than servants of the general good (cf. Williams 1973: section 5) – is patently overstated: for it would be a miserable world (hence not one in which utility was maximised) in which no one was permitted to take a special interest in his own projects that he did not take in others'. But at what point does our psychologically natural, and utility-enhancing, concern with our own projects pass over into immoral self-indulgence? And how self-denying can utilitarianism realistically expect individual agents to be? These issues challenge utilitarians, but they challenge other moral theories too. Only a naive account of the moral life finds no difficulty in answering the question what a person owes to himself and what he owes to others. It is a good test of the quality of any moral conception how persuasively it delimits a sphere of legitimate agent-centred concerns. How well utilitarianism itself does on this test we shall have to see.

**5 Universalist**   This fifth feature of utilitarianism is historically of great significance, though it is scarcely more than a vestigial feature of most contemporary utilitarian theories. Universalism is the idea represented by the second half of the famous formula, 'the greatest happiness of *the greatest number*'. Traditionally, utilitarians have encouraged not merely the creation of the largest amount of happiness, but the distribution of this happiness as widely as possible. Samuel Scheffler has remarked on the important role of utilitarianism in the Enlightenment project of pushing outwards the boundaries of moral concern (a programme which continues to the present day). Utilitarians are not unique in believing, but they share much of the credit for making the belief a commonplace, that 'Any person, no matter how poor, or powerless, or socially marginal, no matter how remote from the centers of influence and privilege, may, by invoking moral principles, assert a claim or express a grievance in the language of a system to which nobody, however rich, powerful, or well-bred, may claim immunity' (Scheffler 1992: 12).

Traditional utilitarian benevolence is of the universalist kind; to the scriptural question 'Who is my neighbour?' the utilitarian answer is 'Everyone'. Universal love was demanded in the fifth century BC by the earliest known utilitarian, the Chinese philosopher Mo Tzǔ. By the eighteenth century, universalism had become a keynote of the works of utilitarians and their sympathisers. In France, Helvétius called on governments to pass laws which would produce a happiness which was *universelle* as well as *égale* (Helvétius 1774: 187, 194). The Scottish philosopher Francis Hutcheson anticipated Bentham's famous slogan as early as 1725 when he wrote that 'that action is best which secures the greatest happiness of the greatest number' (Selby-Bigge 1897: 106–7). Forty years later Cesare Beccaria's influential treatise on the criminal law advocated 'the greatest happiness divided among the greatest number' (Becarria 1764: 61–2). And Bentham himself spoke repeatedly of the 'happiness of the community' which governments should do everything in their power to enhance, claiming that states had a duty to create a 'fabric of felicity by the hands of reason and of law' (Bentham 1789: 1–2). J.S. Mill considered that 'In the golden rule of Jesus of Nazareth, we read the complete spirit of the ethics of utility', and added that 'laws and social arrangements should place the happiness . . . of every individual, as nearly as possible in harmony with the interest of the whole' (J.S. Mill 1861: 218).

Part of what the universalist idea expresses is simply the familiar ethical principle that everyone's interests count equally – that there are no moral second-class citizens. Uncontroversial though this principle may seem to us today, it did not always appear so in the past (for example, in pre-revolutionary France). Yet the attempt to develop a principle of equal concern into a doctrine that we should always act so as to benefit the largest feasible number of people is fundamentally flawed, for a technical reason that is easy to grasp. We cannot coherently pursue the double maximand of the greatest happiness of the greatest number of people, for we must often choose between one action which will provide a lesser utility for a larger population and another which will produce a larger utility for a smaller number. In such circumstances it is *not possible* simultaneously to produce the greatest happiness *and* to benefit the greatest number. Bentham, who was well aware of the problem of the double maximand, declared for maximisation of utility as the more essential utilitarian goal. (In his later career he accordingly abandoned the classic formula 'the greatest happiness of the greatest number' in favour of the simpler expression 'the greatest happiness'.) Yet Bentham also believed that the universalist and maximising goals of utilitarianism, while involving theoretically 'conflicting elements of extent',[9] were rarely divergent in practice. He thought that real life frequently exhibits a principle of diminishing marginal returns, whereby the greater the quantity of some good which a person holds, the less his happiness is increased by each incremental addition. On this view, any limited quantity of goods for distribution will normally produce greater utility if distributed among a larger than among a smaller number of people (provided that the goods are not spread so thinly that their incremental contribution to everyone's utility is close to zero).

It might be thought that the two maximands could be treated as lexically ordered, so that while our first priority should always be to maximise utility, we should break a tie between two equally eligible utility-producing actions or policies by choosing the one which will benefit the larger number of persons. However, this strategy would permit very small variations in the quantity of expected utility to have an unjustifiable impact on distributions. Thus if we faced a choice between actions $A$ and $B$ which would provide, respectively, 10 units of utility to $X$ and 5 units to each of $X$ and $Y$, we ought, according to this strategy, to choose $B$. But if there were a third alternative, $C$, which would provide 11 units of utility to $X$ and none at all to $Y$, then we should choose $C$ in preference to $B$. Yet $Y$ might reasonably wonder why his interests, which determined the superiority of $B$ to $A$, should count for nothing when *B* is weighed up against *C*. We are not therefore assisted to solve the problems of justice which arise from the maximising character of utilitarianism by construing 'the greater number' as a logically posterior maximand to 'the greatest utility'. (For further critical observations on the 'greatest number' principle, see Griffin 1986: 151–5.)

This completes the preliminary sketch of the leading features of the utilitarian family of moral theories. Members of this family have a number of immediate attractions which explain their permanent fascination for many reflective people. They are, as we have seen, concerned with something of primary importance to human beings – our welfare, in a broad sense.[10] Though utilitarians do not all agree in their detailed accounts of what makes lives go well, they concur in the belief that the central concern of morality is that lives should go as well as possible. Even critics who deny that utilitarianism provides an ultimately satisfactory account of morality must concede that it focuses on something of indisputable significance to us, the quality of our lived experiences.

Not only is the possession of a flourishing life of obviously great importance to people: it also provides a basis for moral theory which is remarkably empirical and down to earth. Utilitarianism offers a single rational criterion for appraising actions, practices and institutions: the maximisation of utility. It makes no reference to the law of a divine being (though utilitarians may be religious believers), nor does it posit, as some secularised descendants of religious-based morality do, a moral law without a lawgiver. It likewise avoids the metaphysical and epistemological problems of theories which claim the existence of rights, duties and norms known through an obscure faculty of moral intuition. Utilitarians countenance no experience-transcendent sources of moral knowledge, and represent moral thinking as continuous with other kinds of practical reasoning. In addition, utilitarianism appeals to many people for its impartiality and its emphasis on improving the welfare levels of wide constituencies of human beings; many think this makes it the ideal moral and political philosophy for a modern democratic state.

Nevertheless, utilitarianism, for all its attractions, faces considerable difficulties on several scores. Utilitarianism's welfarist theory of value has provoked objections that it affords no non-arbitrary way of excluding from the category of legitimate satisfactions such morally undesirable pleasures as those of the sadist or the masochist. (Some utilitarians simply disregard all second-order preferences or pleasures; but this device seems remarkably *ad hoc*.) Its consequentialism is criticised for the failure to acknowledge that duty should be done for its own sake and not in order

25

to produce good results; while consequentialists are held to be morally purblind in their failure to recognise the reality of intrinsic rightness and wrongness. The aggregative element is allegedly beset by insuperable difficulties concerning the commensurability of tastes and the basis for interpersonal comparisons of utility. Maximisation raises worries that utilitarians are too cavalier in their attitudes to the rights and interests of individuals, and psychologically unrealistic in the level of self-sacrifice they demand from individual agents.

These, and many other difficulties, substantial and insubstantial, will be discussed in the course of this book. Some of the complaints we shall look at are of quite recent origin; others are of much older vintage. And it is to the history of utilitarianism that we shall first turn. Tracing the development of utilitarian doctrine from ancient times to modern is a fascinating exercise in itself, and helps to set the contemporary debate in context. The history of utilitarianism, like that of many theories, has a tendency to repeat itself, and much that is complacently thought to be original in twentieth-century work can be found prefigured in earlier writings. Utilitarianism is an an age-old intellectual phenomenon, not the invention (as some imagine) of a handful of radical and unconventional men in Hanoverian and and Victorian Britain. Since the dawn of philosophy and social thought, thinkers of a particular cast have gravitated towards some form or other of utilitarianism as a code of justice or a panacea for ills. In the next chapter we shall begin our historical survey by looking at four ancient teachers who in their different ways and to different degrees anticipated what we should now call utilitarian ideas. Of the four – Mo Tzŭ, Jesus, Aristotle and Epicurus – perhaps only the first can be described as a fully-fledged utilitarian; the others anticipated utilitarian doctrine only at certain points. But each, as we shall see, was a powerful proponent of some element or elements of the great tradition with which we are concerned.

# CHAPTER II

# Four Ancient Moralists

## 1 Mo Tzǔ

We know very little about the life of Mo Tzǔ (otherwise known as Mo Ti, or 'Master Mo'), who has been described as teaching 'doctrines which were morally the most sublime of all the ancient Chinese schools' (Fitzgerald 1961: 79).[1] Neither the dates of his birth and death nor the place of his origin can be stated with certainty, but he may have been born in the state of Lu in present-day Honan province, and most scholars believe that he flourished around 420 BC (which makes him a contemporary of Socrates). Living in the period of the 'Warring States' (from 481 to 221 BC), Mo Tzǔ was one of the many prominent sages who sought a philosophical remedy for the endemic strife and disunity of the troubled land we now call China. (Ironically, it was not to be abstract thought which finally ended the political anarchy, but the iron fist of the first Ch'in emperor, Shih-Huang Ti, the notorious burner of books.)

The Mohist school, which survived until the Ch'in conquest (it was not revived again until the Ming Dynasty in the seventeenth century), preached an ethic with two central principles: the all-embracing love of mankind and the judging of the worth of all actions by their fruitfulness or utility (li). Our knowledge of Mohist philosophy is based primarily on the fifty-three surviving chapters of the Mo-Tzǔ Book, a compilation which regrettably does not always distinguish clearly between the sayings of the Master and the glosses and commentaries of his followers. The book, like most committee productions, is undeniably less than notable in a literary sense, though Arthur Waley exaggerated in claiming that 'Mo Tzǔ is feeble, repetitive . . . , heavy, unimaginative and unentertaining, devoid of a single passage that could possibly be said to have wit, beauty or force' (Waley 1939: 164–5). It does, however, succeed in presenting a subtle, well-rounded and humane philosophical position which it is not anachronistic to call 'utilitarian'.

Mo's thinking is, in fact, strikingly similar to Christianity in its advocacy of universal love (*chien ai*) as a solution to all evils. 'Suppose we try to locate the cause of disorder,' says the *Mo-Tzŭ Book*, 'we shall find it lies in the want of universal love' (Motse 1929: 78). In order to bring peace to the earth, men must broaden the scope of their active concern, cease to care only about themselves or a small handful of others, and love everyone as themselves:

> If every one in the world will love universally; states not attacking one another; houses not disturbing one another; thieves and robbers becoming extinct; emperors and ministers, fathers and sons, all being affectionate and filial – if all this comes to pass the world will be orderly (80).

Such love, Mo Tzŭ thinks, should be encouraged by every emperor and leader of men. But all-embracing love must not remain at the level of vague philanthropic sentiment: it must be translated into deeds. As an example of love-in-action, Mo cites the semi-mythical exploits of King Yü of the Hsia Dynasty (*c.* 2000 BC), who was reputed to have laboured for years on drainage and flood-prevention schemes for the good of his subjects (85; cf. Fitzgerald 1961: 14). Moreover universal love, when practised by all, produces mutual aid:

> Whoever loves others is loved by others; whoever benefits others is benefited by others; whoever hates others is hated by others; whoever injures others is injured by others. Then, what difficulty is there with it (universal love)? (Motse 1929: 83).

Mo Tzŭ's emphasis on the practical aspect of love and on the mutuality of benefits is intended to answer the objection that all-embracing love, while fine in principle, is not a real possibility for human beings constituted as we are:

> The gentlemen in the empire think that, though it would be an excellent thing if love can be universalized, it is something quite impracticable. It is like carrying Mt. T'ai and leaping over the Chi River (84).

This objection is the forerunner of that frequently heard today, that utilitarian theories which call upon us to maximise utility and maintain strict impartiality among persons make unrealistic demands of us. How could one, for instance, care as much about a total stranger as about one's own children? A morality which tells us that we should give a hard-earned pound to benefit a stranger's child rather than our own when doing so would produce greater utility, is at best hard to follow and at worst threatens our psychological integrity. 'When every one regards other families as his own family,' asks Mo wistfully, 'who will steal?' (80). But it is neither clear that we ever *could* regard other families as our own, nor, in the view of many philosophers, desirable that we should try.

Yet Mo Tzŭ's contention that love should be practical and aid reciprocal suggests that he may never have intended to require from us love of any psychologically impossible sort. He may have believed not that we should hold all men in a warm glow of sentimental affection like that we feel for ourselves, our families and our friends, but that we should regard other people as valuable beings who exert on us a certain kind of ethical pull. Mo's view would then resemble Kant's in the *Foundations of the Metaphysics of Morals* (1785), where the distinction is drawn between love as affectionate feeling and love as a variety of moral respect. In Kant's opinion

> It is in this manner, undoubtedly, that we are to understand those passages of Scripture . . . in which we are commanded to love our neighbour, even our enemy. For love, as an affection, cannot be commanded, but beneficence for duty's sake may. . . . This is *practical* love, and not *pathological* – a love which is seated in the will, and not in the propensions of sense – in principles of action and not of tender sympathy (Kant 1785: 15–16).[2]

If this is what Mo Tzŭ believed too, then the implausibility of his position is dissipated. It may be easier to carry Mt T'ai than to care for the peasantry of China in the way you care about your own children, but it is not so hard to treat all human beings as having a value which entitles them to your respect and concern. Mo's call to all-embracing love could therefore be closely related to the universalist strand in later utilitarianism which holds that all people possess moral importance and make a claim on one's beneficence.

However, there is another possible construal of Mohist love, which makes it appear less pure and high-minded. Mo constantly denies that all-embracing love is difficult, claiming that it is *mutual* love which inhibits 'calamities, strifes, complaints, and hatreds' (Motse 1929: 82–3). It is tempting to read his affirmations of the ease with which all-embracing love may be practised as premised on the assumption that it is in everybody's interest to extend *ai* to his neighbour, because then his neighbour will extend *ai* to him in return. Yet this transforms Mohist love into a calculating love which we only practise towards others on the understanding (or at least in the hope) that they will reciprocate. It is no longer a love which, as St Paul put it, does not count the cost, but a 'love' which counts it very cannily.

The truth of this cynical reading of Mohist doctrine may appear more likely in the light of Mo's Hobbesian vision of an original state of nature, in which men engaged in a bloody struggle for a limited supply of natural resources. To escape from that state, Mo thought, men had to learn that there was more personal advantage to be gained from cooperation than from warfare, and that a better life was possible under a stable political order than in conditions of anarchy (55–8). But this reinforces the suspicion that Mohist *ai* is love of others neither in a 'pathological' nor a Kantian 'practical' sense, but is merely enlightened *self*-love, a disposition to treat others well in order to be treated well by them. As such, whatever merits it may have as the basis of an effective system of practical politics, it seems to have little to do with genuine utilitarian concern for others.

It is unlikely, though, that this unflattering interpretation of Mo Tzǔ's account of all-embracing love is correct. Even the Confucian Mencius, arch-enemy of the Mohists, candidly conceded that Mo 'loved all men and would gladly wear out his whole being from head to heel for the benefit of mankind' (Fitzgerald 1961: 98). That hardly sounds like a man who believed in doing good to others only so that they would return the good with interest. It is more probable that when confronted by the challenge to give a rational reason why an agent should love other people, Mo unwittingly gave an answer to a rather different question: namely, why an agent should trouble himself to promote the welfare of others. If Mo really meant to entice the person who only cares for himself into caring for others too, he fell into the trap that many subsequent philosophers have done who have tried to talk the egoistic individual out of his self-centredness: he played into the egoist's hands by appealing to *his own interests* in doing well by his neighbours. It is a reasonable hypothesis that Mo's 'all-embracing love' involved at the very least a positive sense of the ethical pull of other human beings, perceived as the valuable subjects of valuable lives; it almost certainly involved also what Kant would have called 'pathological' elements. The vindication of *ai* by reference to the benefits accruing to the self from acting well towards others was perhaps the very earliest instance of a classic philosophical false step: the self-stultifying appeal to self-love to justify the love of others.

In explaining how we should express an all-embracing love of humanity, Mo Tzǔ anticipated the pivotal utilitarian principle that right action is essentially *profitable* action, or action issuing in genuine practical benefits for mankind. Mohists clashed sharply with many other of the 'Hundred Schools' of philosophy, and particularly with Confucianism, by criticising as pointless (or worse) various practices claimed as obligatory within a righteous style of living. Just as modern utilitarians are often accused of sinking the moral in the expedient (an insult, in their opponents' view, both to morality and to human nature), Confucian critics of Mohism objected that Mo Tzŭ's pragmatic attitude to life was disgraceful and demeaning. Mencius declared with characteristic intemperance that 'Mo Tzŭ wished to reduce mankind to the level of wild beasts' (Waley 1939: 181) – a remark strikingly reminiscent of the complaint that the utilitarian doctrine is 'worthy only of swine' (cf. J.S. Mill 1861: 210).

Mo Tzŭ preached a simple and frugal lifestyle, condemning as unprofitable the elaborate ceremonial beloved by the Confucians, the prodigal spending on funerals conventional at that time, luxury in food and clothing, and, above all, the pursuit of military adventures. He urged rulers to work in the service of their subjects rather than squander lives and property in the belligerent pursuit of regal glory.

> In issuing an order, taking up an enterprise, or employing the people and expending wealth, the sage never does anything without some useful purpose. Therefore wealth is not wasted and people's resources are not exhausted, and many are the blessings provided (Motse 1929: 117).

Mo had nothing but contempt for the lavish funerals and the lengthy periods of mourning for parents which Confucius believed expressed the filial principle at the basis of ethics: 'It has never happened, from ancient times to the present day, that benefits are procured, calamities averted for the world, and disorder among the people is regulated by elaborate funerals and extended mourning' (124).

He further ridiculed all those who called the murder of one man unrighteous, yet 'when it comes to the great unrighteousness of attacking states, they do not know that they should condemn it' (99). War, being murder, is wrong for a very simple utilitarian reason: 'Why? Because it causes others to suffer more; when others are caused to suffer more, then the act is more inhumane and criminal' (98–9). War may sometimes benefit a few people, but it never benefits the many:

> It is like a physician giving his drugs to his patients. If a physician should give all the sick in the world a uniform drug, among the ten thousand who took it there might be four or five who were benefited, still it is not to be said to be a commonly beneficial medicine (103–4).

31

Mo Tzŭ also criticised music as a waste of time; this has led one modern historian to remark that 'He does not, in fact, seem to have had a developed artistic nature' (Fitzgerald 1961: 97). Probably what Mo mainly objected to was the contemporary obsession with ritualistic and ceremonial uses of music while more important social needs went unregarded. 'Now suppose we strike the big bell, beat the sounding drum, play the *ch'in* and the *she* and blow the *yü* and the *sheng*, can the material for food and clothing then be procured for the people?' (Motse 1929: 176). Hence Mo Tzŭ said: 'To have music is wrong' (177). Yet there is a certain amount of evidence that the Master did indeed lack a developed aesthetic sense. A Confucian philosopher when asked the reason for performing music told Mo that 'Music is performed for music's sake.' Mo's scornful rejection of this reply – that it was like saying that houses are built for the sake of building houses – indicates a failure to comprehend the important distinction between things which are done as a means to an end, and aesthetically satisfying activities which are practised as ends in them- selves (237). Mo's distaste for artistic pursuits appears to have stemmed from a deep distrust of the emotional nature of man, which he saw as a threat to his reason. Emotional states were 'peculiarities' ('depravities', in some translations), which were best uprooted where possible:

> When silent one should be deliberating; when talking one should instruct; when acting one should achieve something. . . . Pleasure, anger, joy, sorrow, love [presumably, shallow sentimental affec- tion] and hate are to be removed and magnanimity and righteous- ness are to replace them (224).

Like Bentham at a later date, Mo left little room for 'the love of beauty, the passion of the artist; the love of *order*, of congruity, of consistency in all things, and conformity to their end' – in short, for all 'complex forms' of feeling, which he thought of only as 'idiosyncracies of taste' (J.S. Mill 1838: 96). But Bentham at least made room for pleasure. While Bentham's position is a long way from the pantomime utilitarianism of Dickens's *Hard Times*, Mo Tzŭ's official philosophy does sometimes seem close to the grotesque simplifications of Gradgrindery:

> Facts alone are wanted in life. Plant nothing else, and root out everything else. You can only form the minds of reasoning animals upon Facts; nothing else will ever be of any service to them (Dickens 1854: 1).

Mr Gradgrind's declaration of faith would not be entirely out of place in the *Mo-Tzŭ Book*.

Yet in spite of Mo Tzŭ's wariness of the emotional side of human nature, it is hard to see the Mohist philosophy as rooted solely in the thin soil of reason. Mencius' picture of a saintly sage who dedicated himself to the good of humanity suggests a man driven rather by a passionate concern for his fellow men than by any wire-drawn conception of duty. On the most plausible reading, Mohism's crucial distinction was between a laudable affection for mankind, the foundation of magnanimous actions of profit to other people, and frivolous or factitious tastes for things that do not really promote welfare. It was not, in other words, emotion *per se* which attracted Mo Tzŭ's condemnation, but emotional attitudes directed towards the inessential, the time-wasting and the merely amusing.

## 2 Jesus

Mo Tzŭ's advocacy of all-embracing love will remind the western reader of the ethical teaching of Jesus Christ. 'I give you a new commandment,' Jesus announced to his disciples at the Last Supper: 'love one another as I have loved you' (John 13: 34). Moreover, we should love not only our friends, but also our enemies:

> But I say this to you who are listening: Love your enemies, do good to those who hate you, bless those who curse you, pray for those who treat you badly (Luke 6:27–8).

Love can hardly be more all-embracing than this.

To what extent was Christ's teaching utilitarian? This question has received surprisingly little attention from historians of philosophy and religion. It is commonly supposed, without much argument, that Christian ethics and utilitarianism, while sometimes convergent in their value judgements, are very different in their tone and rationale. But this view is open to challenge. Mill, a rare dissentient from the orthodox line, thought that 'In the golden rule of Jesus of Nazareth, we read the complete spirit of the ethics of utility' (J.S. Mill 1861: 218). Christ's religious concerns may tend to disguise from us his status as a proto-utilitarian. Yet it is not difficult to discover some substantial utilitarian strands in his ethical programme.

Old Testament morality, unlike Christian, is distinctly deontological. Moral injunctions like the Ten Commandments are thoroughly non-consequentialist in character: they are rules to be obeyed unquestioningly and without calculating the effect of obedience or disobedience in particular cases. By contrast, Jesus could sum up his moral teaching in two highly generalised prescriptions:

This is the first: ... you must love the Lord your God with all your heart, with all your soul, with all your mind and with all your strength. The second is this: You must love your neighbour as yourself. There is no commandment greater than these (Mark 12:29–31).

Fulfilling these commands calls not for the consultation of a rule book but for imaginative reflection on the practical demands of love. Jesus laid down no detailed regulations for the exercise of charity; instead he taught the meaning of a loving attitude to others through readily comprehensible parables (the Good Samaritan, the Prodigal Son and others) which illustrate the ways in which loving people behave. Moral appraisal is a matter of applying the general law of love to individual cases: we have to consider in a consequentialist way how best we can benefit our neighbour. Loving people entails caring that their lives should go well; so a person who loves his neighbour looks for opportunities to promote his welfare and helps him in times of trouble. Real love, Jesus stressed, is active, useful love, not merely a passive sentiment of benevolence.

The Gospels provide considerable evidence that Jesus shared Mo Tzŭ's impatience with ritualistic observances, the inflexible protocol of religious ceremonial, and all rules of behaviour of an 'unprofitable' kind. The Pharisees who objected to Christ's healing of the sick and picking of ears of corn on the sabbath provoked his particular wrath. 'The sabbath was made for man,' he rebuked them, 'not man for the sabbath' (Mark 2:27–8). St Luke records Christ's question to the Pharisees: 'Which of you, if his son falls into a well, or his ox, will not pull him out on a sabbath day without hesitation?' To this, we are told, they could find no answer (Luke 14:5). Such pragmatic common sense, it is true, is not unique to utilitarians. But the demand that rules should serve a useful purpose, and the refusal to follow even normally useful rules in situations where their observance would do more harm than good, marks a strong resemblance between the ethics of Christ and of many modern utilitarians.

Nevertheless, the view that the Christian ethic has much in common with utilitarianism has recently been denied by two prominent writers of utilitarian sympathies. Anthony Quinton, in his book *Utilitarian Ethics*, acknowledges that Christianity advocates a lively concern for the general good of mankind, but insists that its two central features are nevertheless not utilitarian ones. First:

its conception of the happiness or well-being of mankind was ascetical and non-hedonistic. . . . Man's greatest felicity is the beatific vision of God that is to be enjoyed after bodily death by those who have been saved (Quinton 1973: 12).

34

Second, Christianity 'in its simplest and most rudimentary form bases the validity of the moral principles it enjoins on the fact that they are the commands of God' (13). Similarly, Alan Ryan holds that 'the attempt to pass off Jesus as a utilitarian is special pleading', a view for which he offers much the same reasons as Quinton: that the main purpose of Christian living is to get to heaven, and that 'what constitutes moral goodness is obedience to God's commandments' (Ryan 1987: 22).

However, neither of these claims to identify crucial differences is very convincing. The first – the claim that Christianity's primary interest is in our afterlife, not our terrestrial existence – is dubious because the historical Jesus (as distinct from the Christ of the later Church) seems to have seen his central mission as the realisation of the Kingdom of God upon earth, the institution of a golden age when the two supreme laws of love would be universally observed. Exactly what Jesus thought the Kingdom would be like is obscure; but it is abundantly clear that Christ was at least as intensely concerned with life *before* death as he was with life *after* it, and that he believed that life in the coming Kingdom of God would be grounded on the love of God and one's neighbour. Jesus did not think of earthly life simply as a preparation for the next world, but as a form of existence potentially valuable in itself, although this potential could not be fully realised until the advent of the Kingdom.

Next, Quinton's contention that Jesus could not have been a utilitarian since he did not maintain a hedonist theory of value holds water only if it is assumed that all utilitarians must be hedonists. While most forms of utilitarianism are *welfarist*, concerned that lives should flourish or prosper according to some specified criterion of well-being, not all consider pleasure as the be-all and end-all. There are solid arguments against equating welfare with pleasure, even if it is hard to conceive of a life's going well that contains no pleasure at all. Jesus' vision of the good life is not truly ascetical, despite the fact that it does not give a prominent place to pleasure (unless we extend the term to cover contentment with one's lot and ease of soul). Leaving the religious dimension aside, Jesus' conception of well-being is quite strikingly similar to Mo Tzŭ's: both men proposed a way of life based on frugality, simplicity, friendship and community ties, and an indifference to riches and social eminence. This is a life stripped down to essentials, shorn of all superfluities.[3]

Quinton's second alleged difference between utilitarianism and the Christian ethic (again echoed by Ryan) is that the validity of the latter, unlike that of the former, depends upon divine commandment. It is unfortunately not clear exactly what either author understands by this dependence. Not all Christian theologians have explained right actions as those which God wills or commands. Many have supposed that while God wills only what is right, what is right is so not *because* God wills it but on some independent ground. On this line of thought, God may command us to perform right actions, but the *moral* reason for performing them is something other than the fact that God commands them. But even if 'right' is taken to mean 'commanded by God', *what* God commands (if we take our cue from the Gospels rather than from the Old Testament) is that we should love God and our neighbour; and it has already been suggested that these generalised directives are meant to be unpacked in consequentialist terms. Neither of these alternatives, then, appears to support the idea of a fundamental divide between the Christian and the utilitarian points of view. (If, on the other hand, what Quinton and Ryan really intend is the *epistemological* claim that Christians do not need to engage in consequentialist reasoning to decide matters of right and wrong, but can simply consult a list of God's commandments, this is also rendered unlikely by the generalised character of the commandments of love.)

Finally, it is worth probing a little further into what Jesus meant by the term 'love'. We have seen that Kant thought that Christ can have meant to recommend only 'practical love' – a disposition to act dutifully towards other people – and not 'pathological love' – a feeling of affection for others – on the ground that only the former is under the control of our will. Utilitarian ethics, like Kantian, can indeed be sustained on a foundation of 'practical love', where such love expresses a sense of respect for other persons as valuable beings capable of living valuable lives. But it is hard to resist the impression that Christ, like Master Mo, meant to instil in his hearers something more 'pathological' than a rationalised spirit of respect. Someone who succeeds in loving his neighbour *as himself* must feel something of higher emotional temperature than a mere dutiful disposition towards him; and what both Mo Tzŭ and Jesus seem to have wished to encourage was the extension to all mankind of the *same kind* of love that we naturally feel for ourselves, our close family and friends.[4] None the less, Kant's view that it is impossibly idealistic to demand that everyone should embrace this doctrine of perfection has a lot of human experience to support it; and there is much in the proposal that the best reason for attempting to develop in people a set of moral attitudes based upon respect for others is precisely to compensate for the inevitable shortfall in our natural affection for one another. Christian and Mohist morality can be plausibly regarded not only as the most sublime form of ethics, but as the highest form of *utilitarian* ethics. Yet as 'ought' implies 'can', it may ultimately be more realistic and fruitful for utilitarians to promote a less emotionally demanding, more respect-centred, conception of moral action.

## 3 Aristotle

In a well-known passage near the beginning of the *Nicomachean Ethics*, Aristotle raises the question of what is the highest of all goods achievable by action:

> Verbally there is very general agreement; for both the general run of men and people of superior refinement say that it is happiness [*eudaimonia*], and identify living well and doing well with being happy; but with regard to what happiness is they differ, and the many do not give the same account as the wise (Aristotle *Nicomachean Ethics*, 1095a).

That the common answer is the right answer seems plain to Aristotle because the highest good attainable by action must be something both final and self-sufficient, and nothing but happiness appears to fit that description. Happiness is not something we aim at for the sake of anything else, and once we are happy, we do not think that our lives are deficient in any respect. 'Happiness, then, is something final and self-sufficient, and is the end of action'; it is also 'blessed' and an object to be 'prized' rather than 'praised', praise being more appropriate to things, such as personal excellences, which are goods but not final goods (1097b, 1101b).

This view that happiness is the proper end of life seems, on first encounter, strikingly close to the classical utilitarian position; Aristotle not only presents a teleological account of life, but agrees with utilitarianism's specification of what the *telos* is. In contending that *eudaimonia* is the proper final goal of action, Aristotle appears to anticipate Mill's statement of the greatest happiness principle, 'that actions are right in proportion as they tend to promote happiness, wrong as they tend to promote the reverse of happiness' (J.S. Mill 1861: 210). Also like Mill, Aristotle devoted careful attention to the nature of happiness and concluded that the most fully flourishing, most intensely *eudaimon*, form of life is that achieved by the intellectual who pursues philosophical or scientific investigations, and not by the libertine wallowing in sensual indulgence.

Yet Aristotle, with good reason, is not normally regarded as a utilitarian; he stands to modern utilitarianism more in the relation of a great-uncle than an ancestor in the direct line. Unlike Mo Tzŭ and Jesus, Aristotle saw the fundamental issues of ethics in terms of the agent's obligations to himself rather than his obligations to other people or to humanity in general. On the Aristotelian perspective, the ethical quest takes a strongly first-personal turn: the problem each one of us must address is: how can I live the life which is most suitable to my nature as a human being, hence most fulfilling? Aristotle failed to arrive at a notion of all-embracing love, or even of 'practical love' of the Kantian kind, because he was not raising a question to which any doctrine of altruism for its own sake would have seemed an answer. Someone who lives his life according to Aristotelian prescriptions will in fact tend to treat his neighbours, in practical terms, rather well: he will be generous, just, good-tempered, truthful, friendly, and so on. But his good behaviour towards them is dictated not by the ethical *pull* they exert on him as valuable human subjects capable of living valuable lives, but by his sense of his own ethical *push*, that is, his conception of himself as a being whose value is enhanced by the development of certain excellent dispositions of character (*aretai*, usually and somewhat loosely translated as 'virtues').[5] Fine behaviour expresses and consolidates a fine character; it appeals to the Aristotelian agent for its self-enriching rather than its other-enriching properties. A person who successfully trains himself to be loyal or brave or forbearing or witty can be justly proud of acquiring those excellent traits of character; any warmth of feeling for other people he may have developed in the process is, ethically speaking, incidental. Needless to say, the intense egocentrism of this Aristotelian view of right action has not been followed by utilitarians.

There is a further respect in which Aristotelianism and utilitarianism are significantly different. While both theories take a teleological line on happiness as the ultimate goal of action, Aristotle's is teleological in a further sense: it presupposes that man, like other living creatures, has a function (*ergon*) – that, in other words, there is something that human beings are *for*. Just as a flute-player or a sculptor has a characteristic role or activity – playing the flute or making statues – Aristotle believes that man *qua* man must have a function too. 'Have the carpenter, then, and the tanner certain functions or activities,' he asks, 'and has man none?' (Aristotle, *Nicomachean Ethics*, 1097b–1098a). This function, whatever it is, must be something that arises out of the nature (*phusis*) of man, and represents the most distinctive thing about him. Nutrition, growth and perception are considered as candidates for our essential function, but rejected because they are shared with lower living things. Finally Aristotle settles on rationality as the *ergon* of man: 'we state the function

38

of man to be a certain kind of life, and this to be an activity or actions of
the soul implying a rational principle' (1098a). Aristotle's view of the
place of human beings in the order of nature (at the intersection of
animality and divinity) thus leads him, by a different route, to the same
belief which many utilitarians have held in the pre-eminence of intellectual pursuits within a flourishing human life. But an Aristotelian is
less likely to justify those pursuits by appeal to any subjective satisfactions they yield than by reference to their suitability for beings of our
distinctive *ergon*.

Utilitarianism is not a form of neo-Aristotelianism, but the history of
utilitarianism displays much evidence of Aristotelian influence. This is
hardly surprising in the light of the *Nicomachean Ethics'* unfailingly
instructive discussion of topics of interest to the 'school of utility': the
nature of human motivation; the relationship of the goal of happiness
(*eudaimonia*) to our other goals; the distinction between happiness and
pleasure; the pre-eminent place of intellectual pursuits within the good
life; the importance of seeing one's life in an organic way, where the
whole is more than the sum of the constituent parts; the value of self-
respect and of having a character that one can love and admire. Not every
utilitarian has been persuaded by Aristotle's treatment of all of these
themes, nor have those (such as Mill) who have been most greatly
influenced accepted all his conclusions. Nevertheless utilitarianism has
invariably gained in depth and realism whenever it has engaged seriously
with Aristotelian concerns.

## 4 Epicurus

Two thousand years before Bentham defended the doctrine of utility that
'all things are good or evil, by virtue solely of the pain or pleasure which
they produce' (J.S. Mill 1978: 61), a gentle and cultivated man had
taught in a garden at Athens that the pursuit of pleasure and the avoidance
of pain were the most fitting objectives in the life of the wise man. The
name of this sage, who endeavoured to provide in his own career an
exemplar of his doctrine, was Epicurus. Born on the Aegean island of
Samos in 341 BC, he formed a love of philosophy in his teens, and by
an early date had gathered a group of disciples around him. After several
years of wandering, he settled in Athens in the year 306, where he bought
a house and garden and established his philosophical school. There, with
his pupils and friends (who, unusually for the time, included women and
slaves), he lived a life of semi-seclusion and economic self-sufficiency,
growing vegetables and herbs and discussing the proper conduct of

human life. Diogenes Laertius, the third-century AD biographer of the philosophers, and the more reliable ancient sources describe Epicurus as being of an unusually mild and benevolent disposition, beloved by his followers, and perenially patient under the affliction of a chronic and painful disease (possibly a stone in his bladder or kidneys), from which he died in 271 BC.

On J.S. Mill's reading of history, Benthamite utilitarianism and Epicureanism were essentially identical in their theory of value.[6] But if Epicurus was, as Mill believed, the ultimate begetter of the utilitarian tradition, there was some danger in drawing attention to the fact. From ancient times Epicurean ethics had borne a most equivocal reputation. Its founder had often been accused of advocating a brutish, self-destructive life of pleasure-seeking, quite incompatible with the proper dignity of human beings. Indeed few ethical theories have divided opinion more sharply than Epicurean hedonism. In his own day, Epicurus was worshipped by his followers as the best of men, and reviled by his opponents as the worst. Even by the standards normal to the factious world of the Greek philosophical schools, the advocacy of pleasure as the supreme end of human life had generated passions of unusual intensity. Mill took a diplomatic risk in portraying utilitarianism as simply Epicureanism in modern guise.

But what did the historical Epicurus really teach? First and foremost, that we should live a simple life in accordance with nature, and that we obey her when 'we fulfil the necessary desires and also the physical, if they bring no harm to us, but sternly reject the harmful' (Epicurus 1926: 109). He believed that living well is living pleasantly, 'for we recognise pleasure as the first good innate in us, and from pleasure we begin every act and avoidance, and to pleasure we return again, using the feeling as the standard by which we judge every good' (87). Yet Epicurus was careful never to advocate the unstinted indulgence of our sensual appetites; such a life, he believed, would not, in the long run, prove the most pleasant. Instead he recommended the cultivation of prudence, because 'from prudence are sprung all the other virtues, and it teaches us that it is not possible to live pleasantly without living prudently and honourably and justly, nor again to live a life of prudence, honour and justice without living pleasantly' (91).

Despite the carefully stated moderation of Epicurus' prescriptions for living well, his ideas outraged the sterner moralists of the day, and set up a fierce resistance which medieval Christianity continued. Diogenes Laertius records that misunderstanding of his teaching began at an early date, stimulated by the publication of scurrilous and often fantastic misrepresentations of it. According to his calumniators, Epicurus spent enormous sums on food, and 'used to vomit twice a day owing to his luxurious living'; most damagingly, perhaps, he was said to be 'profoundly ignorant of philosophy' (145). If such tales had contained a grain of truth, there would have been some excuse for the view that the Epicurean philosophy was what its critics contended it was, 'a doctrine worthy only of swine'(J.S. Mill 1861: 210); but Epicurus' own fragmentary surviving writings consistently support Diogenes' very different picture of a saintly sage whose own preference was for 'a most simple and frugal life' (Epicurus 1926: 147).

Epicurus was a prolific writer, but of his works only three letters, a list of 'principal doctrines' and some scattered fragments survive. However, enough is extant of his own writings and those of his followers for us to form a fairly detailed impression of the Epicurean system. Whilst Epicurus' chief concern was with the question of how to live the most flourishing human life, he thought it an important propaedeutic to provide a careful account of the world in which men live. Epicurean natural philosophy maintains that all things come into existence by the chance motions of atoms, that gods of some sort exist but are remote from, and uninterested in, human affairs, and that the human soul (itself a concatenation of atoms) perishes along with the human body. Because there are, to all practical intents and purposes, no gods, and no survival of bodily death, Epicurus taught that people should devote their attention to achieving happiness in this present life, and reject as childish superstition all hopes and fears concering an afterlife. (For his denial of the immortality of the soul, Epicurus was later condemned by Dante to the Sixth Circle of the Inferno, the Circle of heretics.) The essence of the Epicurean philosophy is summed up in the two-word slogan of the poet Horace, *Carpe diem*. But the difficulty is to know in what manner we should 'seize the day'. As Torquatus, the spokesman for the Epicurean point of view in Cicero's dialogue *De finibus* put it, 'The Ends of Good and Evils themselves, that is, pleasure and pain, are not open to mistake; where people go wrong is in not knowing what things are productive of pleasure and pain' (Cicero 1931: 59).

So how did Epicurus himself think that the wise man should live? Not by the frenetic pursuit of wine, women and song, but by seeking health of body and serenity of soul (*ataraxia*). This is the aim of the life of blessedness, when physical and mental disturbance is banished, and 'the living creature has not to wander as though in search of something that is missing, and to look for some other thing by which he can fulfil the good of the soul and the good of the body' (Epicurus 1926: 87). Just

41

as the Epicurean community practised economic self-sufficiency within the walls of its Garden, the Epicurean man cultivates an inner self-sufficiency, a contentment in his own physical and mental states and a suppression of unnecessary desires. Epicurus conceded that the satisfaction of any desire is pleasant, and that no pleasure is bad in itself; but he warned that 'the means which produce some pleasures bring with them disturbances many times greater than the pleasures' (97). Someone who sets his mind on acquiring fame or riches condemns himself to a hectic and anxious life, with no sure hope of reaching his goal. It is better, in Epicurus' view, to seek 'the immunity which results from a quiet life and the retirement from the world' (99).

Achieving serenity does not require that all our desires be satisfied; many are better suppressed altogether as incompatible with *ataraxia*. Epicurus' rough rule of thumb is that the simpler a lifestyle, the more pleasant it is likely to be. He distinguished desires carefully into the categories of 'natural' and 'vain'. Vain desires are for frivolous and unnecessary objects and answer to no real need of our nature; satisfying them normally involves more trouble than it is worth. 'Natural' desires are subdivided into those which are genuinely necessary and those which are 'merely natural', and Epicurus explained that of those which are necessary, 'some are necessary for happiness, others for the repose of the body, and others for very life' (87). Thus the desire for food is not only natural but is also for something necessary to sustain life; on the other hand, a desire for love affairs is entirely natural, but (in Epicurus' opinion) its fulfilment is inessential to the good life. Epicurus recommended that we should suppress our vain desires, and keep our natural non-necessary ones under strict control, to prevent their destroying our serenity. Sexual desires attracted his particular scorn: 'the pleasures of love never profited a man', he asserted, 'and he is lucky if they do him no harm' (115). In brief: 'Nothing satisfies the man who is not satisfied with a little', and 'Self-sufficiency is the greatest of all riches' (137).

The ideal Epicurean leads a frugal life, eschewing luxuries and moderating his bodily desires. But he has a greater appetite for the pleasures of the mind. Mill's doctrine of 'higher pleasures' is clearly anticipated in Epicurus' observation that 'it is not continuous drinkings and revellings, nor the satisfaction of lusts, nor the enjoyment of fish and other luxuries of the wealthy table, which produce a pleasant life, but sober reasoning, searching out the motives for all choice and avoidance, and banishing mere opinions' (89/91). Like Plato and Aristotle, Epicurus held that the life of the philosopher is the most satisfying life of all; though he added characteristically that 'Of all the things which wisdom acquires to produce the blessedness of the complete life, far the greatest is the possession of friendship' (165). The Epicurean idea of perfect happiness is talking philosophy with one's friends, in a secluded garden far from the press of public affairs.

But Epicurus was enough of a realist to know that before a person can give himself whole-heartedly to the pursuit of philosophy, he requires a certain minimal level of physical and mental well-being. No one who is in severe pain or sorely troubled in mind will profit much from a discussion on the proper ends of human life. This was what Epicurus meant when he said that 'The beginning and the root of all good is the pleasure of the stomach; even wisdom and culture must be referred to this' (135); a much misunderstood remark, but one whose irony is evident when we recall its author's chronic stomach ache. Epicurus agreed with the Stoics that the truly wise man who had achieved *ataraxia* could never be wholly robbed of it, for even on the rack he could enjoy the happy recollection of his mastered desires and his well-ordered character; but he also allowed, more realistically than the Stoics, that a man on the rack would cry out and lament (165).

One puzzling feature of Epicurus' account is that he sometimes appears to equate the condition of painlessness with a state of *pleasure*. When someone with a chronic ailment finds himself for an hour without pain, he plainly experiences a very pleasant sense of relief; but, strictly speaking, it is the cessation of the pain, not its simple absence, which gives him pleasure. It seems odd to describe someone who has never endured stomach pain as being in a state of pleasure with regard to his stomach, and more plausible to characterise his case, as Aristotle did, as a neutral one, between pleasure and pain (Aristotle, *Nicomachean Ethics*, 1173a). But did Epicurus really mean to classify all painless states as pleasant ones?

This issue is not merely a verbal one, for it goes to the heart of what Epicurus meant by 'pleasure' (*hedone*). Cicero, a hostile critic, alleged that Epicurus simply displayed his confusion in conflating the ideas of pleasure and of absence of pain (Cicero 1931: 81f.); yet a careful examination of Epicurus' texts suggests that his use of the term 'pleasure' to cover both positive delights and certain pain-free states of body and mind was no confusion, but embodied a substantive and intriguing philosophical thesis about human well-being. Diogenes Laertius tells us that Epicurus distinguished pleasures into two kinds, the *kinetic*, which involve motion, and the *katastematic*, or those pertaining to stability of condition. 'Freedom from trouble in the mind and from pain in the body are static [i.e. katastematic] pleasures, but joy and exultation are considered as active pleasures involving motion' (Epicurus 1926: 169). Kinetic pleasures are those which from an everyday point of view we may think of as the paradigmatic pleasures; they are the ones we secure by putting ourselves into appropriate situations to obtain certain desirable experiences. The pleasures of playing a musical instrument, or tasting the cool spring water, or talking with our friends, require our performance of certain actions; they are essentially pleasures involving physical agency.

Katastematic, or static, pleasure is a little more difficult to understand. One recent writer has characterised it as follows:

> [I]t is the comfortable feeling that follows after the satisfaction of hunger or thirst, the relaxed condition that follows after attending the theater, a public festival or a banquet. Exceptionally, it describes the return to normal after the joy of escape from peril of life (DeWitt 1954: 243).

This account rightly emphasises the origin of katastematic pleasure in a sense of contrast between present and previous conditions of the self, and frees Epicurus from the charge of construing mere painlessness as a species of pleasure. However, it omits one crucial point. Katastematic pleasures are of especial significance in the Epicurean scheme because the best of them make the largest contribution to the state of *ataraxia* which is the prudent man's chief aim (Epicurus 1926: 89). Most important among katastematic pleasures are those reflective satisfactions a person enjoys when he surveys his life as a whole and finds his desires under control and directed on the right objects. (To be sure, reflection is a kind of activity, but it is not the sort of *physical* activity that makes a pleasure a kinetic one.) The most valuable katastematic pleasures are pleasures of a logically higher order than other pleasures; they are pleasures taken in reflecting on the appropriateness of one's lower pleasures and their well-ordering within a life that is stable, coherent and self-sufficient. Such katastematic pleasures, in fact, do not so much cause *ataraxia* as constitute it. True serenity consists in the joyous recognition that one is living the style of life most suitable to human nature – calm, simple and impeded neither by runaway desires nor by serious distresses of body or mind.

Like utilitarianism, Epicurean ethical teaching is anti-mystical, unpuritanical, and informed by a sense that human existence is to be justified internally, by the richness of its constituent experiences, rather than externally by its relation to God, or the cosmos, or some transcendental purpose. And like utilitarianism too, Epicureanism takes a *consequential-*

44

*ist* line on the standard of right and wrong. Epicurus held the feeling of pleasure to be the sole criterion by which we should judge every good (87), though he emphasised, as we have seen, the need for wisdom in choosing the pleasures which make our lives go best. A constant feature of Epicurus' moralising is an implicit denial of any constraints on action of a deontological kind. Thus in a letter to a friend he writes:

> You tell me that the stimulus of the flesh makes you too prone to the pleasures of love. Provided that you do not break the laws or good customs and do not distress any of your neighbours or do harm to your body or squander your pittance, you may indulge your inclination as you please (115).

Conspicuous by its absence here is any rigorist 'Thou shalt' or 'Thou shalt not', the deontologist's categorical imperatives of duty. Instead the focus falls on the likely practical consequences of adopting a particular mode of living. (Predictably, Epicurus suggested that his correspondent would be lucky to avoid all the pitfalls associated with free indulgence in the sexual life, and would do best to avoid it.) Virtues are valued only because they facilitate the life of pleasure. Epicurus rejected as pernicious the praise of virtues which are of no help in improving the quality of life. To another friend he wrote, 'But I summon you to continuous pleasures and not to vain and empty virtues which have but disturbing hopes of results' (127).

There is, however, one striking difference between Epicureanism and classical utilitarian theories. Although in all utilitarian theories freedom from pain is seen as a desirable state, there is no inclination to exalt *ataraxia*, or serenity, as the highest goal of human lives. *Ataraxia* has never been a prominent leitmotif of utilitarianism, because placing the pursuit of personal *ataraxia* centre-stage in one's life makes it difficult to sustain a lively concern for the interests of other people. Utilitarians must find it difficult to give more than one cheer for the pursuit of *ataraxia*, because as a major goal of our lives it is not readily compatible with promoting the general welfare. Like Mo Tzŭ and Jesus, Epicurus was personally noted for the benevolence of his character; and throughout his works, friendship receives the highest praise. 'Friendship goes dancing round the world,' he wrote, 'proclaiming to us all to awake to the praises of a happy life' (115).

Yet Epicurus, like Aristotle but unlike Christ or Master Mo, saw as the starting point of ethical reflection the question: what is the best, and most rewarding, form of life for a human being to live, the life which is most suitable for beings with our nature? Despite Epicurus' warm regard

45

for friendship, there is something distinctly non-utilitarian in the notion of shutting oneself off (literally or figuratively) from the wider community to engage in the single-minded pursuit of the good life in the company of a select band of friends. 'As many as possess the power to procure complete immunity from their neighbours,' Epicurus wrote, 'these also live most pleasantly with one another, since they have the most certain pledge of security' (105). But the idea of trying to attain such security from other people is incompatible with both the universalist and the maximising strands in utilitarianism. It is even possible to start doubting the purity of the motives of Epicurean *friends* in their relations with one another, given Epicurus' admission that, while all friendship is desirable in itself, 'it starts from the need of help' (109). Having friends is valuable, on this view, just because they help us to pursue the good life and achieve serenity. Whatever Epicurus' personal feelings for his friends might have been, his official teaching on friendship seems little advance on the cool-blooded Aristotelian position that rational friendship is rooted in a person's love for himself (Aristotle, *Nicomachean Ethics*, IX). But Epicurus, more than Aristotle or other Greek thinkers, invites a charge of moral solipsism by his advice to withdraw as fully as possible from the turmoil of the world and to seek tranquillity of soul in a place apart. That Epicureans made bad citizens, by their deliberate disengagement from the concerns of their fellows, was a common complaint in antiquity from critics not otherwise noted for a Kantian respect for humanity. It is difficult not to see Epicureanism as smug and self-indulgent in its detachment from the troubles of humanity.

Utilitarians, no less than other people, value peace of mind. They can also pride themselves on achieving a certain mental or emotional equilibrium, or on suppressing a disturbing desire. But they cannot favour the search for a state of ataractic contentment attained through a deliberate exclusion of all aspects of the external world which threaten to disturb their self-complacency. Caring only about one's own serenity argues a self-absorbedness which true utilitarians must deplore. The real Achilles' heel of Epicureanism, then, is not its hedonist theory of value, but its promulgation of a goal of tranquillity in a world to which tranquillity is generally an inappropriate response. Taking refuge in a garden bounded by stone walls or by the limits of the self represents a selfish refusal to be drawn by the ethical pull of others who require our help. The best utilitarian theories are an improvement upon Epicureanism because they preserve its virtues but avoid its key defect. Mill said that people should frame 'an indissoluble association' between their own happiness and that of others; and utilitarian moral education, unlike

Epicurean, tries to ensure that 'a direct impulse to promote the general good may be in every individual one of the habitual motives of action, and the sentiments connected therewith may fill a large and prominent place in every human being's sentient existence' (J.S. Mill 1861: 218).

# CHAPTER III

# Utilitarianism and Enlightenment

'Oh Happiness! Our being's end and aim.'
           – Alexander Pope, *Essay on Man*, Epistle 4, l. 1

Utilitarianism during the Christian Middle Ages was not a philosophy; but it was occasionally a style of argument. St Thomas Aquinas held that a state might legitimately permit prostitution to avert greater ills (he presumably thought the damnation of one prostitute less serious than that of many adulterous wives). And Richard of St Victor employed what we should now call 'rule-utilitarian' reasoning to defend the secrecy of the confessional. Although it might sometimes be *utile* to the confessing person to reveal a sin disclosed under the seal of secrecy, it is more conducive to public good (to which charity gives precedence over individual good) to maintain the absolute confidentiality of the sacrament.[1] Such examples of utilitarian logic are fairly common, but they do not amount to an outlook on life. Whatever Christ himself may have thought, the medieval Church saw the present life as pre-eminently a period of probation determining man's destination for eternity. Happiness in the next world, not this, was what counted; and man's business on earth was to earn that happiness by scrupulous adherence to God's law. Saints took rejection of worldly happiness further still: they endeavoured to earn extra merit by eschewing all earthly comforts and deliberately cultivating hardship. But for ordinary folk, strait was the gate and narrow the way which led to paradise. Even moderate self-denial, thought the noted preacher Robertus Caracciolus in the fifteenth century, was beyond the capacity of most people; consequently almost everybody would be damned. Generally speaking, the Middle Ages was not a period of optimism about human possibilities; the perceived distance between divine perfection and human imperfection was simply too great.

    The Renaissance initiated the long process of transition from a

God-centred to a man-centred universe. Neoplatonist philosophers like Marsilio Ficino and Pico della Mirandola reacted against medieval notions of human worthlessness, and reasserted ancient ideas of the dignity of man, the uniquely rational animal (see Kristeller 1972). The seventeenth century also witnessed a revival of interest in the thought of Epicurus, culminating in France in the apologetic of Pierre Gassendi. Meanwhile in England Thomas Hobbes's *Leviathan* gave serious weight to the fact that people have an interest in being happy in the present life, and proposed political strategies for dealing with the conflicts of interests that inevitably arise from human insecurity, vanity and greed.

But we can move swiftly forward to the next century to resume the main thread of our story. The eighteenth century was the green youth of utilitarianism, as the nineteenth was its prime. Almost all of the character-istic theses of utilitarianism had made their appearance by 1800, many of them before the advent of the term 'utilitarian'. Utilitarianism has been justly called the dominant philosophy of the mature Enlightenment (P. Gay 1973: 459).[2] This was a role for which it had several significant quali-fications. To begin with, it claimed to be rooted in the scientific study of human nature, substituting for ideas based on religion, myth or guesswork empirical theories of sensation, motivation, and the intellectual operations of the mind. It could also be seen as a socially progressive philosophy, for many existing political, social, economic, legal and religious institutions beloved by conservatives appeared plainly defective by the test of public happiness. Utilitarianism embodied, too, a rationalism that, to enlightened minds, seemed admirably fitted to sweep away moribund ideas and the profitless practices they sustained. It gave hope to men like the Marquis de Condorcet, who believed passionately in the perfectibility of man and the possibility (under suitable arrangements) of true human happiness on earth. Writing in the shadow of the guillotine, Condorcet looked forward to a future epoch of the world in which no one would go hungry, when all illnesses could be cured and life expectancy increased without limit, slaves would be freed and women gain equality with men, war would be abolished and the arts and education flourish (Condorcet 1794). This was a more comprehensive scheme of improvement than any dreamed of by Bentham, and a good deal more utopian; but it exemplified a similar impatience with the status quo and the same sanguine belief in the power for change of an energetic good will supported by science.

Utilitarian ideas appealed also for their secular, this-worldly character, their unindebtedness to Jerusalem, Rome or Geneva. They answered (as the Kantian ethic did too, in a different way) to the *philosophes*' demand for a non-religious, rational morality which would treat human beings as ends in themselves and their lives as valuable irrespective of their place in a divine plan. Moreover utilitarians ascribed to all human beings an equal moral status, regardless of race, sex, age or class. Kant defined 'Enlightenment' (*Aufklärung*) as the 'exit by man from his own self-imposed minority', when he begins to rely on his own understanding and rejects the guidance of others (Kant 1793: 34). Utilitarian moral thought was 'enlightened' in this Kantian sense: utilitarians refused to be guided by authority, and insisted on working out their own positions from first principles.

## 1 Chastellux and Helvétius

Jean François, Marquis de Chastellux and Claude Helvétius exemplify perhaps better than any other writers the specific flavour of utilitarianism in pre-revolutionary France. Both were deeply committed to the improvement of the condition of the poor and believed that governments had a duty to foster the general good; both thought that, as Helvétius put it, 'wise laws would be able without doubt to bring about the miracle of a universal happiness' (Helvétius 1774: 187).[3] For these writers, as for others of their compatriots, utilitarianism was primarily a political philosophy and less a theory of personal morality. Further, it was a philosophy which offered what seemed to them a clear-cut and highly practical recipe for political action: governments should first of all find out what makes people happy, then devise appropriate social strategies to bring that happiness about. Subsequent experience of well-meant but often disastrous social experiments from 1789 to the fall of communism may make us question how straightforward this programme really was; but nothing can destroy the credit of the *philosophes* for promulgating it, at considerable personal risk, in the France of the *ancien régime*.

'It is an indisputable point, (or at least, there is room to think it, in this philosophical age, an acknowledged truth)' wrote the Marquis de Chastellux in his essay *De la félicité publique* (translated into English as the *Essay Concerning Human Happiness*), 'that the first object of all governments, should be to render the people happy' (Chastellux 1774: vol. 1, 50). In order to discover how governments could best do this, Chastellux turned to history. What past nation, he asked, had been the happiest? To answer this question called for an investigation of social history from ancient times to the present, a daunting project on which Chastellux duly embarked. Yet the disappointing, if unsurprising, conclusion of his ambitious survey was that no society had yet discovered how to bring about the general happiness; the 'history of happiness' was, in truth, the history of unhappiness. There had indeed been pockets of happiness from time to time, and some promising attempts made to establish it on a systematic basis: early Christianity, for instance, had taught the value of equality, charity, beneficence and the distribution of alms, before the 'spirit of charity' had been submerged by the 'spirit of discussion' and the bickering of theologians (vol. 1, 322–3). But human society was a mere 3,000 years old – hardly long enough, Chastellux thought, for people to learn how to live in peace with one another (vol. 1, xxii). There remained good hope for the future: the mistakes of the past, once understood, could be avoided, while recent developments in industrial and agricultural technology promised to alleviate the terrible drudgery of the poor. Knowledge and liberty were the twin routes to social improvement and would assuredly lead in time to *'the acquisition of the greatest happiness of the greatest number'* (vol. 2, 180).[4]

A more powerful thinker than Chastellux, Helvétius is the most important, and the most forthright, of the Gallic utilitarians. In place of Chastellux's often fanciful and impressionistic history, Helvétius presented in his works *De l'esprit* (1758) and *De l'homme* (1771) a detailed theory of human nature designed to show how men could be made happy through the fulfilment of their fundamental needs. Although some of his early readers objected to the relentlessly egoistic picture of human beings he painted, Helvétius believed that through carefully managed education individuals could be moulded into cooperative citizens of communities enjoying a high level of general happiness. The work of the legislator was itself a species of education: 'It is solely through good laws that one can form good men. Thus the whole art of the legislator consists of forcing men, by the sentiment of self-love, to be always just to one another' (Helvétius 1758: 176). Justice was to be encouraged by convincing people that to be happy one did not need to be rich or powerful. The grounds of happiness exist in everyone, without regard to wealth or status: a person is happy when his primitive physical and social needs, for example, for eating, drinking, sleeping, shelter, sex and friendship, are satisfied. Being nourished is all a man requires, not the synthetic delights of a rich man's table. Wealthy people are in fact often bored, because they do not have to work towards the fulfilment of their own needs, a major source of human contentment; '[t]he man who is occupied,' thought Helvétius, 'is the happy man' (Helvétius 1771: vol. 2, 190). Happiness consists in doing moderate labour in the intervals of satisfying one's basic natural requirements.

Helvétius was under no illusions that the happy society envisaged in his model would be easy to bring about. There were too many sectional interests which stood in the way, as well as unthinking custom and prejudice. Therefore, philosophers must become educators, instructing people in the real nature of happiness and ridding them of false ideas about the good life. No individual or society whose conception of human welfare rested on fantasy could hope to attain happiness. 'Oh truth, you are the divinity of noble souls', Helvétius declared; and when princes can be brought to love truth, 'happiness and virtue prevail under them in their empire' (283–4).

The constructive problem for the philosopher, as Helvétius conceived it, had two main parts:

> The object of the first must be the discovery of laws suitable to render men as happy as possible, to procure for them consequently all the enjoyments and pleasures compatible with the public good. . . . The object of the second must be the discovery of means by which one may insensibly raise the people from the state of misery they now endure to the state of happiness they are capable of enjoying (258–9).

The first was the more general task, calling on a knowledge of universal human nature; the second had regard to the peculiar institutions and conditions of life existing within a particular polity, such as France. Helvétius further hoped that a form of society could be devised in which no individual's private interest would ever be contrary to the general good (294). This utopian result was to be obtained not just by placing institutional constraints on people's ability to acquire powers, privileges and property, but by devising an educational scheme to limit what they should *want* to acquire. Helvétius's programme is both ambitious and disturbing; it not only places extraordinary demands on educators but, more worryingly, it seriously threatens the capacity of persons to live lives which express their own individuality. But in his more realistic moments, Helvétius refrained from condemning private interests which are merely in *potential* conflict with the public good, and required only that people be prepared to relinquish those interests in situations of *actual* conflict. Even this more limited objective, however, would require an educational system capable of turning out saints, and it would certainly not please those present-day critics who find utilitarians much too ready to demand self-sacrifice from individuals in the name of the general good.

But in pressing these criticisms we must take care not to lose our historical perspective. Helvétius's intended target was not individuality, but the gross social disparities of rich and poor in eighteenth-century Europe. French utilitarianism was not so much careless of the individual, as careful of the mass of people whose interests were invariably subordinated to those of rich and powerful minorities. The clarion call of public happiness in a pre-democratic age evoked different emotions, and raised different conceptual issues, than talk of the general utility does in the late twentieth century. Our present worries about the interests of individuals and minorities are premised on the political power of the majority in modern western states. What rightly mattered more to an eighteenth-century utilitarian was the domination of the many by the few. All men, Helvétius believed, had a right to an 'equal felicity' (194); and philosophers should help to ensure that they obtained it.

## 2 Hutcheson

The Scottish philosopher Francis Hutcheson (1694–1746) was the first to speak of the greatest happiness of the greatest number; more importantly, he bears the distinction of being the earliest writer to enunciate a philosophy that can without qualification be termed 'utilitarian'. That this has not always been grasped is because Hutcheson is also a major representative of an approach to ethics which is often considered to be incompatible with utilitarianism, that which maintains that moral truth is revealed not by any form of reasoning but by a special 'moral sense'. In Hutcheson's case, however, there is no real opposition between these positions: moral sense and consequentialist reasoning are assigned different but complementary roles in moral reflection. In his early work *An Inquiry concerning the original of our Ideas of Virtue or Moral Good* (1725), Hutcheson argued that human beings are endowed by nature with benevolent as well as selfish impulses, and that the impulse to benevolence becomes 'the universal Foundation' of 'a Sense of Goodness and moral Beauty in Actions, distinct from Advantage' (Selby-Bigge 1897: vol. 1, 118, 114). A being who was totally indifferent to what happened to others could never approve of a charitable act or disapprove of a cruel one; he would be without the emotional equipment to perceive the beauty of the former and the vileness of the latter. But in Hutcheson's view, a moral sense founded on benevolence focuses specifically on the advantageous and disadvantageous consequences of actions: so 'when we are ask'd the Reason of our Approbation of any Action, we perpetually alledge its Usefulness to the Publick, and not to the Actor himself'. And if we want to defend a censured action, we will argue 'That it injur'd no body, or did more Good than Harm' (118). The picture which emerges from Hutcheson's discussion is of a division of labour, in which the moral sense causes us to look with favour on actions which benefit others and disfavour those which harm them, while consequentialist reasoning determines a more precise ranking order of practical options in given situations. Our moral sense may, for instance, inform us of the beauty in general of acts of telling the truth and of saving innocent lives; but faced with a case in which an innocent life can only be saved by telling a lie, consequentialist reasoning will guide us towards telling the lie.

Hutcheson admittedly did not always make as clear as he might have done the relations of the roles of moral sense and moral reason. This is true even in a passage whose place in the development of early utilitarianism is significant enough for it to be quoted at length:

> In comparing the moral Qualitys of Actions, in order to regulate our Election among various Actions propos'd, or to find which of them has the greatest moral Excellency, we are led by our moral Sense of Virtue to judge thus; that in equal Degrees of Happiness, expected to proceed from the Action, the Virtue is in proportion to the Number of Persons to whom the Happiness shall extend; (and here the Dignity, or moral Importance of Persons shall compensate Numbers) and in equal Numbers, the Virtue is as the Quantity of the Happiness, or natural Good; or that the Virtue is in a compound Ratio of the Quantity of Good, and Number of Enjoyers. In the same manner, the moral Evil, or Vice, is as the Degree of Misery, and Numbers of Sufferers; so that, that Action is best, which procures the greatest Happiness for the greatest Numbers; and that, worst, which, in like manner, occasions Misery (106–7).

In spite of the explicit reference here to the moral sense, it is plain from the passage that Hutcheson means to accord a considerable role to consequentialist reasoning in the evaluation of actions. When we judge and compare actions, we need to weigh up rationally a number of factors: the amount of happiness or misery they will generate, the number of people potentially affected, and the 'Dignity or moral Importance of [the] Persons' concerned (for example, we should avoid benevolence which 'encourages' evil people 'in their bad Intentions, or makes them more capable of Mischief' (106)). Hutcheson adds that we may reasonably judge it right to perform an ill act for the sake of a greater benefit: for 'an immense Good to few, may preponderate a small Evil to many' (107; cf. Hutcheson 1755: vol. 1, 231). These consequentialist reflections are followed by a remarkable anticipation of Jeremy Bentham, when Hutcheson sketches out a 'universal Canon to compute the Morality [i.e. the praiseworthiness] of any Actions', involving the mathematical treatment of several variables including the 'Moments' of good and evil (both public and private), and the degrees of ability and benevolence of the agent (Selby-Bigge 1897: section III. xi). Such appraisal of actions and agents would obviously far outrun the capacities of a purely intuitive moral sense.

Hutcheson's posthumously published book *A System of Moral Philosophy* (1755) repeats, in essence, the utilitarian content of the *Inquiry*, but is notable for its more subtle treatment of the nature of the good life, wherein it anticipates not so much Bentham as J.S. Mill. One important feature of the good life is that it will be a *virtuous* life. In Hutcheson's view, 'to maintain the calm and most extensive affection toward the universal happiness, able to control all narrower affections when there is any opposition, and the sacrificing all narrow interests to the most extensive . . . is the highest perfection of human virtue' (Hutcheson 1755: vol. 1, 243). But Hutcheson displays a kindly tolerance towards those who find such demanding virtue too difficult. When narrower affections overpower wider ones, this is forgivable where the narrower affections are good in themselves: 'any of those tender affections extenuate the guilt more than any merely selfish principle could have done' (243).

Hutcheson believes that we are naturally inclined to want, and to work for, our own happiness and that of other people. As for what happiness is, it consists, for any being, 'in the full enjoyment of all the gratifications its nature desires and is capable of' (100). But he immediately explains that pleasures can be divided into 'higher' and 'lower' categories, and that greater happiness ensues from pursuing the former than the latter. (Indeed we should pursue only as many of the lower pleasures as our enjoyment of the higher leaves us time and energy for (100).) Higher pleasures tend to be more durable and more dignified than lower pleasures, though not always as intense:

> We have an immediate sense of a dignity, a perfection, or beatifick quality in some kinds, which no intenseness of the lower kinds can equal, were they also as lasting as we could wish. No intenseness or duration of any external sensation gives it a dignity or worth equal to that of the improvement of the soul by knowledge, or the ingenious arts; and much less is it equal to that of virtuous affections and action (117).

Such passages look backward to Epicurus, as well as forward to Mill. But Hutcheson is at his most strikingly similar to Mill when he attempts to locate a criterion by which higher pleasures may be distinguished from lower ones. Like Mill, Hutcheson believes that people do not necessarily possess 'equal happiness when each can gratify all the desires and senses he has' (120). Persons enjoy a more profound happiness in proportion to their capacity to appreciate the higher pleasures. And they know that this happiness is greater when they have experienced both higher and lower pleasures, and found the latter wanting in the qualities of the former.

> The superior orders in this world probably experience all the sensations of the lower orders, and can judge of them. But the inferior do not experience the enjoyments of the superior.... we are more immediately conscious that one gratification is more excellent than another, when we have experienced both (120).

Shorn of the gratuitous identification of people of greater discernment with people of higher social status, this is very close to Mill's proposal that

> Of two pleasures, if there is one to which all or almost all who have experience of both give a decided preference, irrespective of any feeling of moral obligation to prefer it, that is the more desirable pleasure (J.S. Mill 1861: 211).

But this is a notoriously problematic criterion, as many critics have pointed out. One obvious objection to Mill's version is that it is very unlikely in practice to yield the answers which he wants it to yield. Suppose we wish to know whether classical music provides a higher pleasure, and thus more happiness, than pop music, or poetry a more profound satisfaction than football. An unbiased survey of popular tastes would undoubtedly show that people in general prefer low-brow to high-brow activities. Few people in contemporary society have heard no classical music, yet the vast majority still firmly prefers pop. Mill tries to tighten his criterion by stipulating that the only persons qualified to judge quality are those who are 'competently acquainted' with both of the pleasures being assessed: people, in other words, who are 'equally acquainted with, and equally capable of appreciating and enjoying, both' (211). But this refinement takes us little further forward; not all football-playing philosophers, for instance, would estimate philosophy superior to soccer in point of *pleasure*. (If, however, Mill's reference to competence is really intended to restrict the pool of judges to persons who are going to give the 'right' verdicts, then it is patently question-begging.) The fact is that no coherent ordering of higher and lower pleasures can be determined by preference-rankings based solely on feelings of pleasurableness. Pleasures can be meaningfully distinguished as 'higher' and 'lower' only by a criterion which makes reference to values other than pleasure alone.

Hutcheson's socially élitist form of the criterion is no more satisfactory. Most eighteenth-century 'superior people' preferred the delights of the hunting field or the ballroom to the pleasures of poetry and art. To be sure, Hutcheson sometimes appears to abandon his social conception of superior beings, and consider them instead as the people who possess 'diviner faculties and fuller knowledge' (Hutcheson 1755: vol. 1, 121). On this account, the ideal assessors are those experienced people (whatever their social position) who have 'their tastes and appetites in a natural vigorous state' and can 'immediately discern what are the noblest [pleasures]' (121). But this strongly suggests that Hutcheson has already decided which pleasures should count as noble; and if so he is begging the question. Moreover, if sound judges are by definition those who prefer noble to ignoble pleasures, then noble (i.e. higher) pleasures cannot be defined as those which sound judges prefer.

Hutcheson's moral philosophy is not always perfectly clear, consistent or cogent, but it is an intriguing and suggestive system worth closer attention than it usually receives. More than any other writer, Hutcheson deserves the title of father of British utilitarianism. His work contains, if sometimes in rudimentary form, most of the ideas which were characteristic of utilitarianism in its early period. All the leitmotifs of utilitarianism can be found in his books. Hutcheson was a consequentialist who believed that well-being (happiness) was the proper target of human action. He never questioned that both happiness and misery were aggregative commodities. And he held that we should always endeavour to maximise the happiness and minimise the misery of the largest number of people whom we are able to affect. Hutcheson did not grasp all the possibilities of utilitarianism, or foresee all of its problems. But his very considerable achievement was to lay the solid foundations on which others could build.

### 3 Hume

David Hume (1711–76) combined, in a highly original way, a theory of moral sense with a rejection of moral realism. Traditionally philosophers who maintained the existence of a moral sense conceived of it as an avenue to knowledge of ethical truth – a kind of 'inward eye', in Shaftesbury's phrase, that 'distinguishes and sees the fair and shapely, the amiable and admirable, apart from the deformed, the foul, the odious or the despicable' (Shaftesbury 1773: vol. 2, 415). Hume thought moral sensibility a real enough phenomenon, but denied it such an epistemic role.

Take any action allow'd to be vicious: Wilful murder, for instance. Examine it in all lights, and see if you can find that matter of fact, or real existence, which you call *vice*. In which-ever way you take it, you find only certain passions, motives, volitions and thoughts. There is no other matter of fact in the case. The vice entirely escapes you, as long as you consider the object. You can never find it, till you turn your reflexion into your own breast, and find a sentiment of disapprobation, which arises in you, towards this action. Here is a matter of fact; but 'tis the object of feeling, not of reason (Hume 1739: 468–9).

Hume did not intend to dispute the reality of vice, but he did mean to deny a particular (objectivist) analysis of it. Although we standardly speak of things as *being* good or bad, right or wrong, moral qualities properly understood are, in his view, projections on to the world of our (natural or socially instilled) feelings of favour and disfavour. By this Hume did not mean that things are determined as good or bad simply according to whether they give us pleasure or its opposite; rather, moral feelings are feelings of a special kind (a distinctive kind of pleasure and pain) which we entertain about certain characters, actions and states of affairs. Moral judgements express these feelings of approbation and disapprobation; they do not ascribe objective moral qualities to things.

Hume's theory of moral judgement has very reasonably been regarded as foreshadowing twentieth-century non-cognitivist theories of ethics. But what chiefly makes him interesting in the history of utilitarianism is his account of the grounds of our moral sentiments of approval and disapproval, praise and blame. Like Hutcheson and Joseph Butler, but unlike Hobbes and La Rochefoucauld, Hume disbelieved that human beings are purely selfish. We are all, he thought, naturally capable of caring about the welfare of others, even if our benevolent and sympathetic sentiments are often overborne by our egoism. 'There is no such passion,' he suggested in the *Treatise of Human Nature* (1739), 'as the love of mankind, merely as such'; yet if we are not capable of loving humanity in the abstract, we are able to feel an altruistic concern even about total strangers once we are brought into contact with them: "Tis true, there is no human, and indeed no sensible, creature, whose happiness or misery does not, in some measure, affect us, when brought near to us, and represented in lively colours' (481).[5] This ability to feel for the happiness and suffering of others Hume believed to be the psychological basis of our moral sentiments: we approve of voluntary actions which increase people's happiness; we disapprove of those which increase their misery.

> Have we any difficulty to comprehend the force of humanity and benevolence? Or to conceive, that the very aspect of happiness, joy, prosperity, gives pleasure; that of pain, suffering, sorrow, communicates uneasiness? (Hume 1751: 220)

Such 'principles of humanity' have a considerable influence on our actions. They likewise 'have *some* authority over our sentiments, and give us a general approbation of what is useful to society, and blame of what is dangerous or pernicious' (226). Thus notions of utility underpin our concepts of virtue and vice: 'we pronounce any *quality* of the mind virtuous, which causes love or pride; and any one vicious, which causes hatred or humility [i.e. humiliation]' (Hume 1739: 575). Hume thought the point especially clear with regard to the 'artificial virtues', that is, those, like justice in the distribution of goods or modesty or good manners, which are not natural to us but are 'human contrivances for the good of society' (577). If, through some changes in circumstances or psychology (say, goods became very abundant or very scarce, or human beings became perfectly humane or wholly malicious), justice ceased to be profitable, it would also cease to be virtuous: 'By rendering justice totally *useless*, you thereby totally destroy its essence, and suspend its obligation upon mankind' (Hume 1751: 188). In short, 'the circumstance of *utility*, in all subjects, is a source of praise and approbation', and 'is constantly appealed to in all moral decisions concerning the merit and demerit of actions' (231).

Hume, unusually among early utilitarians, was a conservative in politics, a Tory who disbelieved that the cause of public happiness required any substantial changes to the social status quo. There were, of course, more ways than one of interpreting the *Enquiry*'s keynote term 'utility', as subsequent writers were to show. But Hume contributed much more than a word to the development of the theory. He demonstrated more forcefully than his predecessors had done how well utilitarian principles fitted into a demystified, naturalised conception of the moral life. His vigorous attack on moral realism and his subtle analysis of the psychology and phenomenology of moral experience indeed seemed to leave moral philosophy with nowhere else to go. Hume thought it a simple 'matter of fact' that sentiments of humanity and sympathy lead human beings to approve or disapprove of actions, virtues and practices on the basis of their utility. Hence utility 'is a foundation of the chief part of morals, which has a reference to mankind and our fellow-creatures' (231). Hume may have been no radical in politics, but he was uncompromising in his support for the central tenet of utilitarianism.

## 4 Priestley and Paley

Not all utilitarians wished to put moral theory on a purely secular footing. Some considered it important to emphasise that happiness is not only what human beings desire for themselves but also what a benevolent deity desires for them. Richard Cumberland in the late seventeenth century and John Gay in the early eighteenth accordingly argued that fostering the general happiness is a duty imposed upon us by God (Cumberland 1672; J. Gay 1731). But 'theological utilitarianism' found its most important defenders in the later eighteenth century, in the persons of two clergymen of strongly contrasting character and outlook, Joseph Priestley (1733–1804) and William Paley (1743–1805).

Priestley was a Unitarian minister of Nantwich in Cheshire, a chemist, philosopher and extreme political radical. His chapel, house and scientific instruments were destroyed in a riot following his celebration of the fall of the Bastille, and popular opposition to his enthusiastic support of the French Revolution finally forced him to seek refuge in America. In his *Essay on the First Principles of Government* of 1768, Priestley looked forward to a 'glorious and paradisiacal' state of human society, in which civil and religious liberty would flourish and enlightened governments would see their role as the promotion of the people's happiness (Priestley n.d.(b): vol. 22, 9–10). The form of government best equipped to bring about this outcome, he argued, was that of an 'equal republic', in which each person would sense his own importance and know himself an equal citizen with every other (26, 48). In a slightly later work, the *Institutes of Natural and Revealed Religion* of 1772–74, Priestley was more explicit about the religious sanction for such political ideals. God, he said, has 'made us, to be happy' – but not selfishly to seek our own happiness and ignore other people's:

> Since ... the Divine goodness is general, and impartial, and he must, consequently, prefer the happiness of the *whole* to that of any *individuals*, it cannot be his pleasure, that we should consult our own interest, at the expense of that of others. Considering ourselves, therefore, not as separate individuals, but as members of society, another object that we ought to have in view is, the welfare of our fellow-creatures and of mankind at large (Priestley n.d.(a): vol. 2, 26–7).

Like other theological utilitarians, Priestley thought that God's moral commandment could be summed up as the utilitarian precept to promote the general happiness:

Strictly speaking, there are no more than two just and independent principles of human conduct, according to the light of nature, one of which is obedience to the will of God, and the other a regard to our real happiness; for another rule, which is a regard to the happiness of others, exactly coincides with a regard to the will of God; since all that we know of the will of God, according to the light of nature, is his desire that his creatures should be happy, and therefore that they should contribute to the happiness of each other (25).

This passage is not without its difficulties. Priestley leaves it obscure exactly how the 'light of nature' is supposed to reveal to us God's will, or the obligation to obey it. And it is doubtful whether he has distinguished clearly between moral and psychological senses of the phrase 'principles of human conduct'. (Is a 'regard to our own happiness' meant to be a *moral* obligation, or merely a natural principle of human psychology?) But Priestley is philosophically at his most interesting when he confronts an issue which was later to worry Sidgwick, and which troubles utilitarians at the present day.

How morally reasonable or psychologically realistic is it to ask that we should think of ourselves, as Priestley puts it, 'not as separate individuals, but [only] as members of society'? If this is what God demands of us, does he require a sacrifice of personal interests of which only exceptional people are capable? Moreover, could a person 'feel his own importance', as Priestley expects the citizens of his ideal republic to do, if he regarded his own interests as no more significant *to him* than the interests of everyone else? It is hard to see how someone could maintain a sense of his importance as an individual if he were allowed no scope to pursue those personal commitments which not only express but in a considerable degree constitute his individuality. Priestley's response to these problems was to suggest that, whatever first appearances suggest, utility *will* in practice be maximised if we regulate our conduct towards others 'according to those connexions in life that are of the most importance to our own happiness' (47). God, he suggested, does not wish us to mortify ourselves: he gave us a taste for pleasures in order that we should be happy; and while we do better to prefer the pleasures of the intellect and imagination to that sensory pleasure which 'sinks a man below his natural level', we are only positively prohibited from indulging in those pleasures which harm other people (47–8). Moreover our beneficence 'should flow the most freely towards those whom we can most conveniently and effectually serve' – in most cases the people closest to us in our daily lives – for 'if every person, without any particular regard to his own limited province, should extend his care to the wants of mankind in general, very little good would, in fact, be done by any' (46).

There is undoubtedly a core of good sense to these proposals. A community of selfless (or, as we might more significantly write it, *self-less*) individuals who consider all human beings, including themselves, with strict impartiality has a poorer prospect of happiness than a society of highly partial Epicureans. Yet Priestley's suggestion that we almost always do most to maximise the general happiness when we seek to enhance our own happiness and that of people to whom we are emotionally attached seems a little too convenient to be entirely convincing. It is easy to think of cases where maximising the general good calls for a sacrifice of such personal interests. The money we spend on the annual family holiday would prevent an African family from starving for a year; the time we devote to our private hobbies and recreations could be spent assisting sick or disadvantaged people to satisfy their basic needs. And there is a further problem about motivation to which Priestley, like all other early utilitarian writers, is oblivious. To the extent that the general happiness calls for individuals to devote special attention to their own interests, the question arises whether they should self-consciously adopt this perspective only as the most effective means of maximising the general good. This question poses an apparent difficulty for utilitarians. An affirmative answer implies that people should not, at the deepest level, think of themselves as other than utility-maximising agents, which seems to render the agent-centredness of their concerns superficial and leave their individuality under threat. On the other hand, a negative answer suggests that utilitarian ends are best served where people do not believe in, or at least do not consider, the maximising demand of utilitarianism This is not a logically inconsistent position, if utilitarianism is conceived as a theory of moral justification rather than as a decision procedure, yet many critics of the theory (and some utilitarians too) have understandably found an air of paradox about it.[6]

Problems about moral motivation surface also in the work of William Paley, in his day a far more popular writer than Priestley. He has been described as 'a most lucid and elegant expositor' of theological utilitarianism (Quinton 1973: 25),[7] but as a reasoner he is seldom impressive. A pillar of the Anglican Church, Paley held many benefices before rising to become Archdeacon of Carlisle and Subdean of Lincoln. He was a political and moral conservative, holding particularly strong views on the proper behaviour of women. While a Fellow of Christ's College, Cambridge, he ordered a student boycott of a theatrical performance because the mistress of a well-known nobleman was expected to attend it; and in the influential *Principles of Moral and Political Philosophy* of 1785 he recommended that adulterous women should have their property confiscated and be treated legally as if they were dead. (Male adultery did not, in Paley's view, merit similar sanctions) (Paley 1819: 241–2).

Paley defined happiness as the state in which 'the amount or aggregate of pleasure exceeds that of pain' (16). But like most other utilitarians, he considered that some kinds of pleasure contributed more to a person's happiness than others. Not much was to be expected, he thought, from the pleasures of the senses, from those pertaining to 'greatness, rank, or elevated status', or even from aesthetic pleasures in the contemplation of 'music, painting, architecture'; all these were too transient and apt to cloy (18–21). More conducive to happiness were pleasures arising from 'the exercise of the social affections', from 'the pursuit of our faculties . . . in the pursuit of some engaging end', from the 'prudent constitution of the habits' and from the absence of bodily and mental distresses (25–30). Happiness does not require wealth, and is perfectly consistent with labour, so it is fairly evenly distributed through the social classes (from which Paley inferred that attempts to eliminate inequalities of status and income were pointless) (31).

'Virtue' he defined as 'the duty of doing good to mankind, in obedience to the will of God, and for the sake of everlasting happiness' (41). Every person has a 'violent motive' for doing good in this world, as the condition of his happiness in the next; '[t]herefore private happiness is our motive, and the will of God our rule' (45–6). Acting well means obeying God's will; and 'The method of coming at the will of God, concerning any action, by the light of nature, is to inquire into "the tendency of the action to promote or diminish the general happiness."' This rule proceeds 'upon the presumption, that God Almighty wills and wishes the happiness of his creatures' (50). What is striking in this account is Paley's appeal to a purely egoistic motive for doing good to others. If Paley believed that men were made in God's image and likeness, he apparently did not think that the similarities extended as far as a benevolent disposition. God wishes human beings to be happy because he is benevolent: *we* should do what we can to make people happy because God orders it, and only by obeying his command will we secure a place in paradise. Although Paley talked of the pleasures of the 'social affections', he did not think that these were sufficiently powerful or extensive to become the basis for moral action; there needed to be a more naked appeal to self-interest, in the shape of a heavenly reward for good behaviour.

Paley's account of moral motivation was not original – it has precedents far back in the Middle Ages – nor was there anything faulty in its logic. But it paints a grim and unflattering picture of human beings when it represents them as finding compelling reasons for action only in the pursuit of their own advantage. This picture is, moreover, highly at variance with the normal spirit of utilitarianism, which prescribes the promotion of the public welfare *because* it is an intrinsically valuable thing for human lives to go well: something that we can all be reasonably expected to care about. Indeed, even without Paley's unblushing appeal to the self-interested hope of heaven, theological utilitarianism can fairly be accused of muddling its moral and religious objectives. Theological utilitarians face the dilemma of whether to take promotion of welfare to be a valuable end only because God wishes or commands it, or as valuable independently of theological considerations. Neither option is unproblematic: if they do not care about human well-being for its own sake, their status as utilitarians is suspect, while if they care about it for its own sake their use of the label 'theological' seems gratuitous. Someone could, of course, be an ordinary utilitarian and believe that God wants human beings to be happy; but theological utilitarians meet difficulties when they try to forge a more intimate relation between the moral propriety of doing good to others and the religious propriety of obedience to God's will.

One further interesting feature of Paley's position is his advocacy, in a rather confused form, of what is nowadays termed a *rule-utilitarian criterion* of right and wrong. Paley, to his credit, saw that a thorough-going application of the maxim that 'whatever is expedient is right' (54) could lead in some situations to actions which many would judge to be morally wrong. If we simply considered the utility-value of individual actions, he argued, we would think it right to assassinate a pernicious tyrant, or make a miser disgorge his useless wealth for the benefit of the poor – in other words, right to perform, respectively, acts of murder and of theft. Therefore we should always consider not just the particular consequences of an act but also its 'general consequences': which Paley explained to mean calculating the utility of the general rule under which the act falls:

> The particular bad consequence of an action, is the mischief which that single action directly and immediately occasions. The general bad consequence is, the violation of some necessary or useful *general* rule (55).

Murder and theft normally have bad consequences: hence they are kinds of act that should *never* be performed, even in those unusual cases where expediency seems to require them. According to Paley, if the violent elimination of a tyrant were once judged permissible, then every other case in which someone willed to kill another 'whom he thinks noxious or useless' would have to be deemed permissible too – 'a disposition of affairs which would soon fill the world with misery and confusion; and ere long put an end to human society, if not to the human species' (56–7).

Rule-utilitarian decision procedures involve selecting from the various available general descriptions of an act the one most appropriate to its moral evaluation. Killing a pernicious tyrant might be regarded as murder – but it could also be seen as the liberation of a people from an evil oppressor. A familiar problem of rule-utilitarianism is that there is no clear procedure for deciding which of the possible descriptions of an action should determine its moral character. But even if we ignore this problem for now (we shall meet it again in Chapter V), Paley's treatment of the assassination example is unpersuasive. He contends that we have either to condemn assassinating a pernicious tyrant as wrong, or else to accept that anyone may kill another person when he judges him harmful or useless. But there is scant reason to accept this assimilation of killing an evil tyrant to killing just anyone who we think takes up too much room on the planet, and Paley does not show why the removal of oppressive tyrants cannot reasonably be held to be a species of legitimate killing even if most other killings cannot. (Killing an occasional tyrant seems in very little danger of leading, as Paley fears, to the extinction of mankind.)

Paley's discussion also manifests a confusing confusion between the consequences of classes of actions (that is, of the totality of actions which fall under some general description) and the long-term consequences of individual actions. Having urged very firmly that we should consider not the consequences of individual actions but the consequences of rules regarding their kinds, Paley reverts disconcertingly to an act-utilitarian stance:

> Whatever is expedient is right. But then, it must be expedient on the whole, at the long run, in all its effects collateral and remote, as well as in those which are immediate and direct; as it is obvious, that, in computing consequences, it makes no difference in what way or at what distance they ensue (60).

To exemplify this principle, Paley proposes that forging a guinea harms not merely the unlucky person who receives the counterfeit coin but, if the practice of forgery were to be commonly adopted, would have the general consequence of abolishing the use of money. But he fails to see that the question 'What would happen if forging money became a normal practice?' is different from the question 'What are the long-term consequences of forging this particular guinea?' Counterfeiting a single guinea, even in the long term, may have a negligible effect on the value of the currency, harming only the person who first has the coin refused when tendering it in payment for goods. Act-utilitarians can certainly concede that the evil of forgery is a cumulative one – that the more widespread the practice, the more serious the effect on financial stability. But only a rule-utilitarian believes that a single act of forgery is wrong *because* if forgery became a general practice the currency would collapse. Paley fails to make up his mind which of these positions he means to adopt.

Further, if Paley had opted more clearly for a rule-utilitarian stance, he would not then have needed to worry about the proper utilitarian response to rule-breaking deeds which are done in secret. The most important objection, in Paley's view, to openly killing a pernicious tyrant is that it gives a bad example to anyone who believes that certain people would be 'better out of the world than in it' (57). But he recognises that such a bad example will not be given if the tyrant's murder is made to look like an accident. To avoid having to admit the moral legitimacy of the secret assassination of a tyrant, he argues that performing bad (i.e. rule-infringing) acts secretly, itself sets up 'a general rule, of all others the least to be endured', that 'secrecy, whenever secrecy is practicable, will justify any action' (58). But it is clear neither why the performance of secret acts should set up any general rule (if acts are secret, they set no example), nor why, if they did, they should set up a general rule justifying *any* secret acts, irrespective of their utility. What Paley fails to grasp is that a thoroughgoing rule-utilitarian can afford to ignore the issue of secrecy altogether: for on rule-utilitarian premises, what ensures that an individual act is wrong is just the truth of the subjunctive conditional that *if* acts of its kind were generally practised, then disutility would result. While rule-utilitarianism is itelf a far from unproblematic position, Paley would at least have simplified his own standpoint by making a plainer choice in its favour. Nevertheless he deserves praise for being one of the first writers seriously to address the important question of the relationship between utility and rules.

## 5 Godwin

The philosopher and novelist William Godwin (1756–1836) is in some ways the most interesting of the eighteenth-century utilitarians; he was certainly the most passionate and radical of them. More imaginative and a sharper reasoner than Bentham, Godwin wrote with verve, insight and a wholly unswerving determination to carry the utilitarian argument to its logical conclusion. His *Enquiry Concerning Political Justice*, published in 1793, enjoyed a *succès de scandale* second only to that of Tom Paine's revolutionary *Rights of Man* of three years earlier; and though Godwin avoided having, like Paine, to flee the country for his left-wing opinions, he narrowly escaped prosecution for seditious libel. He was the husband of Mary Wollstonecraft, whose *Vindication of the Rights of Woman* appeared the year before his own book. Godwin was a lifelong champion of political and social reform, but his earlier reputation for communism and anarchism did not prevent him rising in his later years to the highly respectable office of Yeoman Usher of the Exchequer.

Much influenced by the French *philosophes*, and especially by Helvétius, Godwin held that 'Morality is that system of conduct which is determined by a consideration of the greatest general good.' Furthermore:

> he is entitled to the highest moral approbation, whose conduct is, in the greatest number of instances, or in the most momentous instances, governed by views of benevolence, and made subservient to public utility (Godwin 1793: 67).

At the social level, no regulations may be legitimately enforced by public authorities which do not promote the utility of the people. Moral duty and justice can be jointly defined as 'the impartial treatment of every man in matters that relate to his happiness' (69–70).

Like Bentham, Godwin considered that: 'Pleasure and pain, happiness and misery, constitute the whole ultimate subject of morality. There is nothing desirable but the obtaining of the one, and the avoiding of the other' (106). 'Agreeable sensation, and the means of agreeable sensations' are the first things desired by any thinking person. In Godwin's view, nothing 'that is not apprehended to be pleasure or pain' will have any motivating force whatever, and Epicurus was right to declare pleasure to be the supreme good (180, 185).

But Godwin did not think that people only pursued their own pleasure. Human beings are born egoistic, but acquire benevolence through a natural process of development. Godwin's explanation of this mental transition (suggestive of the influence of Hartley's associationist psychology) was that what begins as a means to our own pleasure becomes in time converted into an end in itself. To start with, we are merely distressed for our own sake by the sight of a man starving or the sound of a baby crying; but gradually we come to care about the termination of their suffering as an intrinsically valuable end. This purely mechanistic process is complemented by the dawning intellectual conviction that other people are creatures much like ourselves, which renders us 'able in imagination to go out of ourselves, and become impartial spectators of the system of which we are part'. We see then that it is baseless to represent 'our own interest as of as much value as that of all the world besides'. In this way disinterestedness becomes a real and powerful motive with us, and we become 'capable of self-oblivion, as well as of sacrifice' (180–3). Godwin also believed that the existence of a common human nature made it possible to construct a 'science of pleasure', though his own contributions to this science were more impressionistic than precise. The labouring man, he thought, is 'in a certain sense happy', being more contented than a stone. The 'gay man of rank and fashion' is somewhat better off, enjoying more amusements, plus the grati-fications of pride; while 'the peasant strides through life, with something of the contemplative insensibility of an oyster'. Happier than all the foregoing is the 'man of tastes and liberal accomplishments', though happiest of all is the 'man of benevolence'. Godwin took Epicurus roundly to task for failing to see that 'No man reaps so copious a harvest of pleasure, as he who thinks only of the pleasures of other men' (186–8).

There is perhaps some wishful thinking behind the claim that nothing pleases so much as the giving of pleasure, but Godwin is quick to press it into service of his highly demanding picture of utilitarian virtue. If people delight in behaving benevolently, then much can be asked of their benevolence. Justice requires that we should do everything in our power to increase public utility – even if this means dying for it (74). Godwin complains that it is often held that people have a right in many situations to do what they want; but this is false, for it is always our duty to do whatever is best for the public good. Indeed, '[f]ew things have contributed more to undermine the energy and virtue of the human species, than the supposition that we have a right, as it has been phrased, to do what we will with our own'. Properly considered, neither our lives nor our goods are at our own disposal: 'We have in reality nothing that is strictly speaking our own. We have nothing that has not a destination prescribed to it by the immutable voice of reason and justice' (86).

It is a fair question whether the pleasure we take in doing benevolent deeds could by itself motivate us to sacrifice all our property and even our lives when the utility sums require it; and the answer may seem firmly in the negative. But Godwin thought that the pleasure we take in benevolence leads us to empathise with the happiness and suffering of other people, until we come to care about our neighbour's prosperity for its own sake. Having achieved that stage of disinterested concern, we then can see that our own interests are of no more objective importance than other people's. That recognition in turn makes us realise that justice must be entirely impartial and no respecter of persons. Our ability to sacrifice our own selves and interests in the service of the public good depends then, not solely on the pleasures of benevolence, but on the sense of justice to which our benevolent feelings give rise.

Although Godwin maintained that duty demands that we pay no special attention to our own interests just because they are our own, he did not think that moral impartiality entails that people are of equal importance and deserve equal treatment. On his strenuously maximising view of utility, we need to take into account both how much happiness those we can affect by our actions are capable of enjoying, and how productive they are of happiness for others. One person is of greater worth than another in so far as 'he is capable of a more refined and genuine happiness' (70). These reflections receive vivid illustration in the notorious thought-experiment of the burning palace inside which Archbishop Fénelon and his valet are trapped (70–1). Godwin asks us to imagine that the archiepiscopal palace at Cambray is in flames, and that we can save only one of the two men within. Which one should we choose? In Godwin's view, we should clearly rescue the Archbishop, because he is a man 'of more worth' than his valet. Fénelon (the famous theologian, educationalist and author of the popular prose romance *Télémaque*) not only enjoyed (Godwin supposes) a life of more refined happiness than his servant, but was more useful, through his writings, to the general public; therefore '[t]he life of Fénelon was really preferable to that of the valet'. On the same grounds, the valet himself had a duty to refrain from being rescued before the Archbishop: 'It would have been just in the valet to have preferred the archbishop to himself. To have done otherwise would have been a breach of justice' (70–1).

Godwin's treatment of the Fénelon case represents an extreme but consistent application of a maximising principle. Not surprisingly, many of his early readers took it to constitute a *reductio ad absurdum* of the utilitarian philosophy. Godwin appears to have been surprised and disconcerted by the amount of hostile criticism his example drew, and tried in a conciliatory pamphlet to turn his opponents' wrath. To the objection of Samuel Parr that his theory was a product of the head and not of the heart, Godwin responded that in saving Fénelon one should ideally act not on the basis of a 'cool, phlegmatic, arithmetical calculation', but from a passionate desire for the welfare and improvement of mankind. Furthermore, if the valet's brother or son had chosen to save the valet rather than the Archbishop, it would be unreasonable to condemn him too harshly for making an immoral decision; for though his decision *was* wrong, he acted in a way which showed his genuine concern for human beings (Godwin 1793: 325–6). Godwin also echoed the point made a few years earlier by Priestley, that in many ordinary-life situations the best way to promote the general happiness is by directing one's utility-enhancing efforts at one's family and friends, these being the people whom one is best placed to help (324).

Even so, Godwin saw very little room in utilitarianism for an agent-centred prerogative. A man is the more perfect in so far as he manages 'to elevate philanthropy into a passion' (324). 'I am bound', said Godwin, 'to employ my talents, my understanding, my strength and my time, for the production of the greatest quantity of general good.' If my neighbour needs £10 which I can spare, he has a 'complete right' to it. In giving to him the £10, I confer no favour on him: 'I can only do him right' (75). The thrust of Godwin's book is that we should not care so very much about individuals (including ourselves), but should do our duty by humanity in the mass. If all utilitarians had taken the same line, there might have seemed to be some justification for Stuart Hampshire's verdict that 'The utilitarian habit of mind has brought with it a new abstract cruelty in politics, a dull, destructive political righteousness' (Hampshire 1978: 4).

Yet Godwin was a less consistent utilitarian than he aspired to be. He could unblushingly declare that 'Few things have contributed more to undermine the energy and virtue of the human species, than the supposition that we have a right, as it has been phrased, to do what we will with our own' (Godwin 1793: 86). But he also claimed that 'Every man has a certain sphere of discretion, which he has a right to expect should not be infringed by his neighbours' (89). Godwin felt a deep respect for individual liberty of thought and action which he never quite succeeded in squaring with his maximising views. 'The universal exercise of private judgement,' he wrote in one place, 'is a doctrine so unspeakably beautiful, that the true politician will certainly feel infinite reluctance in admitting the idea of interfering with it' (96). Yet what if we happen to employ our private judgement unwisely, in ways which do not enhance utility? Godwin considered that our neighbours – 'invited or uninvited' – have an obligation to restrain us from disutilitarian behaviour; he likewise argued that clubs, societies and religious sects should not be allowed to establish whatever absurdities they pleased

(86–7). Freedom was a beautiful thing – but only tolerable when conjoined with a radical, utilitarian conscience.

The tension between Godwin's love of liberty and his maximising criterion of right action shows up conspicuously in his treatment of punishment. The suffering which punishment causes is defensible only if it tends towards the greater public good. Godwin firmly rejected the concept of retribution: punishing people for what is past and irrevocable 'must be ranked among the most pernicious exhibitions of an untutored barbarism' – it is akin to the behaviour of the angry child who beats the table. If punishment is to be justified at all, it can only be for the sake of 'preventing future mischief' (245–6). In fact, the very notions of guilt and innocence are irrelevant to the practice of punishment; Godwin is one of the small handful of utilitarians to have held that even an innocent man may be 'punished' for the sake of utility: 'An innocent man is the proper subject of it, if it tend to good' (245). At his most extreme Godwin went even further, asserting that 'I may put a man to death for the common good, either because he is infected with a pestilential disease, or because some oracle has declared it essential to the public safety' (244).

Yet no sooner did Godwin urge that even the innocent can be 'punished' where the utility calculation demands it, than he expressed a revulsion against the very idea of punishment. Mistreating a person today to deter people from committing crimes tomorrow is 'abhorrent to reason' and tyrannous. Even taking criminals into custody in order to reform them is morally dubious: it only 'alienates the mind of him against whom it is employed' (249–51). No two crimes are ever exactly alike, and punishment is too blunt an instrument to do much good; it rarely produces enough solid benefit to outweigh the harm done in removing an individual's liberty. In an ideal world there would be neither laws to obey nor governments to enforce them; everyone would be free to determine his own actions by his own reason. In the present imperfect state of things, Godwin reluctantly conceded, the abolition of government and law would lead to an increase in 'violence and danger'; therefore it cannot be considered as a practical option (262–3). Nevertheless government is intrinsically a bad thing, because it is antithetical to liberty. The sooner we can do without it, the better.

That Godwin was unable to reconcile the conflicting claims of public utility and individual freedom is unsurprising; later utilitarians have found the difficulties no easier to solve. Godwin's *Enquiry* is important for displaying some of the most serious fault-lines in utilitarianism, which all their author's ingenuity was unable to close. More so than Bentham, Godwin provides a foretaste of those problems concerning the delicate balance between individual and community good which loom so large in contemporary discussion. If not a thinker of the first rank, Godwin was sufficiently bold and original to provoke in his day much lively and constructive debate. He might fairly have claimed, in a paraphrase of Falstaff, that he was not only philosophical in himself, but a cause that philosophy was in other men: in itself a significant contribution to the public good.

## 6 Bentham

Jeremy Bentham (1748–1832) was less important as an original utilitarian thinker than as a systematiser and a publicist of its doctrines. For most people in the early nineteenth century, 'utilitarianism' meant the theory of Bentham, the leader of the 'philosophical radicals' and the walking embodiment of their ideals. Bentham has been described as 'happy, hard-working, benevolent, unimaginative and unmarried, with a mild affection for music, animals and friends' (Plamenatz 1966: 60). But however diffident and gentle he may have been in manner, he was a man capable of inspiring others with his own zeal for reform in all departments of public life. Sir Leslie Stephen has characterised Bentham as posing the question 'What is the use of you?' to every institution and to every law (Stephen 1900: vol. 1, 271). This brings out well the essentially practical character of Bentham as a thinker: he was a theorist who wrote long and complex books on many subjects, but always in the hope of effecting some increase in public happiness. Theorising for the mere sake of theorising would have seemed to him the merest waste of time, an activity without utility.

Bentham was born the son of a prosperous attorney, and was himself called to the Bar after an education at Westminster and Oxford. Soon finding that his personality was unsuited to a forensic career, he turned his back on the law courts and redirected his analytical talents towards jurisprudence and political science. An incident in a coffee house in Oxford in 1768 had a decisive effect on his intellectual development. Chancing to pick up a copy of Priestley's *Essay on Government*, he was fired with enthusiasm by the phrase 'the greatest happiness of the greatest number'. This was Bentham's Damascus Road experience, although the ground for it had been already prepared by his close reading of Hume, Helvétius and Beccaria. From that date he was a committed utilitarian with a clear view of his life's work.

His first important writing, the *Fragment on Government* of 1776, was an attack on Sir William Blackstone's *Commentaries on the Laws of*

*England* (1765–9), a work whose complacent satisfaction in the English statute book and legal system seemed to Bentham intolerable. Bentham's treatise, the opening salvo in his life-long campaign against the irrationalities of the law and the obscurantism and self-seeking of its practitioners, proclaimed on its very first page that 'It is the greatest happiness of the greatest number that is the measure of right and wrong.' The prime task ahead, he wrote, was to carry out a careful and methodical investigation of this 'fundamental axiom' (Bentham 1776: 227). All his subsequent writings were contributions to this central project. With enormous single-mindedness and boundless energy, Bentham devoted the whole of his long career to spelling out the practical implications of the basic principles he had accepted in his youth. In keeping with Enlightenment tradition, he commenced his theorising with an account of the nature of man. Before any proposals could be drawn up for the reform of social institutions, it was essential to have a clearer picture of the kind of creature they were meant to serve. Works like *An Introduction to the Principles of Morals and Legislation* (1780) and *A Table of the Springs of Action* (1815) accordingly discuss the variety of human motivations, and attempt to demonstrate their reducibility to the promptings of the 'two sovereign masters', pleasure and pain (Bentham 1789: 1). Bentham also interested himself in specific projects for criminological and penological reform, of which the most notable was the scheme for a 'panopticon', a model reformatory in which the inmates could be overseen and controlled by their jailers throughout all hours of the day and night.[8]

The essence of Bentham's view of right and wrong, from which he never deviated, was set out in a few brisk sentences of the *Fragment on Government*. For all classes of action, the feature of moral note is always:

> the *tendency* which they may have *to*, or *divergency* . . . *from*, that which may be styled the common *end* of all of them. The end I mean is *Happiness*: and this *tendency* in any act we style its *utility*: as this *divergency* is that to which we give the name of *mischievousness*. . . . From *utility*, then, we may denominate a *principle*, that may serve to preside over and govern, as it were, such arrangements as should be made to the several institutions, that compose the matter of this science [i.e. of jurisprudence] (Bentham 1776: 237).

This was a principle, thought Bentham, which all men could readily see to be true. Moreover: 'The consequences of any Law, or of any act which is made the object of a Law – the only consequences that men are at all interested in – what are they but *pain* and *pleasure*?' (298).

Fortunately we need not follow up in detail Bentham's minute and painstaking application of the principle of utility to almost every aspect of the legal and political structures of his time; though it is worth noting that in J.S. Mill's opinion, Bentham's greatest service was to have 'deduced a set of subordinate generalities from utility alone, and by these consistently tested all particular questions'. In other words, Mill thought Bentham important less for his account of the mainsprings of action than for his practical and commonsensical treatment of specific issues of public interest. (In a more jaundiced mood Mill put things a little differently, and less flatteringly: Bentham's philosophy was best fitted to 'teach the means of organizing and regulating the merely *business* part of the social arrangements' (J.S. Mill 1852: 173; 1838: 99).) But we shall concentrate on examining three theoretical themes in Bentham's philosophy which underpin everything he had to say about practice. These are: (a) his theory of pleasure and pain; (b) the explanation of the possibility of altruistic behaviour; and (c) the rejection of all non-utilitarian standards of moral evaluation.

(a) Bentham's elaborate classification of the 'springs of action' and of the various categories and dimensions of pleasure and pain is wholly typical of him. He was a man who believed that analysis consisted in the making of lists (Stephen described him as 'a codifying animal' (Stephen 1900: vol. 1, 247).)[9] This passion for classifying things is often tedious and occasionally comic; but Bentham believed, with some justice, that a careful account of the species of pleasure and pain was a necessary preliminary to the construction of detailed rules of utility. The basic presupposition of the utility principle, he explained in the first chapter of *An Introduction to the Principles of Morals and Legislation*, is that every person is subject to the empire of pleasure and pain, the only determinants of human behaviour; the utilitarian objective must therefore be to 'rear the fabric of felicity by the hands of reason and law' (Bentham 1789: 1). All actions should be approved or disapproved solely according to their tendency to promote or to oppose the utility (otherwise, the 'benefit', 'advantage', 'pleasure', 'good' or 'happiness') of the persons they affect (2).

Pleasures and pains are the 'instruments' which legislators (as well as other agents) have to work with; therefore it is crucial that they should understand how to measure their value. Bentham considered that there were seven 'circumstances' which determined the value of a pleasure or a pain: its intensity; its duration; its certainty or uncertainty; its propinquity or remoteness; its fecundity (the chance of its being followed by other pleasures or pains of the same kind); its purity (its chance of not being followed by a sensation of the opposite kind); and its extent (the number of people who are affected by it) (16). Bentham thought that numerical values could in principle be attached to these 'circumstances' and an arithmetical operation performed to determine the relative merits of different courses of action. The strategy is to '[s]*um up* the numbers expressive of the degrees of *good* tendency' which an act has with respect to each individual concerned, do the same with regard to its *bad* tendency, then calculate the balance 'with respect to the total number or community of individuals concerned' (16). We saw briefly in Chapter I some of the obstacles facing the construction of a calculus of utility (or a 'felicific calculus' as Bentham called it); we shall return to the topic in Chapter VI when we discuss the views of Richard Brandt. Bentham himself scarcely apprehended the severity of the technical problems involved in plotting the values of pleasures and pains on a numerical scale (particularly when so many 'circumstances' contribute to determining that value); and he underestimated the difficulty of interpersonal comparisons. Yet he did concede, with more realism than he is sometimes given credit for, that 'It is not to be expected, that this process should be strictly pursued previously to every moral judgement, or to every legislative or judicial operation.' The notion of a calculus should, however, always be 'kept in view' as an ideal model of rational deliberation, to which actual deliberations should conform as closely as possible (16).[10]

Ironically, Bentham himself unwittingly supplied a further ground for thinking that a felicific calculus would be at best extremely hard to operate. The more varieties of pleasant and painful activities there are, the more complex the task of measuring and comparing their quotients of pleasure and pain. But Bentham thought that the number of species of pleasure and pain was very large indeed, and in his inimitable style set out to list them. In the *Principles* we learn that there are fourteen kinds of simple pleasures and eleven of simple pains, all of which are carefully enumerated and discussed. Thus the simple pleasures are said to be those of sense, of wealth, of skill, of amity, of a good name, of power, of piety, of benevolence, of malevolence, of memory, of imagination, of expectation, of relief, and those dependent on the association of ideas. The first category, of sensory pleasures, is further distinguished into pleasures of the taste or palate, of intoxication, of smell, of touch, of hearing, of sight, of sex, of health and of novelty; and other categories of pleasures and pains are subdivided in a similar manner (Bentham 1789: 17f.). Even this exhaustive (and exhausting) natural history of human motives was not Bentham's last word on the subject. *A Table of the Springs of Action* contains a still more elaborate taxonomy of motives, supplying among other things fifty-four synonyms of the word 'pleasure' and sixty-seven of 'pain' (Bentham 1817: 205–7).

Despite the extraordinary labour which Bentham spent on displaying the variety of pleasures and pains, he did not attempt to rank them, as some earlier utilitarians had done and many (following J.S. Mill's lead) did later, according to a *qualititative* measure of value. He did not deny that some kinds of pleasant activity were usually more worth pursuing than others: benevolent deeds, for instance, tended to bring a person a greater and more unalloyed satisfaction than malevolent ones, and were therefore preferable in point of pleasantness. The famous remark that pushpin is as good as poetry if it gives as much pleasure does not entail that pushpin *is* as pleasant as poetry (though Bentham, in a rare resemblance to Plato, suggested that poetry, unlike pushpin, could disturb the soul in a way which was rather painful than otherwise) (Bentham 1825: 253). But he never supposed that some activities were necessarily more satisfying than others because the pleasure they offered was of an intrinsically higher grade. For all activities, the only criterion of worth was the balance of pleasure over pain they generated in accordance with the seven 'circumstances' laid down at the beginning of the *Principles*. There is a single-minded consistency about this account which elicits admiration. Bentham refused to 'cook' his theory of value to ensure that intellectual activities like reading philosophy would emerge superior to non-intellectual ones like sex or football. No activities were to be ring-fenced as belonging to a qualitatively better kind (and, by implication, as delimiting a class of qualitatively better people). For philosophy to stake a claim to peculiar worth, it had to demonstrate itself to be an activity of peculiar pleasantness.

(b) However, Bentham's view that pleasure and pain are the 'sovereign masters' of every human being leads to an awkward problem for his account of moral motivation. The very first paragraph of the *Principles* shows his commitment to a thoroughly deterministic picture of human nature. Pleasure and pain

> govern us in all we do, in all we say, in all we think: every effort we can make to throw off our subjection, will serve but to demonstrate and confirm it. In words a man may pretend to abjure their empire: but in reality he will remain subject to it all the while (Bentham 1789: 1).

If the hold of pleasure and pain over us is really as absolute as this, the scope for genuinely moral action would seem to be nil. In everything we do we are simply seeking our own pleasure or avoiding our own pain, and any attempt to break away from these constraining forces and seek another's good instead of our own is futile. To be sure, Bentham also claims that pleasure and pain 'point out what we ought to do, as well as ... determine what we shall do' (1). But if we cannot help doing a thing, there is no point to saying that we *ought* to do it; and the content of morality would in any case be very thin if the sole moral imperatives were to seek happiness and avoid misery for ourselves. So when Bentham holds that the principle of utility is built on the human subjection to pleasure and pain, the sense of the claim is obscure. Human well-being might conceivably consist, as he asserts it does, in obtaining pleasure and avoiding pain; but the Benthamite psychology makes it hard to see how any individual could genuinely care about rearing 'the fabric of felicity' for all mankind.

Bentham offered a somewhat complex response to this problem. Three separate lines of thought can be distinguished. Sometimes he seems inclined to moderate the egoism of his psychological theory and admit, alongside self-interested motives, altruistic ones as well. In the late work *Deontology* (1834) he conceded the existence of a human disposition to philanthropy and self-sacrifice. Even rulers (of whom Bentham had a generally low opinion) sometimes acted in a benevolent manner, in the interests of their subjects. In addition, Bentham recognised the presence of what Bikhu Parekh has termed 'semi-social' motives for promoting the public good (though admittedly these appeal to selfish interests rather than to benevolence) (Parekh 1974: xii). A rational person realises that it is in his own interests to act well towards others, who will act well towards him in return. Men who live in society need the assistance of others to fulfil their needs, and enlightened self-interest dictates that they display a cooperative spirit in order to secure this. Finally, Bentham claimed (as we have already seen) that benevolent actions can reward the actor with pleasure of an unusually intense kind:

> The pleasures of benevolence are the pleasures resulting from the view of any pleasures supposed to be possessed by the beings who may be the objects of benevolence; ... These may also be called the pleasures of goodwill, the pleasures of sympathy, or the pleasures of the benevolent or social affections (Bentham 1789: 18).

If doing good to others makes the agent happy, Bentham thought, then there can be no real opposition between self-interest and the principle of utility: promoting the public happiness is the best way to become happy oneself.

If this multi-stranded story of Bentham's is correct, then living by the principle of utility is no longer the impossibility it seemed on the original premise that human beings are wholly governed by desire for pleasure and aversion to pain. It is sometimes objected that Bentham is too sanguine if he supposes that self-interest and utility will always coincide: no matter how great the pleasure of benevolence, or the return for doing good to others, situations can arise where the personal cost of acting in the public interest will be greater. The complaint is fair, but it fails to show that the 'coincidence thesis' is false in all circumstances, or as a rule. A more serious point is that the coincidence of public and private utility provides no real evidence that people are not always narrowly self-interested; even doing good to others because of the pleasure it gives one seems to be a species, albeit a refined one, of action from selfish motives. The situation would be saved if Bentham's recognition of a spirit of philanthropy in human beings (the first strand in his story), were capable of filling the psychological gap. But while Bentham certainly believed that human beings are capable of forming a disposition to act for the good of others, the true selflessness of that disposition as he conceived it is open to question. Bentham never referred to any benevolent or self-sacrificing spirit without simultaneously emphasising the pleasure to be derived from cultivating it. There were kings, he allowed, who did their utmost to promote their subjects' welfare – but they reaped great enjoyment from doing their duty. Philanthropy, for Bentham, was a real mental disposition, and not particularly rare; but he seems to have seen its essential motivation as the satisfaction it engenders in the philanthropist.[11]

However, there may be a different way of rescuing Bentham from the charge that his picture of man is of an irredeemably selfish creature. This defence turns on an important feature of the phenomenology of pleasure. Many of our pleasures, though not all, presuppose a pre-existing desire for the object in which the pleasure is taken. We could not, to take an obvious case, derive any pleasure from finding a £5 note in the street if we lacked any desire for money. The pleasure of obtaining money is not the origin of the desire for it; rather, we are pleased when we find £5 because the discovery satisfies our desire for cash. To explain that desire may require in its turn a reference to the pleasures we take in the goods which money can buy; but the desire for money explains, rather than is explained by, the pleasure we take in finding the banknote. It is plausible to suppose that the pleasure of benevolence is a pleasure of the same logical kind. A person indifferent to the happiness of other people could reap no satisfaction from helping his neighbour. A purely selfish being might enjoy performing actions for his own ends which happened coincidentally to assist someone else; for example, a man who liked gardening might happily tend an elderly person's garden without caring anything about the owner. But someone who enjoyed digging the garden *because* it helped the elderly person must care about that person's welfare or his pleasure is incomprehensible.

One writer to have seen this point clearly is Hastings Rashdall. To explain benevolent action by the pleasure of performing it was, he argued, to put the cart before the horse. 'Benevolence is a source of pleasure only to the benevolent man – to the man who has previously desired his neighbour's good':

> If the good Samaritan cared about the present feelings or the future welfare of the man fallen among thieves, it would no doubt give him some pleasure to satisfy that desire for his welfare; if he had desired his good as little as the priest and the Levite, there would have been nothing to suggest the strange idea that to relieve him, to bind up his nasty wounds, and to spend money upon him, would be a source of more pleasure to himself than to pass by on the other side and spend the money upon himself (Rashdall n.d.: 18).

If this is right, then the charge that Benthamite man is wholly selfish collapses. Taking pleasure in benevolent action is possible only to the truly benevolent. Nevertheless, some adjustment to Bentham's views is required to make his position consistent. It can no longer be said that our own pleasure and pain are the only stimuli which move us to action; a care about the pleasure and pain of other people must be admitted as a further basic motivation, to explain the pleasures of benevolence. This complicates the Benthamite psychology, but enriches it too: Benthamite man ceases to be an automaton with only two controls. It also releases Bentham from the uncomfortable position of holding that moral principles needlessly tell us to do what we are psychologically determined to do anyway. If egoistic and altruistic inspirations sit side by side in the human breast, morality has the important role of adjudicating the resulting motivational conflicts.

(c) Bentham shrewdly rested the case for the utilitarian principle in part on the poverty of alternative moral theories. Most of these, he claimed, rely not on evidence but solely on their authors' prejudices. The moral-sense tradition in ethics he dismissed as a rhetorical exercise in which fine-sounding and empty phrases supplied the place of arguments:

One man says, he has a thing made on purpose to tell him what is right and what is wrong; and that is called a 'moral sense': and then he goes to work at his ease, and says, that such a thing is right, and such a thing is wrong – why? 'Because my moral sense tells me it is' (Bentham 1789: 85).

Other philosophers used different language to make the same claim: one referred to his *common* sense to show him moral truth; another to his *understanding* or to natural law or to the 'fitness of things'. Bentham thought that all these variant theories were caught on the horns of the same dilemma: either they represented nothing more substantial than the writer's say-so, or they involved a tacit appeal to utility which should have been made explicit. Bentham likewise criticised the language of rights popular with apologists for the American and French revolutions (movements with which he broadly sympathised); this he condemned roundly as 'rhetorical nonsense – nonsense upon stilts' (Stephen 1900: vol. 1, 292). Only by substituting the idea of utility for the high-sounding but meaningless notion of natural rights would one have a reasonable principle which could be supported by experience.

Bentham's acute and often witty attack on rival theories was singled out for praise by J.S. Mill:

Few will contend that this is a perfectly fair representation of the *animus* of those who employ the various phrases so amusingly animadverted on; but that the phrases contain no argument, save what is grounded on the very feelings they are adduced to justify, is a truth which Bentham had the eminent merit of first pointing out (J.S. Mill 1838: 86).

Bentham, Mill said, always 'required something more than opinion as a reason for opinion' (140). Yet one might fairly ask whether the principle of utility is itself grounded on anything more solid than the opinion of utilitarians. Bentham believed that its superiority stemmed from its basis in a sound psychological theory of human motivation; but this is persuasive only if we grant the very dubious proposition that normative judgements can be derived from descriptive ones – that, in other words, an 'ought' can be deduced from an 'is'. That human beings naturally desire happiness (their own and other people's) does not entail that they *ought* to promote that happiness. A man may tell us, said Bentham

that there are certain practices conformable, and others repugnant, to the Fitness of Things; and then he tells you, at his leisure, what practices are conformable, and what repugnant: just as he happens to like a practice or dislike it (Bentham 1789: 8–9).

The question we need to ask is: what prevents our substituting the word 'utility' for the phrase 'the Fitness of Things'? This is a question which Bentham, unlike Mill, never faced squarely.

# CHAPTER IV

# John Stuart Mill

## 1 Early years

John Stuart Mill (1806–73) is the greatest of all utilitarian writers, and also one of the most enigmatical.[1] More subtle, imaginative and self-critical by far than Bentham, Mill grasped more deeply than he or any previous thinker both the strengths and the weaknesses of the utilitarian philosophy, and explored them with unprecedented intellectual vigour. It may seem at first surprising that Mill never attempted a major treatise on moral philosophy along the lines of his massive works on logic and political economy. But his career is characterised by a persisting ambivalence towards the Benthamite tradition in which he had been raised, and his importance as a moral philosopher rests in large part on his candid and insightful exhibition of the tensions lurking within the utilitarian outlook. As a result of this abiding love–hate relationship with Benthamism, his essays and articles on ethics over three decades display some marked shifts of view which make it hard to speak of a Millian 'system'. Fortunately we have his own *Autobiography* (1873), written late in life, to clarify the main movements of his thought – from the unabashed Benthamism of his early years, through the near-rejection of utilitarianism in the 1830s, to the reinvention of a delicately balanced utilitarian theory two decades later. The main product of the last period, the series of popular essays originally published under the title 'Utilitarianism' in *Frazer's Magazine* in 1861, has become the most famous defence of the utilitarian view ever written, and remains one of the most stimulating. Nevertheless it is not, despite its surface lucidity and confidence, an entirely satisfactory little book; it is marred by occasional over-simplification and shaky argument, and it underemphasises some of the finer insights reached in Mill's earlier work. It may to some extent represent its weary author's final attempt to reach terra firma after a strenuous intellectual and emotional odyssey begun many years before, in one of the strangest childhoods of the nineteenth century.

The story of Mill's extraordinary education by his father James under the approving eye of Jeremy Bentham is well known. These exacting mentors sought to make of John Stuart an ideal man after the Benthamite pattern: analytical, well-informed, empiricist, atheistic and unsuperstitious, unimpressed by conventions or traditions (except their own), and emotionally cool about everything under the sun except the betterment of mankind. To this end they made an early start on turning the child into a rational creature. John Stuart under his father's tutelage began learning Greek at 3, and was reading the dialogues of Plato by 7. He was prevented from forming friendships with other boys, whom his father feared would corrupt him by their 'vulgar modes of thought and feeling', and holidays were not allowed 'lest the habit of work should be broken, and the taste for idleness acquired' (J.S. Mill 1873: 39). Knowing little of the world outside the study, John Stuart seems to have accepted with patience, and even enthusiasm, the austerely academic way of life lived beneath the paternal roof. By the time he entered his teens, his knowledge of classics, history, politics, logic, economics and experimental science already surpassed that of most university-educated men ten or fifteen years his senior. With characteristic humility Mill later denied that his personal talents had been anything out of the ordinary, and imputed his precocious development purely to the genius of his father's pedagogy; any other child of ordinary capacities, he thought, could have bloomed as quickly under the same regimen if – God forbid – he had been subjected to it (33).

The spectacular results of their educational programme persuaded Bentham and the elder Mill that John Stuart should be groomed for the role of torch-bearer of Benthamism in succession to themselves – a scheme which the young man's unbounded admiration for Bentham's philosophy and reform projects made seem eminently reasonable. The 16-year-old Mill was firmly convinced that the greatest-happiness principle represented the dawn of a new and more enlightened age in politics and ethics. 'The feeling rushed upon me,' he records in his *Autobiography*, 'that all previous moralists were superseded, and that here indeed was the commencement of a new era in thought' (67). However in 1826, at the age of 20 and following two years of unrelieved hard work as a research assistant to Bentham, Mill succumbed to a serious nervous breakdown, an occurrence which profoundly affected not only the course of his own life but the subsequent history of utilitarianism. This breakdown took the form of a deadening discovery that there was no one and nothing that he cared much about. Awakening 'as out of a dream', he realised that the achievement of all that he had learned to think of as his proper goals in life would afford him no genuine happiness. 'At this,' he tells us, 'my heart sank within me: the whole foundation on which my life was constructed fell down' (139).

What had happened to produce this dramatic change? Mill's retrospective account is very clear. 'For I now saw, or thought I saw, what I had before received with incredulity – that the habit of analysis has a tendency to wear away the feelings.' Favourable to 'prudence and clearsightedness', analytic habits are 'a perpetual worm at the root both of the passions and of the virtues; and above all, fearfully undermine all desires, and all pleasures' (141–2). The common description of Benthamite man as 'a mere reasoning machine', Mill conceded, had been 'not altogether untrue' of himself during two or three years of his life (111). The attempt to live by Bentham's philosophy had reduced him to emotional and imaginative sterility.

The crisis passed as John Stuart learned to develop his feelings as well as his intellect; the reading of romantic writers like Marmontel and Wordsworth convinced him that his capacities for emotional responses were not dead but sleeping, while the music of Weber and Mozart offered delights of whose existence Bentham's philosophy had given no hint. The much admired idol had been found to have feet of clay. 'How much of human nature slumbered in him,' he wrote of Bentham in 1838,

> he knew not, neither can we know. He had never been made alive to the unseen influences which were acting on himself, nor consequently on his fellow creatures. . . . He measured them but by one standard; their knowledge of facts, and their capability to take correct views on utility, and merge all other objects in it (J.S. Mill 1838: 92).

Having suffered so severely in his own person the harmful effects of this Gradgrinding view of human possibilities, Mill was determined to nail as firmly as he could the mistakes which Bentham and his father had made. The crux of their error, he considered, was the 'neglect both in theory and in practice of the cultivation of feeling', from which 'naturally resulted, among other things, an undervaluing of poetry, and of Imagination generally' (J.S. Mill 1873: 115). Mill's determination that the deficiencies of the Benthamite perspective would not be transmitted through his own work marks, by its radical transformation of value theory premised on a richer and more sophisticated understanding of human psychological needs, the beginning of modern utilitarianism.

## 2 James Mill

It is worth pausing at this point to examine briefly the work of the man who was Bentham's most stalwart disciple and defender. James Mill (1773–1836) rose from very humble origins (he was the son of a Montrose shoemaker) to a position of eminence in the East India Company and a reputation as one of the leading radical intellectuals of his day. A man of forceful character and remarkable conversational powers, he was widely praised for his multi-volume *History of British India* (1818) and his numerous writings on political economy and psychology. Despite possessing a proud and prickly nature, he was forced for many years to rely on financial support from Bentham to help sustain his large family of nine children. In return, he became what Bentham with his more diffident nature could never have been, the dominant personality behind a group of utilitarian zealots and proselytisers. From his own children he elicited respect rather than love; and indeed he was not a very lovable man. John Stuart represents him as gloomy, pessimistic and perpetually driven by a sense of duty. Notwithstanding his allegiance to the utilitarian philosophy, his private morality was Stoic rather than Epicurean, and he had, according to his son, 'scarcely any belief in pleasure'. Holding that most pleasurable experiences were scarcely worth bothering about, he 'thought human life a poor thing at best, after the freshness of youth and of unsatisfied curiosity had gone by'. Older people he believed had outlived all their pleasures except those they could vicariously take in the pleasures of the young (J.S. Mill 1873: 49/51).

James Mill's *Essay on Government* (1819), written for the *Encyclopaedia Britannica* in 1820, is a clear but not very original statement of the utilitarian point of view. Government has the purpose of producing 'the greatest happiness of the greatest number', where 'the lot of every human being is determined by his pains and his pleasures; and . . . his happiness corresponds with the degree in which his pleasures are great, and his pains are small' (James Mill 1819: 3, 4). The maximum happiness of society is to be attained primarily by 'insuring to every man the greatest possible quantity of the produce of his labour' (5). This end, Mill declares, can most effectively be accomplished if men combine to establish a government to cater for their common needs; but the biggest problem of practical politics is to ensure that governments, once in being, do not abuse their power – human beings, in Mill's opinion, possessing an insatiable craving for dominion over others. (This jaundiced view of humanity may say much about the author's own character.) The best form of government, Mill decides, is a democratic one in which male householders over the age of 40 elect representatives to sit in a central parliament; women and younger men need take no part in elections as their interests can be adequately looked after by the older males.

Mill's *Essay* presents an undeniably simplified account of human psychology and a naive view of political relationships. It was important, however, in drawing forth one critical response of great acumen and wit which had a profound effect on the younger Mill. T.B. Macaulay's paper 'Mill on government', published in the conservative *Edinburgh Review* in 1829, prefigures in many of its criticisms the objections which J.S. Mill was to make of Benthamism in his writings of the subsequent decade. Utilitarians, suggested Macaulay, were not the 'incarnate demons' which some imagined them to be, but 'in general ordinary men, with narrow understandings and little information'. James Mill was 'an Aristotelian of the Fifteenth Century, born out of due season' – a man who from a few dubious premises about human nature deduces a priori a whole science of politics (Macaulay 1829: 272–3)! In Macaulay's view it is false to suggest, as Mill does, that every man always desires that other men shall do his will, and that the only modes of political control involve the distribution of pleasures and pains; public opinion, for instance, is an independent force which powerfully constrains both rulers and subjects alike (279).[2] Worse, Mill is not only wholly dogmatic in his brash and unshaded analyses of human motives, but frequently inconsistent too. Thus if the lust for power over others is really as boundless as he asserts, how, Macaulay asks, can he trust the middle-aged males not to abuse the rights of the people they are supposed to protect? Is the interest of a Turk the same as that of the women of his harem? And if the interest of an English gentleman is sometimes the same as his wife's, that only serves to show that we are not all 'Yahoos fighting for carrion', driven, as Mill maintains, by self-interest alone, but are capable of genuinely benevolent feeling too. Mill-style generalisation about motives is always foolish, in Macaulay's opinion, because 'Man differs from man; generation from generation; nation from nation. Education, station, sex, age, accidental associations, produce infinite shades of variety' (300–1). Mill oversimplifies greatly when he reasons 'as if no human being had ever sympathized with the feelings, been gratified by the thanks, or been galled by the execrations, of another' (302). The science of politics, Macaulay concludes, is far removed from 'the barren theories of the Utilitarian sophists', whose views are so entirely innocent of fact that they can be safely ignored. Men like Mill can be dismissed as harmless fools. Yet:

They may as well be Utilitarians as jockeys or dandies. And though quibbling about self-interest and motives, and objects of desire, and the greatest happiness of the greatest number, is but a poor employment for a grown man, it certainly hurts the health less than hard drinking and the fortune less than high play; it is not much more laughable than phrenology, and is immeasurably more humane than cock-fighting (303).

This account is not wholly just to Mill, and Macaulay himself later regretted the sneering tone in which much of his article is couched. In the two volumes of his *Analysis of the Phenomena of the Human Mind* of 1824, Mill showed himself capable of a painstaking study of mental events and dispositions, and, within the restrictions of an unapologetically associationist theory of the mind, even attempted to vindicate the existence of genuinely benevolent feelings.[3] Yet John Stuart professed himself 'not at all satisfied with the mode in which my father met the criticisms of Macaulay'. James Mill's blunt reaction was to treat Macaulay's objections as 'simply irrational' – 'an example of the saying of Hobbes, that when reason is against a man, a man will be against reason' (J.S. Mill 1873: 165/7). Some of the younger Mill's worries concerned technical issues in the logic and methodology of the social sciences which he thought that neither his father nor Macaulay had properly understood. But he felt too

that ... there was truth in several of [Macaulay's] strictures on my father's treatment of the subject; that my father's premises were really too narrow, and included but a small number of the general truths, on which, in politics, the important consequences depend (165).

In his son's view, James Mill, like Bentham, held too constricted and naive a view of human nature to be able to offer a really enlightening theory of politics or ethics.

### 3 The importance of character

Personally scarred by the attempt to cast him in the Benthamite mould yet loath to abandon the greatest-happiness principle, John Stuart Mill reflected deeply in the 1830s on the prospects for a more refined form of moral theory. Was utilitarianism capable of revision, or was the only option to abandon it? The peak of his disillusionment with Benthamism was reached in a highly critical essay of 1833 (printed anonymously to avoid offending his father) as an appendix to Edward Lytton-Bulwer's

*England and the English*. The 'Remarks on Bentham's Philosophy' are a classic example of damnation by faint praise. Mill felt able to commend Bentham for 'teaching law as no peculiar mystery, but a simple piece of practical business, wherein means were to be adapted to ends, as in any other of the arts of life'; but he firmly dismissed Bentham's claims to contribute anything of importance to ethical theory (J.S. Mill 1833: 10). Bentham had seen man as a selfish creature, driven only by the hope of his own pleasure and coolly calculating in his pursuit of his ends. This was not merely a travesty of the truth, thought Mill, but a positively harmful doctrine: 'By the promulgation of such views of human nature,' he said, 'and by a general tone of thought and expression in keeping with them, I conceive Mr. Bentham's writings to have done and to be doing very serious evil' (22).

By 1838 Mill had slightly moderated his criticism, and conceded that Bentham had at least done ethical thought good service by advocating a plain and unmysterious criterion for the moral quality of actions in terms of their propensity to produce pleasure or pain; however inadequate this was, it was a great improvement on the vague and unverifiable appeals to moral intuition that were the stock-in-trade of most moral philosophers. Yet the hiatus of omission in Bentham was still vast:

Man is never recognized by him as a being capable of pursuing spiritual perfection as an end; of desiring, for its own sake, the conformity of his own character to his standard of excellence, without hope of good or fear of evil from other sources than his own inward consciousness (J.S. Mill 1838: 95).

At most, Bentham's thought 'can teach the means of organizing the merely *business* part of the social arrangements'; and Bentham 'committed the mistake of thinking that the business part of human affairs was the whole of them' (100). Bentham was a good philosopher, even a great one, within his limits; but those limits were very narrow.

Had Mill, then, ceased to be a utilitarian in the 1830s? The answer to this depends, as he himself explained, on how the term 'utilitarian' is understood. Writing to Thomas Carlyle in 1834, he carefully distanced himself from the Benthamite camp, but without disavowing the label 'utilitarian':

I am still, and am likely to remain, a utilitarian; though not one of 'those people called utilitarians'; indeed, having scarcely one of my secondary premises in common with them; nor a utilitarian at all, unless in quite another sense from what perhaps anyone but myself understands by the word (J.S. Mill 1963: 207).

The 'benevolentiary, soup-kitchen school' of utilitarianism he firmly rejected:

> Though I hold the good of the species (or rather of its separate units) to be the *ultimate* end, (which is the alpha and the omega of my utilitarianism) I believe with the fullest Belief that this end can in no other way be forwarded but by the means you speak of, namely by each taking for his exclusive aim the development of what is best in himself (207–8).

Mill's use of the word 'exclusive' here may represent an exaggeration of his real view, diplomatically intended to emphasise the extent of his agreements with Carlyle (that least utilitarian of sages); it would be hard to argue that a person was a utilitarian in the most minimal sense if he cared *only* about his own well-being and fineness of character. But the statement testifies to a conviction which Mill frequently reiterates in this period, that an individual who develops an excellent character is most likely to be happy himself and to make others happy. For Mill, an excellent character is a well-rounded one in which the intellectual talents valued by Bentham coexist with liveliness of spirit and imagination, and a love of humanity in one's neighbour's person as well as one's own. Developing a character of this sort is a surer way than adopting a felicific calculus of becoming a practically wise agent and an effective promoter of the public happiness. In an 1832 letter to his friend John Sterling, Mill spoke of 'the *spirit* of all morality, right self-culture', adding that 'the culture of man's self, of his feelings and will' fits him 'to look around and see how he is to act' more clearly than any 'express definition' or 'prescribed mode of action' (101). Mill valued excellence of character – or said he did – solely as a condition of happiness; and in this respect he remained squarely within the utilitarian tradition.

An eloquent passage in *A System of Logic* of 1843 neatly sums up his view:

> The character itself should be, to the individual, a paramount end, simply because the existence of this ideal nobleness of character, or of a near approach to it, in any abundance, would go further than all things else towards making human life happy; both in the comparatively humble sense, of pleasure and freedom from pain, and in the higher meaning of rendering life, not what it now is almost universally, puerile and insignificant – but such as human beings with highly developed faculties can care to have (J.S. Mill 1843: 952).

Mill did not mean that having a fine character is valuable purely in the instrumental sense that someone who combines intelligence and imagination with a lively sympathy with others is likely to prove a particularly efficient (because insightful and knowledgeable) creator of happiness. Being of fine character, and having the consciousness that one is, are grounds of happiness in themselves. Yet this raises some subtle issues about the relation of happiness and the things which make a person happy which Mill did not fully apprehend. It is helpful to compare Mill's position with that of modern neo-Aristotelians, who see the acquisition of excellence of character as an intrinsically worthwhile end. Mill's official view, by contrast, was that acquiring a good character is valuable because it contributes to happiness. Part of what Mill no doubt meant here was that the exercise of imagination, benevolence, intelligence, wit, aesthetic sensibilities and the other ingredients of a fine character are pleasant or rewarding occupations in themselves. But he seems to have regarded at least some of the happiness of having a fine character as arising out of the sense *that* one has a character that is fine, and the problem with this is that it apparently conflicts with the utilitarian idea (which he never explicitly rejected) that happiness is the only ultimate value. Mill appears to have seen only hazily that a person could not reap happiness from the recognition of his own fineness of character unless he saw fineness of character as a condition worth acquiring for its own sake – where the value of a fine character explains the happiness to be taken in having it, and not the other way about. Although, as we shall see, Mill later tried to clarify the relationship of happiness with its objects by means of his 'parts of happiness' doctrine, the distinction of his middle-period position from a form of neo-Aristotelianism must be judged less than entirely clear.

## 4 Higher and lower pleasures

After the thesis and antithesis, the synthesis. It is difficult to date precisely the opening of Mill's third period as a moral philosopher. The *Autobiography* records a softening of his views on Benthamism in the 1840s and 1850s under the influence of the feminist Harriet Taylor, whom he married in 1851 after a platonic friendship lasting twenty years.

> In this third period (as it may be termed) of my mental progress, which now went hand in hand with hers, my opinions gained equally in breadth and depth, I understood more things, and those which I had understood before, I now understood more thoroughly (J.S. Mill 1873: 237).

In particular: 'I had now completely turned back from what there had been of excess in my reaction against Benthamism' (237). Harriet caused her husband to recover some of the radicalism of his youth after the relatively conservative years in which he had been 'much more indulgent to the common opinions of society and the world' (237). Once again Mill took keenly to heart Bentham's concern for social justice and his insistence on subjecting all institutions to the test of utility.

It was in these changed circumstances that Mill drafted, in the early 1850s, two essays on utility and justice which came to form the basis of the *Frazer's Magazine* articles of 1861.[4] 'Utilitarianism', as it finally appeared in the pages of *Frazer's*, is a highly puzzling work. Many of its ideas and arguments could have flowed from the pen of Bentham himself. Mill begins with an unblushing statement of pure Benthamism:

> the Greatest Happiness Principle, holds that actions are right in proportion as they tend to promote happiness, wrong as they tend to produce the reverse of happiness. By happiness is intended pleasure, and the absence of pain; by unhappiness, pain, and the privation of pleasure (J.S. Mill 1861: 210).

Moreover:

> pleasure and freedom from pain, are the only things desirable as ends; and ... all desirable things (which are as numerous in the utilitarian catalogue as in any other scheme) are desirable either for the pleasure inherent in themselves, or as means to the promotion of pleasure and the prevention of pain (210).

These formulations resemble closely the summaries of Bentham's position in the essays of the 1830s; the difference is that Mill now appears to accept them! Bentham's 'fractional truths', previously dismissed for their metaphysical and psychological inadequacy, are presented in 'Utilitarianism' without disapproval or qualification (cf. J.S. Mill 1833: 5; J.S. Mill 1838: 94). In 1838 Mill had heavily criticised the serious deficiencies of Bentham's view of human beings:

> He saw in man little but what the vulgarest eye can see; recognised no diversities of character but such as he who runs may read. Knowing so little of human feelings, he knew still less of the influences by which those feelings are formed: all the more subtle workings of the mind upon itself ... escaped him (J.S. Mill 1938: 93).

And he had thought Bentham ignorant, too, of the pursuit of other ideals for their own sake: honour and personal dignity, beauty, order, action, power and 'the love of *loving*' (96).

What had happened to cause Mill so completely to change his mind?

Why had he withdrawn his objections to a conception of man he had once condemned as not only facile but even dangerous? A possible answer, persuasive because it saves Mill from the charge of gross inconsistency, is that he had not really withdrawn his objections at all: he had merely discovered a way of incorporating a richer theory of man within the Benthamite terminology of pleasure and pain. The key to this development (on this interpretation) was Mill's arrival, sometime between the late 1830s and the early 1850s, at the belief that pleasures can be distinguished on qualitative as well as on quantitative grounds. To quote his explanation in 'Utilitarianism':

> It is quite compatible with the principle of utility to recognise the fact, that some *kinds* of pleasure are more desirable and more valuable than others. It would be absurd that while, in estimating all other things, quality is considered as well as quantity, the estimation of pleasures should be supposed to depend on quantity alone (J.S. Mill 1861: 211).

Distinguishing higher and lower pleasures, Mill suggested, offers a means of rebutting the common objection that utilitarianism (like Epicureanism), with its fixation on pleasure, is 'a doctrine worthy only of swine' (210). If an appropriate 'rule of life' for creatures with 'a human being's conceptions of happiness' is very different from one which would be suitable for a pig, then the fear evaporates that utilitarianism confines man to a degrading existence: 'Human beings have faculties more exalted than the animal appetites, and when once made made conscious of them, do not regard anything as happiness which does not include their gratification' (210–11).

An adequately satisfying human life must thus contain 'pleasures of the intellect, of the feelings and imagination, and of the moral sentiments', which have 'a much higher value as pleasures' than those of 'mere sensation' (211). 'Lower' pleasures generally require less expenditure of mind and need to be taken in strict moderation; they include (depending on tastes) activities like sunbathing on a warm beach, eating a pizza, holding hands with one's favourite person, or (an example of G.E. Moore's) throwing the crockery around when drunk. People of higher tastes spend more of their time reading Shakespeare or Kant, listening to Beethoven and writing poetry. Once we realise that pleasures can be placed in a hierarchy of quality, we need no longer resist as boorish or implausibly reductive the proposition that 'pleasure, and freedom from pain, are the only things desirable as ends'. Mill added, with more hopefulness than realism, that when people recognise one pleasure to be superior in quality to another, they will tend to prefer a very small amount of the higher to a large amount of the lower (211).

This account calls for a number of comments. To begin with, the distinction between superior and inferior pleasures was not an original discovery of Mill's, though it is often popularly represented as his most striking innovation in utilitarian theory. The distinction had always been deeply embedded within the utilitarian tradition, and Mill himself correctly ascribes it to the Epicureans (210). To be sure, Mill added that the superiority of mental over bodily pleasures consists in more than merely such 'circumstantial advantages' as the greater 'permanency, safety, uncostliness, etc.' of the former which the Epicureans had stressed; and some commentators have taken this to mean that Millian higher pleasures possess some kind of non-utilitarian value which is absent in lower ones. This interpretation, however, is quite uncertain; Mill may simply have meant that higher pleasures, apart from their 'circumstantial advantages', are also more deeply pleasing pleasures than the rest. But it is notable that almost all the writers we have considered in our historical survey have believed some pleasures to be more worth seeking than others; and most (like Mill) have valued intellectual and aesthetic pleasures, and the pleasures of sympathy, more highly than those of the 'animal appetites'. Even Bentham, though he undervalued the pleasures of the imagination, thought intellectual pleasures generally greater than bodily ones (John Stuart Mill's education was intended to turn him into a scholar, not a playboy). Mill's own way of explaining the higher–lower distinction is foreshadowed most closely by Hutcheson, who anticipated his criterion for determining the place of pleasures in a qualitative hierarchy. Both men believed that the most worthy pleasures are the ones, whichever they may be, which the most competently equipped judges prefer – a proposal whose problems we have noted in the previous chapter.

Mill may not have invented the notion of a qualitative scale of pleasures, but on the view we are considering his originality consisted in grasping the use that could be made of it to encompass an adequate theory of human ends within the standard utilitarian formula. Yet if this reading is right, it is surprising that Mill did not explain his intentions more plainly. Only three or four pages are devoted to the subject of higher and lower pleasures, and most of the discussion is concerned with the specific problem of identifying a workable criterion of quality. If the distinction of higher and lower pleasures is Mill's long-sought-for philosopher's stone, the fact is very well concealed. There are, besides, substantial philosophical objections, as Mill knew better than anyone, to identifying all species of human fulfilment with forms of *pleasure*. Bentham's pivotal mistake, as Mill had diagnosed it in the 1830s, was not to underestimate the kinds and varieties of pleasure, but to think that pleasure was the *only* worthy goal of human activity. Mill saw clearly in his middle period that no amount of arranging pleasures in hierarchies of quality would overturn the fundamental fact that human well-being did not consist solely in the acquisition of pleasures and the avoidance of pains. Bentham had forgotten (if he had ever known) that fulfilled lives manifest 'spiritual perfection' and self-respect, and the love of external objects like beauty, order and truth. It is certainly possible that Mill, in the season of his happy marriage to Harriet, had become more generously disposed towards pleasure, and readier than formerly to grant to it a central position among human goods. But it is hard to believe that he had abandoned his old opinions so completely as to think that happiness was nothing more than pleasure (even pleasure of the higher kinds) and the absence of pain. Attaining spiritual perfection or a love of beauty may give pleasure, but it is not, and logically cannot be, that anticipated pleasure which motivates the pursuit of them as goals. They must first be seen as autonomously valuable components of a human life that is going well before their attainment can please, or the failure to attain them give pain.

Recent years have witnessed an increasing and welcome tendency among commentators to emphasise the value of the ethical writings of Mill's middle period. Sir Isaiah Berlin's essay 'John Stuart Mill on the ends of life' (1969) and Fred Berger's book *Happiness, Justice and Freedom: The Moral and Political Philosophy of John Stuart Mill* (1984) are perhaps the most influential of several works which have rightly given centre stage to Mill's ideas on the ethical centrality of self-development. More problematic, however, has been the tendency in some of this new writing to interpret Mill's ideas on higher and lower pleasures in the light of his second-period views. According to Elizabeth Anderson, Mill's higher pleasures are those which are 'taken in the realization of excellence' (Anderson 1991: 13); in Susan Feagin's opinion they are 'felt in response to an idea more "noble and majestic" than anything met with in sense experience' (Feagin 1983: 251). Rem Edwards considers them to be the 'distinctively human' pleasures (Edwards 1979: 113); while Berger's own suggestion is that they are 'more crucial to our happiness than others', because particularly important in the development of our 'human capacities' (Berger: 1984: 40, 38). These interpretations are probably reading more into the text than is really there. Mill's higher–lower distinction is presented in an entirely traditional form: there are said to be, on the one hand, the bodily pleasures corresponding to the 'animal appetites', on the other, the pleasures of the intellect, of sympathy, of the feelings and the imagination; but the importance of the latter pleasures is not referred to the role they may play in developing a fine character. Mill even expressed a doubt 'whether a noble character is always the happier for its nobleness', and this genuine reminiscence of his earlier views indicates how great he still thought the conceptual distance between the goals of pleasure and of self-development (J.S. Mill 1861: 213). Although by the 1850s Mill had softened in his opposition to Benthamism, it is not easy to believe that he had abandoned the central insight of the middle period that there is more to life than pleasure, and that conceptions of happiness like Bentham's which do not recognise this truth rest on a one-dimensional view of human experience.

What, then, is the point of Mill's discussion of higher and lower pleasures? A likely, if rather dull, explanation is that Mill wished to keep the discussion simple in what was meant to be a popular defence of utilitarianism rather than a text for professional philosophers. Voicing his personal doubts about the adequacy of a pleasure-centred theory of welfare might have been more candid philosophically, but would not have helped to sell utilitarian ideals to a sceptical public. Utilitarianism had never enjoyed a good press, and it had lately been subjected to unjust attack by the most prominent novelist of the day. Jeremy Bentham may have been, as Mill called him, 'a boy to the last', with too great a reverence for 'facts' (J.S. Mill 1838: 92), but whatever the deficiencies of his character, his fundamentally hedonistic philosophy was worlds away from the bleak Gradgrindery of *Hard Times*. In the context of the 1850s debate, Mill probably thought it more important to convey the fundamental humanity of the greatest happiness principle than to worry his readers with a family quarrel between himself and Bentham over the relation of pleasure and well-being. The ancient distinction of higher and lower pleasures lay ready to hand as the ideal instrument for persuading his audience that utilitarianism was neither a 'doctrine fit only for swine' nor a system for turning out automata. Mill readily availed himself of it.

There are other passages in 'Utilitarianism', however, which more nearly resemble the writings of the middle period. Mill's sketchy but intriguing analysis, in the fourth chapter, of happiness as a complex end composed of a number of separate ends manifests his settled conviction that happiness, as the goal of life, is a multi-dimensional affair, in which beauty, truth, virtue, personal excellence and other ends exist alongside that of pleasure. Admittedly, he immediately added that 'desiring a thing and finding it pleasant, aversion to it and thinking of it as painful, are phenomena entirely inseparable' – indeed, they are 'two different modes of naming the same psychological fact' (J.S. Mill 1861: 237). This obscures the fact, as Mill must have realised, that the attainment of desirable ends gives us pleasure *just because* we ascribe an independent value to those ends, and so are pleased to see them accomplished. But despite the simplifications which Mill no doubt felt it necessary to make for a popular audience, the chapter as a whole manifests clearly his conviction that there are other valuable goals in life besides pleasure and the absence of pain. But we can appropriately postpone a more detailed examination of Mill's 'parts of happiness' doctrine to Chapter VI, when we shall turn to the broader question of the definition of utilitarian goals.

## 5 The 'proof of utility'

Bentham believed the principle of utility to be incapable of proof; it was too ultimate a principle for its truth to be demonstrated by reference to anything else: 'Is it susceptible of any direct proof? It should seem not: for that which is used to prove every thing else, cannot itself be proved: a chain of proofs must have their commencement somewhere' (Bentham 1789: 2). Bentham added that giving such a proof was not only impossible but needless – presumably because he thought it incoherent to speak of requiring a thing which logically could not be supplied (2).

Mill was dissatisfied with this position, and with good reason. If nothing could be said to vindicate the greatest happiness principle, then its proponents were in no better case than those intuitional philosophers whom Bentham derided – the people who erected 'every inveterate belief and every intense feeling of which the origin is not remembered' into 'its own all-sufficient voucher and justification' (J.S. Mill 1873: 233).[5] Utilitarians should if possible avoid similarly insisting on the self-evidence of a principle they were unable to verify. But Mill conceded Bentham's point that 'questions of ultimate ends do not admit of proof, in the ordinary acceptation of the term', any more than do 'the first principles of our knowledge'. Nevertheless just as ultimate questions of fact can be 'made the subject of a direct appeal' to the sensory basis of our knowledge, so too, he thought, ultimate questions about ends can be defended by appeal to the basis of natural desires (J.S. Mill 1861: 234).

Mill's 'proof of utility', in the third paragraph of the fourth chapter of 'Utilitarianism', has received little praise, and it is indisputable that as it stands it is deeply flawed; identifying the two serious fallacies it contains has been a popular training exercise for generations of undergraduates. But whether the passage is the irredeemable tissue of errors and confusion which its fiercer critics like Bradley and Moore have asserted it to be is less easy to decide. Mill begins by affirming that questions about ends are questions about what is desirable, and that the utilitarian doctrine is that only happiness is desirable as an end. But why, he asks, should this doctrine be believed?

> The only proof capable of being given that an object is visible, is that people actually see it. The only proof that a sound is audible, is that people hear it: and so of the other sources of our experience. In like manner, I apprehend, the sole evidence it is possible to produce that anything is desirable, is that people do actually desire it (234).

The mistake in this reasoning is evident. While the proof that something is visible or audible is that people see or hear it, the proof that something is desirable cannot be that people desire it, because 'desirable' means not '*able* to be desired' but rather '*worthy* to be desired'. Happiness may be what all or most people want; but it does not follow that it is what they *ought* to want. Maybe people should desire instead to do their duty, or to obey the law of God.

Mill makes bad worse by his supplementary argument to show that not only one's own happiness, but the *general* happiness, is a desirable object:

> No reason can be given why the general happiness is desirable, except that each person, so far as he believes it to be attainable, desires his own happiness. This, however, being a fact, we have not only all the proof which the case admits of, but all which it is possible to require, that happiness is a good: that each person's happiness is a good to that person, and the general happiness, therefore, a good to the aggregate of all persons (234).

Mill's purpose here is to show that the general good (the utilitarian goal) is a rational goal for individual agents. But this proposition is not entailed by the premise that each individual's happiness is a good for that individual. In a letter of 1868 to Henry Jones, Mill admitted that the argument was badly stated, but insisted that all that he had meant to prove was that 'since A's happiness is a good, B's a good, C's a good, etc., the sum of all these goods must be a good' (J.S. Mill 1972: 1414). This conclusion, however, is patently weaker than the one which Mill initially aimed at. If each individual's happiness is a good *to him*, the happiness of all is, in one sense, a good to 'the aggregate of all persons'. But that is not the same as saying that the *general* happiness is a good to each individual – the premise needed to vindicate the principle of utility.

Let us return to Mill's assertion that 'the sole evidence it is possible to produce that anything is desirable, is that people do actually desire it'. Granted that this is not justified by the suggested analogy between 'desirable' and 'visible'/'audible', can any more cogent argument be offered for it? In fact the proposition becomes more plausible when considered in the light of Mill's thoroughly naturalistic view of human values. There are two essential aspects to this. First, Mill would not have considered it probable (he may even have considered it meaningless to suppose) that something could be a worthwhile objective for human beings if it were a thing that would never be chosen by persons in possession of all the relevant empirical facts. Things that fully informed people find no reason to desire are unpromising candidates for objects we *ought to* desire. People do not as a rule, for instance, desire to turn three somersaults before breakfast. Any claim that we *should* perform this athletic feat strikes us as senseless unless it comes with some persuasive reasons. (Maybe someone will find one day that turning somersaults before breakfast improves the digestion.) Things which people do not desire, because no one has yet found a reason for desiring them, cannot sensibly be proclaimed to be desirable;[6] and only mystics or irrationalists would claim a thing to be valuable without having an explanation of how it answers to human interests.

Second, a naturalistic conception of value can make little room for the idea that things which are normally desired by well-informed people may nevertheless be worthless. Certainly there can be misguided desires for things which are in reality rather bad for us: for example, people may falsely believe that taking a particular drug assists longevity or sexual performance when its only effect is to destroy the kidneys. Such errors are in principle discoverable ones. But it would be hard to believe that the universal desire for happiness could be similarly founded on ignorance of its actual worthlessness. If people generally desire happiness, it is scarcely coherent to suppose that what they want may nevertheless be bad. In short, an adherent to a naturalistic conception treats with scepticism two sorts of claim: first, that a thing may be valuable which rational and informed persons find undesirable, and second, that a thing which rational and informed people desire may really be valueless. A naturalistic philosopher like Mill takes the actual pattern of human desires to be the strongest possible evidence as to what is genuinely desirable from the human point of view (the only one which matters to us).

Mill can hardly be said to argue for such a naturalistic perspective; he takes it very much for granted. But for anyone who shares that perspective, Mill's claim that happiness is not only a desired object but a desirable one has much to commend it.[7] Given the empirical and anti-mystical character of the naturalistic point of view, it could reasonably be held that the onus of argument falls on anyone who rejects it. But reliance on the naturalistic perspective alone will not suffice to save the second part of Mill's case. To establish that the *general* happiness is a rational objective of *individual* agents requires a different kind of argument.

There is little hope of rescuing Mill's own defence. From the premise that an individual person has an *agent-relative* reason for desiring his own happiness, it cannot be inferred that he has an *agent-neutral* reason for desiring the happiness of anyone, or of everyone, else. But a more sophisticated argument to the same conclusion appeared a few years later in Henry Sidgwick's *The Methods of Ethics* (1874), and a form of this argument has recently been restated by Thomas Nagel in *The View from Nowhere* (1986). Sidgwick begins, in an echo of Mill, by speaking of the 'Universal Good' as a whole of which the goods of all individual human beings are the 'integrant parts'. By then 'considering the relation of integrant parts to the whole and to each other', we are able to obtain the 'self-evident principle that the good of any one individual is of no more importance, from the point of view ... of the Universe, than the good of any other'. With this first 'self-evident' premise Sidgwick conjoins a second: that 'as a rational being I am bound to aim at good generally, – so far as it is attainable by my efforts, – not merely at a particular part of it'. Thus:

[f]rom these two rational intuitions we may deduce, as a necessary inference, the maxim of Benevolence in an abstract form: viz. that each one is morally bound to regard the good of any other individual as much as his own, except in so far as he judges it to be less, when impartially viewed, or less certainly knowable or attainable by him (Sidgwick 1874: 382).

Mill attempted the hopeless task of justifying an impartial concern for human welfare on the basis of the partial concern of each individual agent for his own welfare; Sidgwick's, on the surface less illogical, strategy is to defend the impartiality of moral concern as an intrinsically reasonable position from the point of view of the universe. But are individual human beings capable of occupying this self-transcending perspective? Sidgwick believed that they are; and his belief is shared by Nagel. In Nagel's opinion, none of us is condemned to a permanent subjectivity of consciousness; we are also able to form an objective view of the world (a 'view from nowhere') that takes in ourselves and our own subjective viewpoint. Objectivity 'allows us to transcend our particular viewpoint and develop an expanded consciousness that takes in the world more fully'. And significantly 'this applies to values and attitudes as well as to beliefs and theories' (Nagel 1986: 5). Nagel finds it 'self-evident' that pleasure and pain have 'neutral value' – that is, value which is irrespective of their subjects – and not merely 'relative value' to those subjects themselves. But '[i]f we assign impersonal value to pleasure and pain, then each person can think about his own suffering not just that he has reason to want it gone, but that it's bad and should be got rid of.' When the 'objective self' (that is, the self taking the objective perspective – Sidgwick's 'point of view of the universe') contemplates pain, it regards it as something to be eliminated regardless of whose pain it is.

> The desire to be rid of pain has only the pain as its object. This is shown by the fact that it doesn't even require the idea of *oneself* in order to make sense: if I lacked or lost the conception of myself as distinct from other possible or actual persons, I could still apprehend the badness of pain, immediately. So when I consider it from an objective standpoint, the ego doesn't get between the pain and the objective self. . . . There's a reason for me to be given morphine which is independent of the fact that the pain is mine – namely that it's awful (160–2).

Considerations like these support the claim that the general happiness can be a rational object of concern to each individual agent – once he takes up the objective point of view. From this standpoint, happiness is a good, irrespective of its subject, and the more happiness there is around, the better. (Hence the idea of pleasure and pain having neutral value offers some support to the maximising strand in utilitarianism.)

But if the objective point of view is only one of the perspectives available to a person, the question remains whether anything rationally compels him to take it up. Imagine that you and I are both suffering from headaches, and that the only available aspirin tablet is locked in my medicine cabinet. From an objective viewpoint I may grant that my pain has no better claim to be alleviated than yours; I may even allow that, to judge by your moans and groans, your headache seems to be worse than mine and so (objectively speaking) is a more regrettable event in the history of the universe. But should I give you my aspirin tablet when from my subjective point of view only *my* headache hurts me? If I swallow the tablet in front of your eyes, you can accuse me of meanness, but scarcely of irrationality. Neither Sidgwick nor Nagel commit the naive error of supposing that because the objective perspective is a legitimate one for an individual, he cannot rationally refuse to assume it. 'The relation between agent-relative and agent-neutral reasons,' writes Nagel, 'is probably the central question of ethical theory' (159); it is one we shall have to return to in Chapter VIII. Mill's contention that the general happiness is a good to the aggregate of persons, and so to each member of the aggregate, is warranted on the basis of the objective perspective. But unless some reason can be shown why the objective point of view should trump the subjective, it remains to be established that a rational individual should prefer to promote the general happiness in preference to his own.

## 6 Utility and justice

Mill acknowledged in the fifth and final chapter of 'Utilitarianism' that a common and persistent 'obstacle to the reception' of the doctrine of utility is that the expedient is not the same as the just, and that the demands of justice possess more moral force (are 'far more imperative') than those of utility (J.S. Mill 1861: 240–1). Mill clearly felt some sympathy with this objection, which seemed to him to be noteworthy for two reasons. In the first place, he himself accepted that there was a meaningful distinction between the positively wrong and the merely inexpedient. But if utility was the sole ultimate criterion by which the value of actions could be assessed, some subsidiary principle was needed to determine where that distinction fell. Second, popular conceptions seemed to imply the possibility of clashes between the demands of justice and those of utility. For example, breaking faith with anyone, or violating an agreement, were normally thought to be unjust; yet on exceptional occasions they might enhance the public good. It was an important question, then, whether utilitarianism really did sometimes sanction injustice.

To resolve these issues, Mill began by making a distinction between two senses of the term 'unjust'. Sometimes when we describe a thing as unjust we mean that it violates the *legal rights* of a person, those which are secured to him by the laws of the state of which he is a citizen. But we also employ the notions of justice and injustice in a further sense, in which we mean by calling a thing unjust that it 'consists in taking or withholding from any person that to which he has a *moral right*' (242). Not all human laws are just in the moral sense, and an individual may sometimes possess legal rights which belong to him only by virtue of a morally bad law. Such ill-founded rights cannot be regarded as 'absolute', in Mill's opinion; they may properly be 'overruled by a stronger obligation of justice', though Mill allows some force to an argument from expediency, resting on 'the common interest of mankind, of maintaining inviolate the sentiment of submission to law', against breaking even a bad law. Such laws should ideally be repealed rather than broken (242). (Mill is thus a kind of qualified rule-utilitarian about laws of the land.)

Mill's view of the relationship between utility and justice is that justice in the moral sense is fundamentally one and the same with utility, while the justice of laws should always be determined by the criterion of utility (that is, a good law is a *useful* law). It is an illusion, he thinks, to suppose that utility and justice in the *moral* sense can conflict, for a thing cannot be at odds with itself. But it can sometimes happen that what is just 'in ordinary cases' fails to be just because of some peculiar disposition of utilities:

> Thus, to save a life, it may not only be allowable, but a duty, to steal, or take by force, the necessary food or medicine, or to kidnap, or compel to officiate, the only qualified medical practitioner (259).

This, Mill stresses, is not to permit utility to triumph over justice. In cases like these, justice itself demands that we do the thing which it would normally be wrong to do. It is clear from this that utilitarian justice is quite different from Kantian. Kant would not permit the interests of one person to be sacrificed for the greater good of others, for this would be to treat him as a means to others' good rather than as an end in himself. Mill's view is that such sacrifices, in a well-ordered society, will be rare but not unknown.

But Mill is prepared to accede to the popular belief that an unjust act is worse than a merely inexpedient one. The inconsistency here is more apparent than real. Moral injustice, in Mill's view, is nothing other than disutility; but disutility comes in degrees, and there is something to be said for the popular habit of reserving the term 'unjust' for the more seriously harmful acts or states of affairs – specifically for those which are bad enough to be worth discouraging by institutional or some other form of sanctions:

> We do not call anything wrong [i.e. unjust], unless we mean to imply that a person ought to be punished in some way or other for doing it; if not by law, by the opinion of his fellow-creatures; if not by opinion, by the reproaches of his own conscience. This seems the real turning-point of the distinction between morality and simple expediency. . . . Duty is a thing which may be *exacted* from a person, as one exacts a debt (246).

No doubt this is partly intended to point up the measure of convergence of utilitarianism and ordinary morality. But Mill probably has in mind, too, the common objection that utilitarianism is an unreasonably rigorous doctrine because it condemns as immoral even the most trivial failures to promote the good. Mill attempts to render utilitarianism less demanding by suggesting that no moral blame attaches to actions (or inactions) insufficiently serious to merit 'punishment' (understanding that term broadly enough to include the unpleasant reproaches of the agent's own conscience). But this proposal is more problematic than he realises. Although any rational utilitarian will recognise that some harmful things are trivial in comparison with others, he cannot – as a theorist who accepts the logical dependence of the right on the good – lay down by fiat that things which are only slightly harmful are morally neutral. Slightly harmful things must be slightly immoral; and if they are guilty to only a small degree, they deserve at least the punishment of self-reproach. It would have simplified Mill's theory considerably if he had ceased to insist on a distinction between the unjust and the merely inexpedient, and adopted a 'sliding-scale' account of guiltiness instead. Defining wrongness in terms of punishability may seem to reverse, in any case, the correct logical order. To decide whether, and how severely, a person should be punished for something he has done, we normally think that we must first determine the moral quality of his action. The concept of punishment is posterior, not prior, to the concept of wrongdoing.

But it might be suggested in Mill's defence that he is not really saying that it is actions which are *worthy* of punishment that are bad, but only that those actions are to be judged as bad whose deterrence by sanctions enhances utility. This is the way he has been interpreted in an influential article by David Lyons. On Lyons's reading, Mill thinks that a particular act is wrong if, and only if, the establishment of a coercive social rule against doing acts of its kind would yield a positive balance of utility (Lyons 1976: 103).[8] Provided that we can make the relevant comparative judgements of utility, we should have little difficulty in applying the label 'wrong' to those deeds we see good reason to discourage. But the question arises of what the term 'wrong' can mean if its use is explained in this way. There are many kinds of act we customarily regard as morally bad but do not seek to deter by coercive rules. Such rules are normally applied not to prevent morally culpable deeds but those in the different category of the socially unacceptable – breaking a contract, for example, but not simply failing to keep a promise. Socially unacceptable deeds are not even a subset of morally culpable ones; some socially unacceptable practices are not intrinsically immoral, such as driving one's car in

Britain on the right-hand side of the road. Mill's own formulation makes a fairer bid to capture the category of morally wrong deeds, operating as it does with a broader notion of punishment; Millian sanctions include adverse public comment and the recriminations of the agent's own conscience, as well as the sort of coercive rules employed to deter acts of a socially unacceptable type. As it stands this must be too wide as a criterion of the morally wrong, implying the inclusion of socially unacceptable but not immoral actions within the category of the unjust. But its main problem is that the only sanction appropriate to many kinds of deed is the bite of a bad conscience; and one cannot know when it is appropriate to feel conscience-stricken about something one has done without already knowing that one's act was wrong. The concept of moral guilt, like that of punishment, is logically subordinate to the concept of moral fault.

Mill's attempt to make punishability the criterion of injustice in the moral sense must be judged unsatisfactory. But the criterion construed in Lyons's way, where Mill's term 'punishment' is understood to refer to the application of socially coercive rules, is a plausible rule of thumb to guide the construction of a system of laws. To determine what duties and rights to ascribe to the citizens of a state, it is reasonable to ask what kinds of practice should, on grounds of utility, be deterred by social sanctions; and anything not worth forbidding may be considered as permitted. Mill himself proposes that the notion of legal constraint is the essence of law and the 'generating idea' of the notion of justice (J.S. Mill 1861: 246). He plausibly adds that the concept of justice is a progressive one, and that it is the mark of an enlightened state to assign legal sanctions on the basis of the public utility rather than on that of private or sectional interests. (It is only at the next stage that Mill's account becomes less convincing, when he asserts that 'the idea of penal sanction ... enters not only into the conception of [legal] injustice, but into that of any kind of wrong' (246).)

Mill readily admits that much more remains to be said about the shape of a utilitarian system of laws; there are many particular questions to be settled about such issues as the entitlement to hold property or to reap superior remuneration for superior talents, the obligation to pay taxes, and the extent of a citizen's required services to the community. As a paramount guiding principle, he suggests that institutions should be suitably devised to ensure a high degree of personal security to individuals, 'to every one's feelings the most vital of all interests':

> All other earthly benefits are needed by one person, not needed by another; ... but security no human being can possibly do without;

on it we depend for all our immunity from evil, and for the whole value of all and every good, beyond the passing moment; since nothing but the gratification of the instant could be of any worth to us, if we could be deprived of anything the next instant by whoever was momentarily stronger than ourselves (251).[9]

Unfortunately Mill never seriously tackles the question of how far an individual's security can be guaranteed in a social dispensation organised on utilitarian principles. We have seen him concede that individuals may sometimes have to suffer hardship where considerations of social welfare demand it. It is not, of course, inconsistent with this admission to claim that such enforced sacrifices should be kept to a minimum; no society could be happy whose members went in constant fear of becoming sacrificial victims on the altar of utility. Mill quotes with approval Bentham's dictum of equal treatment, 'everybody to count for one, nobody for more than one' (58). But more discussion is needed than he provides of where, and how, the line should be drawn between the satisfaction of public needs and the protection of individual interests.

# CHAPTER V

# Some Later Developments

## 1 Intuitional utilitarianism: Sidgwick

A good case can be made for regarding Henry Sidgwick's *The Methods of Ethics* as the most important work on moral philosophy to be published in English in the nineteenth century. A text of great richness, it has illuminating things to say on almost all the major issues of theoretical ethics: the nature of motivation, the justification of first principles, the problem of egoism, the reality of benevolence, justice, the virtues, the meaning of happiness and the shape of the good life for man. No attempt will be made here to summarise more than a few of Sidgwick's arguments and conclusions; readers who wish for a more detailed survey of his ideas may consult J.B. Schneewind's excellent study *Sidgwick's Ethics and Victorian Moral Philosophy* (1977). Sidgwick (1838–1900) published *The Methods of Ethics* in 1874, one year after Mill's death and nine before his own appointment as Knightbridge Professor of Moral Philosophy in the University of Cambridge; the book went through several extensively revised editions in his lifetime. An exceptionally careful and fair-minded thinker, Sidgwick was influenced by several schools of moral thought without becoming a partisan of any. But his final if somewhat tentative position is a utilitarian one, though it depends on an intuitional account of moral knowledge which would have disconcerted Bentham and J.S. Mill.

Utilitarianism (or 'Universalistic Hedonism') Sidgwick defined as the theory that

> the conduct which, under any given circumstances, is objectively right, is that which will produce the greatest amount of happiness on the whole; that is, taking into account all whose happiness is affected by the conduct (Sidgwick 1874: 411).

But Sidgwick marvelled at the ease with which most utilitarian writers had combined the principle that everyone ought to seek the happiness of all with the quite different principle of 'Psychological Hedonism', that each ought to seek his own happiness. The contrast between the two propositions was 'so obvious and glaring', that it was hard to understand 'how the two ever came to be confounded, or in any way included under one notion' (411–12). Even if universalistic hedonism and psychological hedonism could be held together without offence to reason (and it was not obvious that they could), it was certain that the former could not be logically derived from the latter – so Mill's 'proof of utility' was a plain *non sequitur*. Sidgwick's moral philosophy can in fact be seen as an extended meditation on the relationship between self-interest and altruism. In some posthumously discovered manuscript notes for a lecture he explained with great clarity how his mature views developed out of a growing dissatisfaction with the standpoint of Mill.[1] Initially attracted both to the 'frank naturalness' of the claim that people seek their own happiness as well as to the 'morally inspiring' 'dictate of readiness for absolute self-sacrifice', he came gradually to the disturbing conclusion that these two positions were in much more tension than Mill had recognised. This, he thought, was the conflict, rather than that between 'Intuitions or Moral Sense Perceptions, and Hedonism, whether Epicurean or Utilitarian', which philosophers of a utilitarian persuasion most urgently needed to resolve (xvii–xviii).

Sidgwick saw that it was of little use to say, with Mill, that individual self-sacrifice in the interests of others was 'heroic'; this evaded the question how self-sacrificing action could ever be *rational*, if the 'natural end of action' was always the agent's happiness.

> I put to him in my mind the dilemma: – Either it is for my own happiness or it is not. If not, why should I do it? – It was no use to say that if I was a moral hero I should have formed a habit of willing actions beneficial to others which would remain in force, even with my own pleasure in the other scale. I knew that I was not the kind of moral hero who does this without reason; from *blind* habit. Nor did I even wish to be that kind of hero: for it seemed to me that that kind of hero, however admirable, was certainly not a philosopher. I must somehow *see* that it was right for me to sacrifice my happiness for the good of the whole of which I was a part (xviii).

There was no difficulty in accounting for the rationality of self-interest, with its basis in the natural psychology of human beings. Sidgwick admitted that there was room for debate about the precise nature of the good for man (for example, whether it is pleasure, or self-preservation, or self-realisation), but thought that there was little room for disputing the reasonableness of an individual's pursuit of his own ends. The harder question is whether it is ever reasonable for him to seek the good of others. Sidgwick readily accepted the view, urged by previous writers, that there are considerable pleasures to be gleaned from benevolent activity. The wholly selfish man 'misses the sense of elevation and enlargement given by wide interests'; he forgoes the 'peculiar rich sweetness ... which is always found in services rendered to those whom we love and who are grateful'. And he is made to feel 'the discord between the rhythms of his own life and of that larger life of which his own is but an insignificant fraction' (501). Nevertheless, the appeal so far is only to the unselfish agent's *own* interests; he is a gainer by his benevolence. It is still unclear why he should perform any altruistic actions which leave him a loser. Yet people do sometimes do genuinely self-sacrificing things; and the pleasures of benevolent action are frequently outweighed by the painfulness of the sympathetic emotions we feel for other people's unhappiness (especially where we cannot relieve it). It is also to the distressful rather than to the more pleasing forms of benevolent activity that 'Duty' seems most sharply to summon us (503). The central problem, then, is to discover some reasonable ground for putting ourselves out for our neighbour, some rational basis for genuinely disinterested behaviour.

It seemed to Sidgwick that there was only one possible way out of the difficulty: to 'recognise the need of a fundamental ethical intuition' that it was right for an individual to sacrifice his happiness for the greater good of others: 'The utilitarian method – which I had learnt from Mill – could not, it seemed to me, be made coherent and harmonious without this fundamental intuition' (xviii–xix). Sidgwick was well aware how heretical such a view would have seemed to an anti-intuitional thinker like Mill, for whom a chief merit of utilitarianism was its ability to dispense with quasi-mystical and question-begging appeals to a faculty of intuition. But if utilitarianism needed an intuitional basis, it was crucial to demonstrate the rational cogency of the intuitions on which it rested. In J.B. Schneewind's words, Sidgwick's axioms 'are obtained not by mental inspection of esoteric entities, but by considering what reason requires of action under the conditions set by the most basic facts of human life' (Schneewind 1977: 303). Sidgwick proposed four conditions 'the complete fulfilment of which would establish a significant proposition, apparently self-evident, in the highest degree of certainty attainable' (Sidgwick 1874: 338). First, 'the terms of the proposition must be clear and precise'. Second, 'the self-evidence of the proposition must be ascertained by careful reflection'. (Sidgwick warned that 'most persons are liable to confound intuitions . . . with mere impressions or impulses', especially in the area of morals.) Third, 'the propositions accepted as self-evident must be mutually consistent'. Fourth, 'since it is implied in the very notion of Truth that it is essentially the same for all minds, the denial by another of a proposition that I have affirmed has a tendency to impair my confidence in its validity'. (Sidgwick added the comment that it is the absence of dissent by those who have properly understood the proposition which matters, not the agreement of the ignorant) (338–42).

As to what the axioms are, Sidgwick suggested that we should begin by looking at the evidence offered by 'common morality', and the considerable measure of agreement on principles found 'at least among moral persons of our own age and civilisation' (215). But many of the generally accepted maxims of everyday morality are 'deficient in clearness and precision' and philosophical techniques are needed to correct and refine them. Sidgwick's proposed 'self-evident' maxims are supposed to be the fundamental principles which underlie the more specific maxims of 'common morality'. Sidgwick's list of them testifies to the eclectic nature of his reading. Kant impressed him with the principle of universalisability, that 'whatever is right for me is right for all persons in similar circumstances' (xix; cf. 378–80). Butler's *Sermons* (1726) convinced him of the existence of 'disinterested' or 'extra-regarding' impulses to action, alongside the motives of self-interest. The recognition of this 'Dualism of the Practical reason' made it essential to locate a principle which would unify and reconcile the two mainsprings of action, and Sidgwick found it in a maxim he drew from Henry More and Samuel Clarke, that 'I ought not to prefer my own lesser good to the greater good of another.' This, together with the related maxim that 'I ought not to prefer a present lesser good to a future greater good', appeared to him equally self-evident with the mathematical axiom that 'If equals are added to equals the wholes are equal'; and both depended on the more basic principle that 'as a rational being I am bound to aim at good generally' (382–3).[2]

Sidgwick believed that this set of maxims was sufficient to vindicate an ethic of a utilitarian kind, impartial, universalist and maximising. (Aggregativeness he accepted with few qualms, believing that 'in all ordinary prudential reasoning . . . the assumption is made that all the pleasures and pains that man can experience bear a finite ratio to each other in respect of pleasantness and its opposite' (124).)[3] We have already seen, in examining Mill's version of the 'proof of utility', how Sidgwick considered the moral point of view to be 'the point of view of the Universe' rather than that of the individual agent. From this radically impersonal perspective Sidgwick's fundamental maxims have a great deal of force. If, as he and Nagel believe, we are capable of transcending our limited, subjective viewpoints and assuming a stance of pure objectivity, the proper attitude to the good would seem to be – as Sidgwick claimed – to promote it, irrespective of who wins and who loses in the process. The critical question from the objective point of view is never 'Whose good?' but always 'How much good?' To quote Schneewind again:

> Why, then, are we to *maximise* goodness? This seems to follow [for Sidgwick] simply from the definitions of rightness and goodness. Goodness is by definition a concept allowing of degrees or of comparability, and rightness is defined in terms of bringing about the greatest good within the agent's power (Schneewind 1977: 307).

It seems likewise to follow from the definition of *evil* that it is something to be eliminated or reduced, wherever it is found. (Compare Nagel's remark that pain does not need to be *my* pain for me to have a reason to get rid of it (Nagel 1986: 159).) Sidgwick's basic principles thus rest on firmer ground than do many allegedly self-evident principles, in ethics and elsewhere. They are not mere 'impressions and impulses', but rather constitutive principles of the objective view of good and evil, from which abstraction has been made of the identities of agents and patients.

However, Sidgwick was forced to acknowledge that there seems to be 'an ultimate and fundamental contradiction in our apparent intuitions of what is reasonable in conduct' (Sidgwick 1874: 508). Although he did not express it in just these terms, it is clear that he saw this 'contradiction' as arising from the duality of objective and subjective perspectives which human beings are able to take on their lives. The conflict, he suggested in the final paragraph of the book, may possibly be soluble; but whether it is or not remains a 'profoundly difficult and controverted question' (508). A person may grant that, objectively speaking, his own good is only a part of the general good, and that there is no justification for him to prefer a smaller benefit for himself to a larger benefit for others. Yet from his subjective point of view the balance of interests appears quite differently. 'It would be contrary to Common Sense to deny,' Sidgwick admitted,

> that the distinction between any one individual and any other is real and fundamental, and that consequently 'I' am concerned with

the quality of my existence as an individual in a sense, fundamentally important, in which I am not concerned with the quality of the
existence of other individuals (498).

Someone may, for instance, find that a regard for 'Utilitarian Duty'
demands from him a sacrifice of his life. There may be some people he
cares about so much that he would not wish to gain a longer life by
sacrificing their happiness to his own. But there are few individuals,
'however strongly and widely sympathetic', who feel for mankind in
general 'a degree of sympathy at all commensurate with their concern
for wife or children, or lover, or intimate friend' (498). To experience
this conflict of practical reason is the mark not merely of the egoist but
of every normal human being.

These acute if inconclusive reflections on the 'antinomy of practical
reason' (as it might be termed) are of more lasting philosophical interest
than Sidgwick's attempt to press his utilitarian principles into support of
the conservative moral system of his day. His discussion of the relationship of utilitarianism to 'the morality of Common Sense' is disappointing partly because of the very limited scope he allows for the
theory of utility to function in a critical role – his prim instruction that
the utilitarian 'must repudiate altogether that temper of rebelling against
the established morality, as something purely external and conventional'
and do all in his power to sustain the established *mores*, is reminiscent
of Paley and quite alien to the reforming spirit of Mill (275). But
Sidgwick's account is more seriously unsatisfactory because his maximising utilitarian axioms do not accord well with the generally non-
maximising temper of the Victorian moral code.

Sidgwick is not the only utilitarian to have thought that 'middle
axioms' are required to guide the advancement of happiness. It would
make the moral life excessively complicated if act-utilitarian evaluation
had to be applied to every fresh moral dilemma. Human experience over
generations has evolved rules for dealing with classes of cases, and
Sidgwick believed that these rules were incorporated in a well-nigh
perfect form in the moral code of 1870s England. Mill, too, he pointed
out, had accepted the need for '*media axiomata*', though he disputed
Mill's qualification that 'the "rules of morality for the multitude" are to
be accepted by the philosopher [only] provisionally, until he has got
something better' (461).[4] In Sidgwick's opinion, 'the utilitarian, in the
existing state of knowledge, cannot possibly construct a morality *de novo*
either for man as he is ... or for man as he ought to be and will be'
(474). To be sure, he should refrain from treating the conventional rules
with superstitious awe, as an 'absolute or Divine code'. Still:

111

he will contemplate it with reverence and wonder, as a marvellous product of nature, the result of long centuries of growth, showing in many parts the same fine adaptation of means to complex exigencies as the most elaborate structures of physical organisms exhibit (475–6).

This rhapsodic enthusiasm for the prevailing code is the attitude of a man who fears that moral chaos is just around the corner. Every breach of the rules, Sidgwick warned, 'seems to give a certain aid to the forces that are always tending towards moral anarchy in any society'. Even Mill could not be absolved from the charge of laxness: the claim in *On Liberty* that people should be permitted to pursue their own choice of lifestyle provided that they did no harm to others 'is certainly opposed to common sense: since (e.g.) it would exclude from censure almost all forms of sexual immorality committed by unmarried and independent adults' (482, 478; see Mill 1861: ch. 4). In principle it was possible that improvements could be made to the existing rules; but Sidgwick thought that, in practice, very few changes were for the better; a new rule was normally 'too subtle or refined, or too complex and elaborate' to have a genuinely beneficial effect (481). In very rare circumstances 'persons defined by exceptional qualities of intellect, temperament, or character' might legitimately break the rules where a careful calculation of utility justified their doing so, but ordinary people should be encouraged to follow the dictates of the moral code without ever questioning them.[5] Sidgwick even thought that the cause of moral stability might warrant restricting knowledge of the utilitarian theory to an enlightened minority:

a Utilitarian may reasonably desire, on Utilitarian principles, that some of his conclusions should be rejected by mankind generally; or even that the vulgar should keep aloof from his system as a whole, in so far as the inevitable indefiniteness and complexity of its calculations render it likely to lead to bad results in their hands (490).

In the Sidgwickian universe, moral reflection is an occupation for an élite band of highly rational and thoughtful people; the unthinking masses should obey the moral law in a spirit of blind and respectful obedience.

Sidgwick's conviction of the importance of 'middle axioms' led him, in one place, to claim that breaching a standard rule is permissible only when the rule-breaking behaviour coheres with some 'more complex and delicate rule' which the utilitarian 'should desire to be universally obeyed' (485). However, this contention seems inconsistent with the contrast elsewhere drawn between the 'exceptions' to normal rules permitted to the reflective few and the obedience to those same rules demanded of the unreflective many; for on the alternative account, the many would presumably no longer be rightly considered to be under an obligation to obey the original rule once the few had discovered a better one. Sidgwick offered the example of the utilitarian who thinks, on grounds of public welfare, that we should generally tell the truth, but may lie when asked how we have voted at a political election where the voting is by secret ballot; he accordingly adopts a refined rule of veracity with a caveat to cover this special case (485). But Sidgwick gave conflicting signals as to whether he believed that ordinary folk, or only the reflective minority, should follow a modified rule like this one instead of the original unqualified version.

There is also a deeper problem about Sidgwick's account of rules. Given his reluctance to allow more than a limited degree of plasticity to rules, situations are unavoidable in which his 'middle axioms' will come into conflict with his fundamental utilitarian principles. This is because the fundamental axioms, as Sidgwick expounded them, are maximising in character, whereas the unadjusted rules of Victorian 'common-sense' morality are generally not. The problem has a more general and a more particular aspect. The more general is that any rules which specify the *right* can run counter in practice to principles which tell us to maximise the *good*. Determining the proper action by reference to rules of right and wrong is an essentially different process from determining it by consequentialist reasoning in accordance with the fundamental axioms of utility. Even where a rule is selected on the basis of its expected propensity to promote the good, circumstances can arise in which strict adherence to the rule will counter production of its intended effect. This fact is well exemplified by Bernard Williams's story of the hostages in the South American town, where one innocent person must be shot in order that the lives of nineteen other innocent persons be spared (Williams 1973: 98–9). Any plausible system of 'common-sense' morality will prohibit the killing of innocent people, a prohibition which can readily be justified on utilitarian grounds. Yet if we apply a maximising axiom directly, killing the innocent hostage seems plainly to be required in this special case. Only if rules are considered infinitely adjustable to the contours of utility are we guaranteed never to have to break a rule of right in the interests of the good; but in that case – as we shall see in Section 3 – we might as well abandon all rules but rules of thumb and stick to act-utilitarian reasoning.

The more specific aspect to Sidgwick's problem is that many features of the Victorian moral system were conspicuously disutilitarian in character. For instance, the gross disparities in the distribution of wealth and privileges in the nineteenth century were poorly calculated to maximise the public happiness; yet the contemporary moral code emphasised to the poor the virtues of patience, a deferential acceptance of the social *status quo*, and contentment with one's lot. Similarly, the socially subordinate position of women, their exclusion from the franchise, the inability of wives to divorce a cruel or unfaithful husband and to control their own goods, are reflections of Victorian bourgeois morality which are hard to justify from the perspective of the universe. Such examples, which could be multiplied, suggest that Sidgwick's admiration for the perfections of the Victorian moral code is far more at odds than he realised with the fundamental axioms of utility. Only a far less grudging willingness on his part to allow those rules to be bent, broken or replaced in the interests of utility would render his position tenable.

## 2 Ideal Utilitarianism: Moore and Rashdall

Whether we call G.E. Moore (1873–1958) a utilitarian or not depends on how elastically we are prepared to use the term. His highly influential book *Principia Ethica* of 1903 contains a fierce attack on the hedonistic utilitarianism of Bentham and Mill, which Moore believed to travesty human nature in its reduction of all we can care about to species of pleasure.[6] Yet Moore's own account of morality is consequentialist, and it differs from earlier versions of utilitarianism chiefly in its more capacious theory of value. Moore maintained that the good consists not just in pleasure, nor in any other merely human states or qualities, but also in the existence of certain objective features of the universe, pre-eminently the beauty of its constituents.[7] This position is often nowadays termed 'Ideal Utilitarianism', though it was not so called by Moore and the label originally meant something different to its inventor Hastings Rashdall.

If Moore rather unreasonably despised Mill, he had considerable respect for Sidgwick. *Principia Ethica* displays the influence of *The Methods of Ethics* at many points, even where it disputes its conclusions. Moore was particularly struck by Sidgwick's account of value, which he quoted and criticised at length. Sidgwick had argued that 'ideal goods' such as beauty and knowledge, while 'commonly judged to be good', would not be good 'out of relation to human existence, or at least to some consciousness of feeling':

For example, we commonly judge some inanimate objects, scenes, etc. to be good as possessing beauty, and others bad from ugliness: still no one would consider it rational to aim at the production of beauty in external nature, apart from any possible contemplation of it by human beings. In fact when beauty is maintained to be objective, it is not commonly meant that it exists as beauty out of relation to any mind whatsoever: but only that there is some standard of beauty valid for all minds (Sidgwick 1874: 114; quoted in Moore 1903: 81–2).

Sidgwick did not, however, hold that a quality like beauty is good only because its contemplation gives pleasure. In a significant move beyond hedonistic utilitarianism, he allowed that beauty is good also because it can 'conduce' to 'the Perfection or excellence of human existence': that is, beings who are capable of aesthetic sensations have potentially richer lives than beings who are not. And 'if there be any Good other than Happiness to be sought by man, as an ultimate practical end, it can only be the Goodness, Perfection, or Excellence of Human Existence' (Sidgwick 1874: 114, 115).

But Moore believed that this revision did not go far enough. Sidgwick still linked the value of beautiful things more closely than Moore thought proper to their impact on human beings, denying that beauty had any intrinsic worth out of relation to human subjects. Yet Sidgwick's position is in some respects unclear. It is hard to be sure whether he would have said that a desert sunset which no one enjoys fails to be beautiful, or that it is beautiful but with a valueless beauty. Or he may have rejected both these alternatives and held that the sunset's beauty *and* the value of that beauty depend only on the existence (somewhere) of potential appreciators – or even that the existence of potential appreciators is sufficient for a sunset to be beautiful, but the presence of actual spectators is necessary for that beauty to be valuable. Whatever Sidgwick's precise view may have been, Moore's position is unambiguous: he held that it is intelligible to speak of the beauty of a phenomenon, and right to regard that beauty as valuable, even on the assumption that no one ever will or can experience it. To persuade his reader to this view, Moore devised a somewhat bizarre thought-experiment. He invites us first to imagine a world which is exceedingly beautiful, full of admirable things 'combined in the most exquisite proportions, so that no one thing jars against another, but each contributes to increase the beauty of the whole'. Next we have to imagine a world of exceptional ugliness, which is 'one heap of filth, containing everything that is most disgusting to us, for whatever reason, and the whole, as far as may be, without one redeeming feature'.

115

Moore asks us to suppose that no human being ever lives in or perceives, or can live in or perceive, either of these worlds, to enjoy the beauty of the one or hate the ugliness of the other. He then poses the question whether it is 'irrational to hold that it is better that the beautiful world should exist, than the one which is ugly?' (Moore 1903: 83–5).

Moore admitted that the beautiful world would be an even better world if there were human beings in it to appreciate its beauty. But that, he said, was beside the point. The issue is whether 'the existence of a more beautiful thing is better in itself than that of one more ugly'. In his view, the answer is yes; and so if we were able to produce the beautiful unperceived world or the ugly unperceived world, we would have a reason to produce the former rather than the latter. 'I hope', Moore added appealingly, 'that some may agree with me in this extreme instance' (84). But many readers of *Principia Ethica* have not agreed with him, and it is a serious weakness of his case that it relies so heavily on purely intuitive responses to a highly *outré* example. Some people have intuitions which are more Sidgwickian than Moorean, and fail to see how it matters whether an object is beautiful or ugly if no one of aesthetic sensibility is ever going to see it. Others find that their intuitions give them no clear lead one way or the other on Moore's question.

Thomas Baldwin has recently commented that 'there are real issues which connect with Moore's intuition that there are intrinsic goods which do not concern human life, arising from conflicts between human goods and the needs of other species'; and he criticises Moore's failure to identify these issues properly and to relate them to an ethical context within which they can be rationally handled (T. Baldwin 1990: 131–2). But while Moore's case makes excessive and unsatisfactory appeal to intuition, it is misleading to represent his distinction between human and intrinsic goods as a distinction between human and *non-human* goods. The welfare of a dolphin or a white rhino is not a human good, but it is not an intrinsic good either, in Moore's sense; it depends on the existence of consciousness or a point of view, albeit of a subhuman kind. Moorean intrinsic goods are objectively good, in the sense that their goodness is not relative to *any* conscious perspective; the beauty of an object would be valuable, on this account, even if the world were permanently devoid of any creature to enjoy it. Moore need not have denied that the preservation of a certain kind of environment is a good from a rhino's point of view. But his assertion that beauty is an intrinsic good needs to be distinguished from the claim that there are things which are good from the point of view of creatures other than humans.

A more serious weakness of Moore's position is that he assumes without argument that beauty is a property of an objective rather than of a perceiver-relative sort. Many philosophers would dispute this assumption, seeing beauty as a kind of secondary property, analogous to properties of colour or sound. On this view, if humans (and other beings) lacked aesthetic sensibility, things would not merely fail to be *seen as* beautiful, but would not *be* beautiful; for beauty is ontologically dependent on the mode of seeing as well as on the thing seen. Consequently, if beauty is a perceiver-relative property, it is as unintelligible to suppose that there could be beautiful objects in a world lacking subjects to sense them as beautiful as it is to suppose that there could be green objects in a world lacking percipients with colour vision.[8] Whether or not this analysis of aesthetic properties is correct, it is unsatisfactory for Moore to leave it without discussion.

Curiously enough, Moore appears in the years after 1903 to have reverted to a more Sidgwickian standpoint. In his introductory textbook *Ethics* published in 1912 he made the unexpected remark that:

> it does seem as if nothing can be an intrinsic good unless it contains *both* some feeling and *also* some other form of consciousness; and ... it seems possible that amongst the feelings contained must always be some amount of pleasure (Moore 1912: 129).

This is not quite 'the characteristic Bloomsbury view that it is only states of consciousness that have intrinsic value' (T. Baldwin 1990: 132); but it does implicitly contradict the *Principia Ethica* contention that the beautiful world which no one ever perceives would be intrinsically good. On the later account, a beautiful world needs to be experienced in a way that yields satisfaction in order to be good. The 'intrinsic good' is not the beautiful world by itself, but the complex whole or 'organic unity' consisting of the world together with the pleasurable sensations it induces in actual subjects.[9] Even in the closing pages of *Principia Ethica* Moore had softened his criticism of Sidgwick to the extent of admitting that the value of beauty in itself is 'negligible, in comparison with that which attaches to the *consciousness* of beauty' (Moore 1903: 189). Nine years later this 'negligible' value has been reduced to zero. Moore's final ethical position is justly described by Baldwin as a form of 'refined hedonism' (T. Baldwin 1990: 132). It is a good deal closer to Mill's theory than its author would have cared to admit, though in contrast to Mill, Moore regarded aesthetic satisfactions as more important than intellectual ones.

The term 'Ideal Utilitarianism' is perhaps less confusingly applied to the views of an author whose conception of the ideal was less hedonistic than Moore's.[10] Hastings Rashdall's treatise *The Theory of Good and Evil* (1907) has suffered in late years an undeserved neglect. Rashdall (1858–1924) was a scholar of many parts (his other books include theological works and a history of the medieval universities), a clear-headed and lucid writer, and a defender of a moral theory which, in his own words, 'combines the utilitarian principle that Ethics must be teleological with a non-hedonistic view of the ethical end' (Rashdall 1907: vol. 1, 184). Rashdall thought more highly of Sidgwick's philosophy than of Mill's, though he considered *The Methods of Ethics* to lack 'the peculiar unction which makes Mill's *Utilitarianism* so persuasive a book to young students of Philosophy' (vol. 1, 50). His own theory of 'Ideal Utilitarianism' was indebted at least as much to Aristotle as to his precursors in the British utilitarian tradition. 'According to this view,' Rashdall wrote, 'actions are right or wrong according as they tend to produce for all mankind an ideal end or good, which includes, but is not limited to, pleasure' (vol. 1, 184). The anti-hedonist nature of Rashdall's utilitarianism emerges clearly in his treatment of virtue. He sharply dissented from the Epicurean idea that virtues (which he thought of in the Greek fashion, as personal excellences) are valuable merely in so far as they subserve pleasure. Being rich in virtues is a goal worth seeking for itself:

> I must observe that even those virtues which are most obviously altruistic in their tendency are, according to our view, also ends in themselves – having a value independent of, and in some cases much greater than, the mere pleasure which they cause in others. Hence it becomes rational to encourage the cultivation and exercise of these virtues even in ways which cannot always be shown to produce a net gain in pleasure on the whole (vol. 1, 189).

Honesty, industry, kindliness, family affection, loyalty, courage and other excellences of character are not merely instrumentally important, but their very possession makes a life more valuable. The same goes, of course, for the excellences of mind.

Rashdall explained with some care the relationship of Ideal Utilitarianism to other teleological moral theories. He noted that there are three leading rival conceptions of the good for man: pleasure, moral well-being (that is, perfection of the moral character), and *eudaimonia* or 'total Well-being including Morality, intellectual and aesthetic good, &c., and recognizing a distinction between higher and lower pleasures'. There are also two views on the moral constituency, some philosophers affirming that the proper goal of action is the good of the agent alone, others that it is the good of mankind in general. There are thus three times two, or six, possible theories of ethics, which Rashdall labelled respectively Egoistic Hedonism, Universalistic Hedonism, Individualistic Perfectionism, Universalistic Perfectionism, Individualistic Eudaemonism and Ideal Utilitarianism (Rashdall n.d.: 48). The last of these – Rashdall's own theory – maintains that we should always promote as fully as we are able the 'total Well-being' of humanity. That human good should be maximised seemed to him intuitively evident, and there is a strong echo of Sidgwick's 'fundamental axioms' in his own statement of principles:

> It is self-evident to me that I ought (where it does not collide with the greater good of another) to promote my own greatest good, that I ought to prefer a greater good on the whole to a lesser, and that I ought to regard the good of one man as of equal intrinsic value with the like good of any one else (Rashdall 1907: vol. 1, 185).

But to know which acts are right and which are wrong, we need a clear conception of *what* we should maximise. Rashdall argued that well-being (*eudaimonia*) involves more than simply happiness, and that happiness involves more than just pleasure. Happiness he characterised as a subjective state of 'satisfaction with one's life as a whole – with the past and the future as well as with the immediate present'. It is naive, he thought, to suppose that happiness can be identified with pleasure, even with pleasure of the higher or more valuable sorts. The reason is that a person can get a lot of pleasure into his life yet be 'on the whole unhappy through the presence of desires which are unsatisfied, dissatisfaction with the past, anxiety as to the future, unfulfilled aspirations, baffled hopes and the like' (vol. 2, 57). At the same time, it is paradoxical to suppose that a life can be happy if it contains no pleasant experiences at all, or a large number of painful ones. But even happiness cannot be the whole of the ideal good for man. To attain the highest degree of well-being, a person needs to have more than merely subjective satisfactions, however intense or profound. (It is at this point that Rashdall parts company with Sidgwick.) The ideal life requires not only happiness but also virtues and a good will; and in addition 'knowledge, thought, the contemplation of beauty, love of other persons and of what is best in them' (vol. 2, 60).

Rashdall's position is appealing for its sophisticated account of the good. Bentham would scarcely have recognised as utilitarianism a theory which proclaims virtue to be an end in itself and enjoins us to pursue the ideal! More than any of his predecessors, Rashdall refused to treat the forms of human value as reducible to a common denominator, whether pleasure or subjective satisfaction or the fulfilment of preferences. To love and be loved, to be courageous or loyal or just, to be skilled as a pianist or an engineer, to know a lot about Plato or astronomy, to have the satisfaction of winning a race or taking a degree, to enjoy listening to a symphony or basking in the sunshine – these exemplify the variety of independently valuable conditions, virtues, attainments, possessions and pleasures which combine to constitute the good life. Rashdall conceded that many of these states and achievements are accompanied by a keen sense of satisfaction: we are happy at doing a brave deed or passing an examination or playing our first solo on the tuba. But in Rashdall's view it is only because we see these things as valuable in themselves that they can yield us this satisfaction; the value explains the satisfaction, and not the satisfaction the value.

Ironically the feature which forms the greatest attraction of Rashdall's Ideal Utilitarianism – its multi-stranded, non-reductionist account of human good – is also the source of its major difficulty. Rashdall largely overlooked the fact that if there is no common denominator of human good, it is unclear how we are supposed to evaluate the relative merits of actions productive of different species of benefit. The injunction to maximise the amount of ideal human existence is virtually a dead letter if there is no principled way of comparing the relative worth of the different ingredients of the good. How, for instance, should an Ideal Utilitarian decide between the Stoic and the Epicurean models of the good life? Should he aspire to develop a character rich in excellences, or aim instead to be a person of refined tastes with a proper appreciation of the higher pleasures? How, again, ought he to respond to the mythical Choice of Hercules between the lives of enjoyment and honour, or the real-life choice of the painter Gauguin between the roles of artist and of family man? Rashdall's utilitarianism, with its multi-dimensional account of well-being, offers no clear-cut procedure for evaluating decisions in either private or public life.

If Rashdall was insufficiently sensitive to this problem, the reason may have been that he was at heart less a utilitarian than an Aristotelian virtue theorist. Consequentialism appealed to him chiefly because it avoided the implausible notion of absolute deontological constraints. 'No sane man', he wrote, 'ever does really pronounce upon the morality of an act in *entire* abstraction from its consequences.' Kant's proposition that we should tell the truth even to a homicidal maniac who demands that we divulge the hiding place of his victim seemed to him manifestly absurd (Rashdall n.d.: 58–9). But Rashdall's Aristotelianism was evident in his belief that the most important right-making feature of actions was that they should be expressions of virtues; for virtuous behaviour he considered not only an intrinsically valuable thing but the most significant of the several components of the good life.

To identify the virtues, Rashdall relied on a frankly intuitional approach. Consider as an example his account of 'purity'. This could be known to be a virtue because it corresponded to 'a state of feeling ... of intrinsic value – a state of feeling which the clearest moral insight and the highest spiritual experience of the race have decided to be incompatible with sexual indulgence outside a relatively permanent monogamous union' (Rashdall 1907: vol. 1, 197). But because purity is of such outstanding importance in itself, it becomes unnecessary to calculate the consequences of relaxing the marriage vow; no adulterous liaison, even one without other harmful effects, could compensate by the pleasure it afforded for the amount of life-enriching virtue it eroded. In Rashdall's view, then, considerations of virtue trump all other considerations, and moral dilemmas should be resolved by determining which among the various available options for action is the most virtuous. Such a theory, however, is no longer utilitarian. There is indeed a conceivable form of consequentialism which treats virtue itself as the practical maximand – that is, which takes the proper end of action to be the maximisation of virtuous behaviour. But this is not Rashdall's theory, and it is hard to recognise it as a species of utilitarianism. It has the disconcerting implication that individuals may sometimes be morally called on to refrain from performing virtuous actions which would maximise well-being. Suppose that by giving generously to a charitable cause, a millionaire renders superfluous the donations of thousands of ordinary people who would otherwise have given of their hard-earned cash. If virtuous behaviour is the end to be maximised, the millionaire would be morally obliged to exercise restraint in his own giving, in order not to discourage generosity in the general public: a conclusion which would have greatly surprised both Aristotle and Mill.

In any case a purely virtue-centred account of the criterion of right action is a significant departure from the Ideal Utilitarianism which identifies virtue as only one among the many ingredients of the good life. Even if virtue is accorded first place among those ingredients it cannot be the only one allowed to carry weight in the process of moral evaluation, or be permitted always to win in the event of a conflict of considerations, without an implicit rejection of the original theory. Pleasure, beauty, knowledge, love and the other constituents of the ideal either do, or do not, contribute to the value of a life. If they do not, then Ideal Utilitarianism gives way to neo-Aristotelianism or (perhaps) to a virtue-maximising consequentialism. If they do, then the virtuousness of actions is not the sole basis on which to make our moral judgements, and the Ideal Utilitarian still faces the baffling question how to determine the relative weighting of the different value-imparting factors. This problem we shall meet again in Chapter VI, when we discuss further the relationship between utility and our valued ends.

## 3 Rule-utilitarianism

The early decades of this century were the wilderness years of utilitarianism. Ethical thinking in English-speaking lands came to be dominated by an intuitionist orthodoxy. Many philosophers believed with H.A. Prichard and W.D. Ross that the rightness of actions was knowable through an intuitive faculty, and that consequentialist reasoning was both unnecessary for moral decision-making and apt to yield conclusions running contrary to the grain of ordinary moral thought (cf. Prichard 1949; Ross 1930). Utilitarianism was criticised for its readiness to allow exceptions to generally accepted rules; its proponents were thought 'ripe for treasons, stratagems and spoils', provided that the pay-off in utility was high enough. And they were said to justify the unjustifiable by reference to a crudely hedonistic theory of value more becoming to savages than to civilised men. To a generation of readers who knew little about Mill and less about Sidgwick, utilitarianism by the second quarter of the century seemed to be going the way of the dodo.

R.F. Harrod's 1936 paper 'Utilitarianism revised' was an important attempt to restore a fairer view. Harrod was an Oxford economist who believed that the chief defect of utilitarianism was its failure to acknowledge the fact, familiar to 'common moral consciousness', that 'certain types of act are obligations' (Harrod 1936: 80). Most people believed it to be their duty to speak the truth even where doing so would cause more pain than pleasure. Utilitarians could accommodate this conviction only by taking a Kantian turn and granting that 'morality requires action on a maxim that may be made a general law' (80). Harrod therefore proposed that utilitarianism should judge actions to be right or wrong, not on the basis of their individual impact on the public utility, but by reference to the utility of the general performance of actions of their kind. So if dire consequences could be expected from the general breakdown of the practice of truth-telling, then all individual acts of lying were wrong. Harrod argued that while a single lie might do negligible harm to the habit of telling the truth, widespread lying would seriously undermine the practices and institutions which relied on it: 'codes of honour, truthfulness, honesty, discharge of debt, performance of promises, etc.'

More precisely, the 'Kantian principle' is applicable where 'the loss due to $n$ infringements [of a rule] is greater than $n$ times the loss due to one' (83). Thus telling a lie, even for a good end, is breaching an obligation, because general mendacity would be intolerable.

This position came later to be known as 'rule-utilitarianism' (Brandt 1959). Harrod thought that 'the substantial point' of his theory had sometimes been glimpsed by earlier writers, but 'not argued with precision' (Harrod 1936: 86).[11] His paper had the immediate effect of reviving the waning interest in utilitarianism, and convincing at least a section of moral philosophers that the doctrine of utility was not beyond redemption. Not all utilitarians, however, have been convinced that rule-utilitarianism marks an improvement on utilitarianism of the act variety. Some have thought that utilitarianism has no business truckling to Kantian notions of moral obligation.[12] It has also often been held that rule-utilitarianism, in its only plausible form, yields exactly the same moral judgements as an act-utilitarian decision procedure does. Yet some eminent utilitarians, among them Brandt and Harsanyi, have argued that social advantages accrue from the general adoption of certain kinds of rule-governed conduct which would not be obtainable if everyone lived by an act-utilitarian standard. Thus Harsanyi lays stress on the enlarged possibilities for social cooperation and the coordination of individual efforts, and on the increased predictability of others' actions, where people accept common rules of behaviour (1977: 36 and *passim*).

The long-running debate between act- and rule-utilitarians has achieved an intricacy which makes it hard to summarise in a few pages. One complicating feature is that several different rule-utilitarian theories have been defended, and each has its particular strengths and weaknesses. While all the versions appraise individual actions by reference to their conformity, or lack of it, with utility-promoting rules, they differ in regard to the conditions under which they are prepared to permit deviations from those rules. We shall examine three important forms of rule-utilitarianism, in descending order of rigour.[13]

(A) *Idealistic rule-utilitarianism*: this, the strongest form, holds that actions are right if, and only if, they accord with a set of rules whose general acceptance would maximise utility. An individual is not permitted to break a rule in any circumstances, provided that *if* everyone were to follow it, utility would be maximised; so the fact that not everyone abides by it, or even that no one else does, is no excuse for him to break it. If the general utility would be maximised by everyone paying their debts and keeping their promises, a person should pay his debts and keep his promises no matter what other people do. This is probably the form of rule-utilitarianism which Harrod had in mind, and it has more recently been advocated by Brandt. In Brandt's view, a set of rules 'is justified if it is what it would be if facts and logic were brought to bear on its "choice" to a maximal extent – that is, if fully rational persons would tend to support it in preference to any other system and to none'; and in no other sense can a moral system be said to be 'justified' (Brandt 1979: 304). (Brandt adds the intriguing suggestion that 'philosophers, psychologists, and other social scientists could co-operate in determining what a welfare-maximizing moral code would be' (293).)

But some writers have thought it unreasonable to expect that people should live by a code which, however optimal it might be in the view of enlightened social scientists, has not been generally accepted in the actual world. The person who fulfils his promises and keeps his hands off other people's property would be a hostage to fortune in a society of liars and thieves. Indeed, the attraction of rule-utilitarianism to many philosophers is precisely that individual agents can enhance their own utility by participating with others in certain kinds of rule-governed practices; and from this point of view it would be worse than pointless for a person individually to follow 'rules' which, however eligible in the eyes of fully rational agents, were not much favoured by actual ones. These philosophers prefer a weaker form of rule-utilitarianism, such as (B).

(B) *Actual-state rule-utilitarianism*: this holds that actions are right if, and only if, they conform to rules such that (1) their general acceptance would maximise utility; and (2) they are generally accepted by the relevant social group. Depending on context, this could be the whole society or some special subset whose members are mutually benefited by their common consent to regulative principles of behaviour, for example, the subset of drivers of motor vehicles who agree to rules like 'Give way to the right at roundabouts.' Rules about keeping promises and telling the truth are not merely justifiable from an idealistic utilitarian perspective but are, by and large, rules which people actually observe. So, given that people mostly fall in with these socially advantageous practices of keeping their promises and telling the truth, we should individually do the same.

Gertrude Ezorsky, who defends a view of this kind, argues that an individual should not think himself entitled to lie even in the exceptional case in which more immediate utility would be produced by telling the truth than by lying. Although (she claims) an act-utilitarian would advise him to lie in this situation, the objection to his doing so is that a contradiction is involved in the supposition that the telling of such lies could become a general practice while most assertions are true (Ezorsky

1968: 539–40). But even if, as Ezorsky asserts, '[t]he generalized consequences of doing *that* [i.e. lying] are disastrous' (540), one may question whether it would have any seriously bad consequences for the general practice of truth-telling if a few utility-enhancing lies were told. (Indeed, in real life some utility-promoting lies *are* told, yet the practice of truth-telling survives.) Moreover the category of permissible lying could be carefully circumscribed under general descriptions (for example, 'lying in order to spare other people's feelings', 'lying in order to save a life', etc.), while lying in all other cases remained forbidden. Reflections like these have led some rule-utilitarians to favour a weaker position than (B), namely (C).

(C) *Conditional rule-utilitarianism*: on this version, an act is right if, and only if, it conforms to a rule whose application always maximises utility. In most circumstances following the simple rule 'Tell the truth' produces more utility than telling lies. But there are some exceptions. Imagine that you are asked by Angelo, a very bad painter, for your opinion of his latest picture. Knowing Angelo to have been deeply depressed recently, you disguise your real view of his daub and try to sound convincing as you tell him how much you like it. Following the rule 'Tell the truth' in this situation would patently have failed to promote utility; it might even have driven Angelo (who respects your opinion highly) to suicide. But you could still claim to have been following a rule, namely the rule 'Tell the truth, except where doing so may hurt someone's feelings, in which case you may tell a benevolent lie.' But your rule will need to be complicated quite a bit more than this if it is to cope with other potential circumstances where following the bare rule against lying would produce bad results. If the acceptability of rules is conditional on their maximising utility on every occasion, then clauses will need to be added permitting the telling of lies for a very large number of benevolent motives.

Conditional rule-utilitarianism nevertheless rescues the utilitarian agent from the paradoxical situation of having sometimes to refuse to perform a utility-maximising action because it conflicts with a normally utility-maximising rule. It seems odd for a utilitarian – someone who purports to see the object of action as the promotion of human well-being – to have to condemn a lie in the exceptional instance where telling it enhances rather than diminishes well-being. Similarly, shooting an innocent hostage breaks a generally beneficial rule against taking human life; yet if shooting one hostage is, as in Williams's story, the only means of saving nineteen, it is hard to recognise someone as a genuine utilitarian who refuses to sanction the killing (cf. Williams 1973: 98–9). As J.J.C.

Smart has observed, to plead that a rule is a generally advantageous one, or that it would be better that everyone should abide by it than that nobody should, seems irrelevant in such cases. It is much more characteristic of a deontological than of a consequentialist point of view to place more importance on observing a moral rule than on securing the best possible outcome. Refusing to break a rule when it would be beneficial to do so indicates a state of mind which Smart has tellingly termed 'rule-worship' (Smart 1973: 10).

A conditional rule-utilitarian will deal with the hostages dilemma by refining the simple rule against killing to something like 'Do not kill people, except when killing a smaller number prevents the killing of a larger number.' But as Smart and Lyons have pointed out, rule-utilitarians who are prepared to refashion their rules like this are effectively being driven by *act-utilitarian* considerations. A rule-utilitarian determined to avoid all rules which can ever fail to maximise utility need not go to the trouble of endlessly elaborating his rules to accommodate all the 'exceptional' circumstances which can possibly arise: he needs only to attend to the deeper principle which governs all his adaptations of those rules, namely 'Act always so as to maximise utility.' But this is just the principle of act-utilitarianism. Version (C) of rule-utilitarianism is therefore, according to Smart and Lyons, extensionally equivalent to act-utilitarianism in the sense that it yields exactly the same set of moral judgements (Smart 1973: 10–11; Lyons 1965: ch. 3).[14]

Lyons goes to some trouble to show that this equivalence thesis is not unsettled by the claim of rule-utilitarianism to do more justice than act-utilitarianism to the common conviction that moral principles have a universal binding force. The question 'What if everyone did that?' is sometimes employed to persuade people that they should not perform some act which, though it would have no bad effects if performed a few times, would have ill consequences if done more often. For example, one person walking across the lawn may not damage the grass, but many people walking across it will certainly do so. For rule-utilitarians like Harrod, and for other philosophers in the Kantian tradition, it is wrong for one person to walk across the lawn if it would be wrong for everyone to walk across it; and act-utilitarianism is defective in permitting things which are incompatible with such universal rules. But Lyons remarks that as no harm will be done to the lawn until more than a certain threshold number of people have walked over it, a better rule than 'You must not cross the lawn' is 'You may cross the lawn provided that no more than the threshold number of people have crossed it.' This rule is applicable to everyone, but it permits exactly as many crossings of the lawn as an act-utilitarian, anxious about the state of the grass, will permit. Therefore extensional equivalence is preserved.

Neither idealistic nor actual-state rule-utilitarianism, on the other hand, are extensionally equivalent to act-utilitarianism. Although this makes them more distinctive positions, one should note two further problems which they face in addition to those already mentioned.

(1) Rule utilitarianism often fails to determine a clear answer to a question about the morality of a given action because the action appears to be right under one description but wrong under another. Consider the case of Tom, who works in a factory making poison gas for a bellicose government. If Tom knows (or suspects) that the government means to use the gas against its neighbours in an evil war of conquest, his behaviour contravenes the moral principle that one should not wittingly assist in the waging of unjust wars. But there is another description of what Tom is doing: he is working hard to earn the money to support his family. Clearly Tom faces a moral dilemma which he needs to resolve. This resolution will be particularly painful if there is a shortage of alternative employment for him to turn to: should he cease to work for the government even if this means that his family will go hungry? An act-utilitarian would recommend him to tackle his dilemma by a careful comparison of the consequences of retaining or of resigning his job. Rule-utilitarian approaches (A) and (B) proceed by evaluating the general practices which his behaviour exemplifies. But unfortunately this produces *conflicting* moral advice depending on whether Tom's action is described as working to support his family or as helping the government to prosecute an unjust war; a dilemma concerning the choice of acts has been transformed into one concerning the choice of rules. It might be suggested that the rule-utilitarian could break the impasse by deciding which of the two descriptions of Tom's activity is morally the more salient. Yet it is hard to argue that it is either more or less important for people to care about their families than for them to care about the international peace. A different strategy would involve looking more closely into the actual facts of Tom's predicament. Maybe Tom has only a very minor role in the gas-production process, though his resigning his post would reduce his family to certain beggary; this may incline us to think that it is better for him to retain his job than to give it up. But consideration of such details is more characteristic of an act-utilitarian than of a rule-utilitarian approach.

Lyons has proposed, in response to this difficulty, that rule-utilitarians should consider only the most complete relevant description of acts. If a person tells a lie to save a life, it is not the utility of lying or of saving a life which should determine the moral judgement, but the utility of telling-a-lie-to-save-a-life (Lyons 1965: 52; ch. 2, *passim*). It would be perfectly coherent, Lyons argues, for a rule-utilitarian to hold that lying is in most circumstances wrong, but right when it is lying-to-save-a-life. So consider the 'complete' description *making-poison-gas-in-order-to-earn-enough-money-to-support-one's-family*. Could a rule-utilitarian approve of actions of this kind? It seems clear he still could not, for making poison gas is in principle a very bad way of earning money to keep one's family: there are many more innocuous jobs which a bread-winner could do instead. But this judgement ignores the fact that in practice there may be no other employment available; Tom's resignation may cause his family to starve. Rule-utilitarianisms (A) and (B) seem intrinsically less well-equipped than act-utilitarianism to deliver judge-ments sensitive to the nuances of particular cases. To be sure, we could complicate the rule-utilitarian's description still further – in effect, move on to version (C) – and assess the utility of practices of *making-poison-gas-in-order-to-support-one's-family-where-there-is-absolutely-no-other-means-of-acquiring-that-money*. But this is evidently little more than an attempt to dress up act-utilitarianism in rule-utilitarianism's clothes; for the point of making reference to the utility of a practice is progressively lost as that practice is more narrowly defined.

(2) Imagine that Jim wishes to lead a celibate life. What should a utilitarian think of this? If everyone led a celibate life, then human beings would die out; but Jim's celibacy in an already crowded world seems beneficial rather than not; at least it is morally inoffensive. Yet according to Harrod, there is a moral obligation to conform with a particular practice when 'the loss due to *n* infringements is greater than *n* times the loss due to one'. By this criterion, Jim's celibacy is *immoral*, for the consequence of *everyone's* not marrying and having children would be the extinction of the human race; Jim's solitary failure to follow the practice may seem harmless enough, but a universal failure would be disastrous. Hence Jim should marry and have children! It can be argued in a similar way that Jim should also grow fruit and vegetables and keep a pig. For if no one bothered to produce food, the result would be universal starvation; therefore, on Harrod's principle, Jim and all of us are under a moral obligation to cultivate our gardens.

Lyons has suggested that the rule-utilitarian can avoid these absurd conclusions by treating all general rules as having *ceteris paribus* clauses attached to them. Lying is wrong, other things being equal – but other things are not equal if we need to lie in order to save a life. In the same way people are free not to marry, or to grow food, *ceteris paribus*; but this freedom lapses if too few other people marry, or grow food (1965: ch. 2). Lyons's efforts on behalf of the rule-utilitarian are designed to relate what an individual is permitted or forbidden to do to empirical facts about the patterns of social behaviour. Conditional rule-utilitarianism, like act-utilitarianism, is able to represent celibacy as a permissible option for Jim *provided that* a sufficient number of other people are maintaining the species. (Act-utilitarianism implies this because it holds that we should always fashion our behaviour to the practical exigencies not just of our neighbour but of the human race.) Conditional rule-utilitarianism and act-utilitarianism are still, therefore, very demanding doctrines. Many would question whether it would really be fair to demand that Jim should abandon his celibacy if a general tendency towards celibacy developed, or become a farmer if too few other people grew food. Admittedly neither of these predicaments is at all likely to arise. But the prospect that, if they did, this is what utilitarians would have to say, reminds us of the common charge that utilitarianism is too strenuous a moral doctrine for ordinary mortals, requiring from us not only that we should make up for other people's deficiencies but, more broadly, that we should always look for opportunities to maximise utility, whatever the cost of doing so to our own favourite projects, commitments and relationships.

The discussion so far may seem to support the opinion of many philosophers that rule-utilitarianism, which seemed so promising in 1936, is an unnecessary and ultimately unhelpful deviation from the mainstream (act-)utilitarian tradition. Whatever the problems that tradition faces, they are not productively addressed by switching to a variant of that doctrine which in its only plausible version delivers identical moral judgements. There seems, besides, little need to refer to the breaking of rules to explain why many wrong deeds are wrong. 'The immorality of, let us say, inflicting great suffering on someone in order to enhance one's fortune, is apparent in a single case. The evil of one such act tells the story well enough' (Ezorsky 1968: 538).

Yet there are good reasons for not leaving the matter here. Consider again a practice like promising. It benefits all of us to be the makers and recipients of promises ('Lend me £5, and I promise I'll pay you back tomorrow', 'Thanks for promising to make my excuses at the party'). But if people do not generally keep their promises, the practice must inevitably decay. Individuals may also reap bad personal consequences from breaking their promises. Consider the case of Smith, who has promised to babysit for the Joneses one evening while they go to the theatre. Early that same evening he has a phone-call from Robinson, who is feeling low and asks Smith to come round and cheer him up. Smith weighs up the utilities of his different options. He doubts whether the Joneses will enjoy the play very much (the critics have slated it as sleep-inducing). Moreover he would much rather spend the evening chatting to his friend than minding Baby Jones, and his conversation always lifts Robinson out of the dumps. So he decides to disappoint the Joneses and go round to Robinson's instead. Most people would say that Smith has acted very badly. But can an act-utilitarian make the same judgement? On act-utilitarian principles, shouldn't promises be broken whenever more utility can be produced by breaking than by keeping them?

Few would quarrel with the view that promises may *sometimes* be broken without any blame attaching to the promisor. If Smith (who happens to be a doctor) had decided to keep rather than break his promise, but on the way to the Joneses had come upon a bad road accident, he would have been wrong to refuse to tend the victims on the basis that it would make him late for his babysitting. But act-utilitarianism is often alleged to recognise no binding force to promises *at all*, and to hold that promises should be kept only when doing the thing promised is likely to produce more utility than any alternative actions.

Yet would a sensible act-utilitarian really be so cavalier about breaking a promise? When Smith is wondering whether to keep his appointment with the Joneses, he ought to reflect on the *long-term*, as well as the immediate, effects of breaking his promise on such slight grounds. He will not only make himself unpopular with the Joneses, but risks excluding himself from the benefits which the practice of promising provides. (People will not trust his promises once they learn how he behaves; and they may feel under less obligation to keep any future promises they make to *him*.) An adequate consideration of the relevant utilities, therefore, should persuade Smith to honour the promises he makes even when shallower (short-term) utility calculation warrants breaking them. And what holds true of promising holds true of many other useful kinds of rule- and convention-governed behaviour, for example, in regard to the making of contracts, the entitlement to hold, bequeath and inherit property, and obedience to properly constituted authority. Individuals can only expect to benefit from participation in the utility-enhancing practices and institutions of a society if they consent to abide by their constitutive rules. Such rules derive, as Hume phrased it, from 'artifice' rather than from 'nature'. They arise from

> a general sense of common interest; which sense all the members
> of the society express to one another, and which induces them to

regulate their conduct by certain rules. I observe, that it will be for my interest to leave another in possession of his goods, *provided* that he will act in the same manner with regard to me (Hume 1739: 489–90).

Harsanyi has argued that act-utilitarianism is unable fully to explain what is wrong with breaking promises. For while the act-utilitarian decision-maker can consider 'the unfavorable *causal consequences* of any individual act of promise breaking, including the effects that such an act would have on other people's expectations and incentives', those causal effects will be 'very, very small, because people will not infer – and cannot rationally infer – from *one* such act that promise breaking has suddenly become a *general* practice in their society' (1977: 38). But this is to neglect the other kind of causal consequences which are likely to flow from an individual broken promise, to wit the bad effects on the promise-breaker who loses his reputation for trustworthiness. By breaking his promise to the Joneses, Smith may do little harm to the general practice of promising, but he stands to do considerable harm to himself. Act-utilitarian reasoning can readily take this potential harm into account, and it is only a very crude form of the doctrine which would permit us to break our promises lightly.

However, it must be admitted that even a sophisticated act-utilitarianism has difficulty in explaining why promises should not normally be broken without very good reasons indeed. The underlying problem is that act-utilitarian styles of justification do not take seriously the real dynamics of a practice like promising. Hume's account of useful practices which are dependent on 'artifice' suggests a much more satisfactory way of explaining the binding force of promises. Promising functions as a useful practice only if people desist from thinking about the advantage to be gained or lost by keeping particular promises, and agree to abide by the rules which are constitutive of the practice.[15] Of course, if it is clear that some very great harm will result from keeping a promise, the promise may be broken; but it is out of keeping with the spirit of the practice to seek to appraise the utility of individual promises, given the utility of the practice as a whole. That keeping a particular promise we have made looks likely to create a balance of harm over benefit is not normally even a prima-facie reason to break it; we show that we have misunderstood the nature of promising if we apply act-utilitarian calculation to determine the rightness or wrongness of keeping our word, no matter how extensive the causal consequences we consider.

The most defensible utilitarian position, therefore, may well be a hybrid one, compounded out of act-utilitarian and rule-utilitarian elements. Most of the time we should reason as act-utilitarians; but we should accept the utilitarian value of such products of human 'artifice' as the rule-governed practice of promising. The rule-utilitarian component of this compound position may be termed *Restricted-range rule-utilitarianism*; it becomes version (D) in our listing. Adopting such restricted-range rule-utilitarianism is entirely compatible with continuing to think in an act-utilitarian way about all those aspects of life not covered by special utility-promoting conventions. As Ezorsky observed, we do not need any rules to explain the wrongness of murder, cruelty or rape; and we certainly cannot say that the more killings there are, the less unjustified any further killings become; for killing – that ultimate utility-destroying act – remains wrong irrespective of how many or how few killings occur. But we *can* maintain that if so many promises are broken that the practice of promising collapses, then the rules forbidding promise-breaking will lose their moral force. Promising is an example of a practice devised by human ingenuity to promote mutual advantage by means of common consent to constitutive rules.[16] If participating persons fail to abide by those rules, the practices will cease to deliver the social benefits which justify them. (Act-utilitarian reflection, which estimates actions individually for their utility yield, would thus be a constant threat to their integrity.) 'Promises', wrote Hume, 'have no natural obligation, and are mere artificial contrivances for the convenience and advantage of societies.' But once the 'contrivance' is in place, whoever makes a promise 'is immediately bound by his intent to execute his engagements, and must never expect to be trusted any more, if he refuse to perform what he promis'd' (1739: 525, 522).

# CHAPTER VI

# Happiness and Other Ends

Among the reasonable demands we make of any moral theory is that it should provide us with a view of the good that is both coherent and attractive. A theory which fails to present an attractive account of the good is uninspiring, but one which lacks a coherent account of it is impossible to live by. Both these demands apply, of course, to utilitarianism. But utilitarianism imposes a special condition of its own on the nature of the good. The good, whatever it is, must be an aggregative commodity, something which comes in greater or lesser amounts, so that moral decision can rest on a basis of comparative quantitative judgements.

The question to be raised in this chapter is how successful utilitarianism is in providing a coherent, attractive account of an aggregative good in the light of some fundamental features of our customary phenomenology of values. In particular, how satisfactory is utilitarianism's identification of the proper goal of action with the satisfaction of preferences, or with happiness, in the light of our common disposition to regard good lives as focused on a variety of valued pursuits, objectives and ideals? This disposition is in fact the source not of one but of two problems for utilitarianism, the first arising from the sheer number of ends to be found in human lives normally judged to be going well, the second stemming from our ascribing to at least some of these ends a value that is apparently intrinsic rather than instrumental.

## 1 Preference and happiness

We turn first to what may be ultimately the least sustainable form of utilitarian value theory, that which identifies a person's utility with the satisfaction of his preferences. We glanced briefly in Chapter I at one of the most cogent versions of this theory, that of John Harsanyi. Preference utilitarianism, in Harsanyi's view, is 'justified by the biblical – as well as the Kantian – principle that *we should treat other people, in the same way as we want to be treated by them*' – that is, 'in accordance with *our* own wants and preferences' (1977: 27). It is not what other people think is good for us, but what we think good for ourselves, that should enter the moral calculation. Yet, as we saw, preference utilitarians usually allow that ignorant or foolish preferences should be disregarded by benevolent agents: there is no moral call on us to satisfy an addict's craving for heroin, or a child's demands for a quantity of sweets that we know will make him sick. Harsanyi's proposal that we need to identify a person's 'true' preferences, namely those he would manifest 'on due reflection and in possession of all relevant information' (1976: 32), however, runs into the difficulty that not everyone is capable of such critical reflection. If the child who requests for his birthday present some expensive toy of which we know he will soon tire, had been more rational, he would have chosen some other gift which would yield him longer-lasting satisfaction; but if he had been more rational he would not have been the child he is (and perhaps would not have been a normal child at all). It might therefore be suggested that we should be content to define individual utility in terms of a person's 'corrected' preferences, whatever they may be (that is, those preferences which a person has thought through as well as he is able, in the light of all the relevant information he is capable of grasping). But this would still leave us sometimes under an apparent moral obligation to assist a person to satisfy preferences which reasonable people would deem unwise. Presumably Harsanyi would not wish to identify such preferences with a person's 'true' preferences. But the whole idea of 'true' preferences hints that a covert step has been taken in the direction of an objectivist account of utility.

There are also serious difficulties with the notion of maximising the satisfaction of a person's preferences. Wants operate over very different time-scales: some of a person's desires are directed on immediate or short-term satisfactions, others on long-term goals. Preference utilitarians talk about maximising the satisfaction of a person's preferences for objects both near and distant. But as Richard Brandt has explained, it is not clear that this conception is intelligible (1979: 249f.). People's desires change with time, and some of the things that we think that we shall want at a later stage of our lives we turn out not to want when that stage arrives. Some of our desires may, in fact, undergo complete reversal over time. Brandt considers the example of a religious sceptic who has boldly protested throughout his life that he wants no priest to be present at his deathbed, yet who in his dying hour weakens and requests that one should be summoned. Is his welfare maximised if we call the priest, given that while this is what he wants *now*, he has spent most of his life preferring that a priest should *not* be called? Is the length of time that we want something more or less important than what we want at the time when the want can be satisfied? Brandt claims that no clear criterion has yet been produced for determining 'in principle, and generally' which of two possible courses of action would produce more desire- (or preference-) satisfaction, 'even if we can predict the impact of the events on the individual, and how long and how intensely each of the several outcomes has been or will be desired [preferred]' (250–1). Needless to say, the problems are compounded when we turn from the one-person to the many-persons case. If it is hard to know how to maximise one person's preferences, it is harder still to know how to maximise the preferences of a number of people whose welfare is at issue, particularly if their preferences clash. (Should we, for instance, give more weight to preferences which are more intensely held? Or would this be unfair to people of phlegmatic disposition who want things less intensely? And how should we cope with the fact that some people want more things than others do (251–2)?)

In Brandt's opinion, utilitarians would do well to revert to the classical view which represents *happiness*, rather than desire- (or preference-) satisfaction as the proper goal of action. The objection that happiness theories involve (as Harsanyi complains) 'dictation to others about what they should do' is 'seriously mistaken': for it fails to acknowledge that any plausible view of happiness must leave ample room for self-determination; people are, by and large, happiest when they are free to make their own decisions (252). Brandt further appeals to the phenomenology of moral experience for evidence that we care about people getting what they want or prefer *just because* we care about their being happy rather than miserble. The only reason we see for helping others to attain their goals is that doing so will produce a net increase in their happiness (147–8). T.M. Scanlon has recently written in similar vein that

> Preferences are important when we are selecting a gift, baking a birthday cake, or deciding where to take a friend to dinner because what we are aiming at in such cases is a person's happiness. Preferences are important because they show us *what* is likely to make someone happy, and because a person is pleased when we take the trouble to find out his wants and satisfy them (1993: 194).

More questionable is Brandt's predilection for a view of happiness which is virtually Benthamite in its focus on the elements of pleasure and pain. Brandt's hedonism is explained largely by his desire to construct a manageable calculus of utility, a project which requires happiness to be reducible to terms simple enough to allow it to be treated as a measurable commodity. For Brandt's scheme to work, we must be able to 'assign numbers to the degrees of enjoyment of the elements' of particular experiences. We begin by selecting a pair of experiences *A* and *B*, such that *A* is very slightly more enjoyable than *B*. Unit value is arbitrarily assigned to the degree of enjoyment by which *A* exceeds *B*. (The inspiration behind this idea may be Edgeworth's proposal that we should define a unit of utility as the smallest perceptible improvement in welfare (cf. Edgeworth 1881).) We can then give the same number to other cases of equal increments, and the number 2 to any increments 'just equal to that of the joint increment of two elements already assigned the number 1' (255). Neutral states (those which are neither pleasant nor unpleasant) are assigned the number 0, while unpleasant ones receive negative numbers. Experiences can then be plotted on an enjoyment graph, whose two axes represent the pleasantness of an experience and its duration. Two experiences plotted on the graph can then be compared in respect of happiness by computing and comparing the areas under their curves (255–6).

This method can next be extended to the many-persons case, provided that we can devise a sound way of making interpersonal comparisons. Brandt argues that behavioural evidence often produces good reason to suppose that one person obtains more pleasure from a particular experience (say, from drinking cider) than another does; and if we can light on a plausible example of an 'interpersonally equally pleasant/unpleasant experience' (Brandt's suggestion is taking a drink when chemical tests show that two individuals are in an equal state of dehydration), then we can 'calibrate their pleasure assignments with each other, just as we calibrate two thermometers' (260–2). Brandt concedes that in some complex cases of interpersonal comparisons, no assignment of cardinal numbers may in practice be possible, but this will not always preclude our judging that one of two feasible acts would increase the total happiness more: for instance, if one act would leave at least one person better off and no one worse off, while the other would leave everyone's happiness level unaltered (264).

An obvious objection to Brandt's calculus is the enormous practical difficulty of assigning the cardinal numbers and carrying out the interpersonal comparisons. Brandt suggests, for instance, that in order to decide whether punishing a criminal does more harm than good we should 'determine the (probable) net increase or decrease of happiness for each individual involved' on the two alternatives of punishing and not punishing him, 'add them up, and sum' (265). No doubt many people with 'broad experience and sensitivity' could, as Brandt says, make some rough and ready predictions about the likely effects of the two strategies – which may indeed be all that a less ambitious utilitarianism requires. But his claim that the matter can, in practice as well as in theory, be reduced to a precise mathematical calculation is very hard to believe. It would, for example, be difficult to determine exactly how many people would run an increased risk of harm from the criminal if he were released into the community, how great that risk actually was in each of their cases, and how much their utility would be diminished by their *fear* of being harmed by him.

In any case, there is more to happiness than enjoyment. Scanlon remarks that there are 'cases in which a true benefactor will aim at a person's overall good at the expense of what would be pleasing (or at least be torn between the two objectives)' (1993: 194). Even where a wise benefactor aims specifically to make a person *happy* (or happier), he will not always proceed by trying to increase his pleasures and reduce his pains. The point here is not just that a certain amount of struggle, pain and disappointment is necessary in every life if a person is to have the satisfaction of overcoming obstacles and surviving hardships, and to learn to appreciate the good things of life at their proper worth (cf. Scarre 1991). It is also important to see that happiness involves more than the experience merely of what Brandt refers to as states of high hedonic tone. Our ability to be happy crucially depends on there being things in the world which we value besides our own pleasures and pains: a matter to which we turn next.

## 2 Dominant- and inclusive-end conceptions of happiness

J.S. Mill thought that the utilitarian value theory could be summed up very simply: 'happiness is desirable, and the only thing desirable, as an end: all other things being only desirable as means to that end' (J.S. Mill 1861: 234). Yet for Mill, as for Aristotle, saying this was only a start: the important task was to spell out the nature of that happiness which constituted the ultimate objective of rational action; and like Aristotle, Mill believed that living well and happily required wisdom in the selection of our specific goals. An end was not necessarily eligible just because it was pleasant. But Mill was well aware that many people denied that happiness was the only, or the most important, goal in life. Some,

137

for instance, affirmed that *virtue* was a more proper end of human conduct (235). Mill's response to such objections was ingenious. Utilitarians, he suggested, need not be embarrassed to admit that virtue and other ends are worth pursuing 'disinterestedly', as ends in themselves.[1] For pursuing them this way need not be an alternative to pursuing happiness. One can pursue virtue, health, wealth, power, fame, physical enjoyments, artistic and literary achievement, and so on, as 'parts' – that is to say, as constituent elements – of happiness. Such objects are not pursued in order to further some end beyond themselves, a more ultimate end called 'happiness'; their pursuit for their own sakes *is* the pursuit of happiness; they are not instrumental but intrinsic goods, components of our happiness:

> The ingredients of happiness are very various, and each of them is desirable in itself, and not merely when considered as swelling an aggregate. The principle of utility does not mean that any given pleasure, as music, for instance, or any exemption from pain, as for example health, is to be looked upon as means to a collective something termed happiness, and to be desired on that account. They are desired and desirable in and for themselves; besides being means [Mill has in mind here the way in which one good, such as health, can assist the pursuit of another, for example, working at some valued task], they are a part of the end (235).

In keeping with the standard Benthamite line that happiness is 'pleasure and the absence of pain', Mill added that pursuing an end like virtue for its own sake, as a part of happiness, means pursuing it 'either because the consciousness of it is a pleasure, or because the consciousness of being without it is a pain' (237). This explanation need not be taken too seriously if our earlier suggestion is right that Mill espouses Benthamite hedonism in *Utilitarianism* more to satisfy the reader's expectations than from any personal conviction. There is, it is true, an Aristotelian precedent for the idea that things chosen for pleasure are things which are chosen for their own sakes (Aristotle, *Nicomachean Ethics*, 1176b), yet Mill's gloss is not very convincing. Pursuing things for their own sake is more plausibly explained as pursuing them for the sake of their value than for the pleasure to be derived from them (note that the pleasure one takes in doing a virtuous deed arises precisely from the consciousness that one has done something *worthwhile*). But Mill could justly look on his 'parts of happiness' doctrine as superior to Bentham's one-dimensional account of human psychology; it allowed for the multiplicity of motivations where Bentham had supposed 'mankind to be swayed by only a part of the inducements which really actuate them' (J.S. Mill 1833: 17). Whether or not the parts of happiness are valuable only because they afford us high-quality pleasures, the recognition of the variety of ways in which human lives attain fulfilment is a step towards realism.

It is a significant question, however, whether Mill's distinction of a plurality of projects, interests and ideals within a life makes talk of *happiness* as a goal redundant. If virtue, self-respect, honour and a love of beauty are the ends which a person pursues for their own sake, why regard them as parts of his happiness? Why not simply say that they are the ends which make his life worth living? Mill himself denied that happiness is any kind of reward or pay-off for following one's various goals; and this renders the point of treating it as the ultimate end obscure. Was it mere atavism which impelled him to echo the traditional formula that happiness is the only thing desirable in itself? Yet it is more probable that Mill grasped that if utilitarianism is to be a tenable theory of morality, there needs to be some commodity or condition or organising feature of experience which functions as the common denominator of good. Happiness, he thought, would serve this purpose: it was the necessary unifying good about which some form of quantitative judgements could be made. While a person's specific goals may deserve to be promoted on their own merits, happiness provides a conceptual linkage among them and a medium of comparative appraisal. Unfortunately Mill said too little about the nature of happiness for it to be clear exactly how he thought it filled this role. But it is doubtful whether he believed that happiness was to be equated with high-grade pleasure; thus the famous remark that it is 'better to be Socrates dissatisfied than a fool satisfied' (J.S. Mill 1861: 212), clearly gestures towards a *non*-hedonistic conception of happiness in which spiritual or intellectual perfection is more important than pleasure. It is at least a reasonable supposition that Mill thought the happy life to be a life with a certain kind of shape and unity to it. The 'parts' of happiness are the various significant ends which a life contains, yet happiness is more than the simple sum of those parts.

Mill's 'parts of happiness' doctrine is an example of an 'inclusive-end' conception of happiness. An inclusive end is one which incorporates a set of individual goals pursued for their own sake, none of which is valued substantially more than the rest. (The constituent goals may possess a ranking order, but no one goal possesses a peculiar pre-eminence.) Inclusive-end conceptions of happiness are to be contrasted with 'dominant-end' conceptions, in which happiness is identified with some particular goal to which the other goals are radically subordinated. Both Bentham and Aristotle in their different ways supported dominant-end views of happiness. Bentham thought that happiness meant the attainment of a balance of pleasure over pain. Aristotle argued that happiness for human beings consisted, above all, in the pursuit of philosophical wisdom. Unlike Bentham, Aristotle believed that other goals besides this main goal, and especially the excellences of character, were of some intrinsic worth, but philosophical wisdom remained the dominant element in *eudaimonia*. (Aristotle's position shows that a dominant-end view of happiness does not have to be a *monolithic*-end view, where only one goal is regarded as having intrinsic value, all secondary goals being ascribed a merely instrumental importance.)[2]

There are two important points to note about inclusive-end theories of happiness. The first is that an inclusive-end analysis of happiness need not be, or involve, an inclusive-end view of *life*. Indeed it would be hard to recognise as a happiness-*utilitarian* theory one which failed to accord the dominant status among life's goals to the pursuit of happiness. But deciding that happiness is the main (or the only) worthwhile object in life does not settle the question whether happiness itself consists in the pursuit of a dominant end or of a number of ends of roughly equal importance. Bentham took a dominant-end view of life and a dominant-end view of happiness. Mill believed that happiness was the dominant end of life but was itself an inclusive end having several components.

The second point is that a plausible inclusive-end theory of happiness will not be a mere unsorted list of goals. According to Kekes, an inclusive end 'is not a specific value but a way of ordering the various specific values that we should like to realize in our lives' (Kekes 1993: 133). On an inclusive-end view happiness is more than the sum of its parts, the various constituent goals which it incorporates: it is a particular selection and arrangement of these. A life directed on happiness can scarcely be a random combination of uncoordinated elements, but needs to possess internal coherence. Happy people avoid the selection of ends which cannot be easily realised within the same life or the same phase of a life, whatever their individual appeal. Happiness also requires the choice of objectives which are perceived to lie within our grasp, even if there are other objectives which we would prefer to have chosen had our talents or our circumstances been different.[3] Yet happiness cannot consist solely in the pursuit of a carefully selected and ordered set of ends chosen for their own intrinsic worth. Pursuing a set of valued objectives for their own sake can be said to make one happy only if it produces personal satisfaction. Elizabeth Telfer has rightly remarked that being happy involves, among other things, being pleased with one's life (Telfer 1980: 8–9). A person may lead a very happy life without deliberately trying to be happy, but satisfaction with the general content and shape of one's life is a necessary condition of happiness. (This satisfaction can come in degrees; some happy lives are happier than others.) One source of satisfaction is that of seeing one's favoured objectives positively promoted, regardless of who promotes them. But deeper satisfactions come from being oneself an effective promoter of one's valued ends; knowing that one is an agent of the good contributes to one's happiness by enhancing one's self-respect.

There is no need to retreat so far from Benthamism as to deny an important place for *pleasure*, too, in the happy life. It may be possible to lead a life which is happy to some degree even though all one's satisfactions arise out of the fulfilment of one's valued projects. But more normally happy lives contain pleasurable experiences which are not logically dependent on the application of concepts of value. One can enjoy eating cream buns or listening to jazz without believing that there is anything intrinsically valuable about cream buns or jazz – their value lies in their capacity to please. Pleasures like these do not constitute, for normal people, the *whole* of happiness, but they can plausibly be seen, as Mill saw them, as a *part* of their happiness. An inclusive-end view of happiness singles out neither pleasure nor any other individual element as the whole of happiness, but sees happy existence as a coherent construction out of a variety of complementary parts – a construction on which the subject can look with satisfaction.

### 3 Problems about multiple ends

This leads us to the first of the questions for utilitarianism posed at the beginning of this chapter. Can utilitarianism provide an adequate guide to action if the ingredients of happiness are many and diverse, and vary from person to person? What sense does it make to prescribe the maximisation of happiness, when there is neither a single nor a simple blueprint for human happiness? There is much less of a problem for dominant-end accounts of happiness. If happiness is reducible to pleasure, then right actions can be straightforwardly identified as those which produce as much pleasure as possible. Or if the development of philosophical wisdom is the key to happy existence, we should do the best we can to turn people into philosophers. But if happiness has many parts, the utilitarian goal appears to defy precise specification. To say only that we should help people to live the *happiest possible lives* seems unhelpfully vague; yet it is hard to give any more detailed content to the injunction to assist people to live happily, when happy lives can be lived in so large a variety of ways. Nothing like a Benthamite or Brandtian calculus looks remotely feasible here.

Yet this difficulty for utilitarianism may, I think, be more apparent than real. Our practical opportunities for making people happy are often quite easy to identify; they are also more limited than we might imagine. Many of the most important 'parts of happiness' are things which individuals can only attain for themselves. An aspirant to Millian qualities like excellence of character, spiritual perfection or eminence in some field of scientific or artistic endeavour will look to other people mainly for moral support and encouragement. And plainly a person can only develop his self-respect as an agent of the good to the degree that his agency is autonomous and unassisted. At the social level, the best way to assist individuals to be happy is to create the basic political, economic and educational conditions which permit their chosen life-styles to be realised. The most fruitful happiness-enhancing service which utilitarians can render is generally to facilitate individuals' own efforts to live the lifestyle of their choice. This can be achieved by ensuring that people have political rights and liberties, suitable education and training, economic independence and a guaranteed minimum stand-ard of material well-being. Happiness is elusive for those who are starving, ignorant, in bondage to others or devoid of all leisure. There is much to be said for thinking of utilitarianism in essentially eighteenth-century terms, as a programme for political action dedicated to providing an optimal social framework within which people can pursue their special conceptions of the good. Utilitarians will also wish to perform more specific acts of assistance to people in need.[4] But the most effective modes of enhancing the general utility involve action on broader fronts, aimed at securing a political and social environment conducive to the realisation of private ends.

Utilitarians like Mill, then, who see happiness as life's dominant end but itself as an inclusive end, need not be stumped by the question of how to promote happiness in the light of the variety of its potential parts and the range of individual preferences. But this brings us to the second, and harder, of our two questions for utilitarianism. This was the question of whether utilitarianism can adequately accommodate the fact that many of the ends which people actually pursue are valued intrinsically, as things worth pursuing for themselves, and not instrumentally, as sources of happiness. It may seem at first that there should be little difficulty here, once we have adopted an inclusive-end view of happiness. On this conception, the pursuit of happiness is the pursuit of an ordered complex of valued ends in which we can take an overall satisfaction. Although happiness would not be happiness without the element of satisfaction, the several 'parts of happiness' are not pursued instrumentally for the sake of the satisfaction they individually cause. So utilitarianism – it seems – has no real problem with the idea that some things besides subjective satisfaction are pursued as ends in themselves. However, it does not follow from the premise that an end is not being sought for the satisfaction it individually yields that it is not being sought because of its capacity to contribute to a complex of ends that satisfies. In fact, it is not easy to see much point to speaking of a goal being pursued as a 'part of happiness' *unless* its pursuit is motivated by the thought of its contribution to a satisfying whole. A constituent end would thus be valuable in the kind of way that a brick in a wall is valuable: as an object of no particular worth in itself but significant in a structured combination with others. If utilitarianism nevertheless insists on maintaining that *happiness* is the be all and end all (the dominant end *in life*), this remains at odds with the familiar fact of moral phenomenology that many of the ends which people pursue are valued for their own sake rather than as constituents of a satisfying complex called 'happiness'. Political, religious, domestic, social, artistic, sporting and other goals, singly or in combination, provide the *raison d'être* of many lives, rather than the search for happiness. Ironically enough, were this not so, the possibilities of human happiness would be fewer than they are: for if we did not regard many ends as valuable in themselves, we could hardly reap much satisfaction from promoting them.

Consider, for example, an ecologically-minded person who believes *biodiversity* to be a valuable goal. He thinks that the world is a richer and better place the more plant and animal types it contains, and that every disappearance of a species is a tragedy. (He may make a few exceptions in the case of really harmful species like tsetse flies.) One day he reads in the newspaper about the creation of a safe haven for white rhinos. Why should he be pleased by this news? Partly because he is glad to think that future generations of people will be able to enjoy these exotic beasts. But also because he believes that preserving a threatened species is a good in itself. (It would be a good, in his opinion, even if the protection of the animals required that humans were debarred all future access to them.) Because success in the attainment of one's goals is satisfying, it is easy to make the mistake of supposing that the value of pursuing those goals is instrumental: that they are worthwhile objects just because they contribute to making one's life more satisfying. Yet the biodiversifier could not coherently say that he would care nothing about the saving of the rhinos if this did not help to make his life go better. Preserving the species pleases him precisely because he sees it as an intrinsically valuable thing. This example suggests that classical utilitarianism fails to do justice to the mode in which many of our actual ends matter to us, when it attempts to impose a covering conception ('happiness') to justify them.

## 4 Two contrasting responses

There are two quite different ways in which utilitarians could respond to these difficulties. They might either accept the objections made to classical (happiness-centred) utilitarianism, and attempt to remodel their theory to make room for intrinsically valued ends besides happiness. Or they could reject the objections and argue that, in the final analysis, nothing really does matter except happiness. We must examine the merits of each strategy.

(A) The first option for utilitarianism is to grant the existence of other valuable ends than happiness and to hold that *all* valuable ends are worth promotion. Thus a person should not only pursue happiness (his own and other people's): he should also promote such ends-in-themselves as biodiversity or the production of a fine book on philosophy or the painting of a beautiful picture. This might be considered a form of *Ideal Utilitarianism*, according to which we should seek to bring into being valuable conditions or states of affairs, of which human satisfactions are only one kind. Such a theory reflects the richness and the complexity of the value systems of normal human beings, and it avoids representing all our ends as merely 'parts of happiness'. But it faces serious problems.

The most obvious of these is the difficulty of how to determine a criterion to enable us to make comparative value judgements about potentially very diverse ends. The need for a meta-value to serve in this role is particularly acute if the theory is construed, in the classical manner, as enjoining us to *maximise* and not merely to *promote* valuable states of affairs. Consider some practical dilemmas. How should a benevolent government decide whether to spend its spare cash on building a sports complex or a concert hall? Are great disparities of wealth among members of the same community to be allowed in the name of liberty or disallowed in that of equality? Should developing countries with expanding populations set aside areas of land for wildlife which could be used for farming? Is it better to allow people unrestricted freedom of expression or to curb the dissemination of pornography? Should the religious and social traditions of ethnic minorities be tolerated where they involve the oppression of women or of other constituent groups? Does the philosopher or the physician, the popular novelist or the politician contribute the more to public utility? These questions are difficult for both classical and for preference-satisfaction forms of utilitarian theory. But for the kind of Ideal Utilitarianism we are now envisaging they appear unanswerable. How are we supposed to decide rationally which of our values to prefer in the event of a clash? No doubt some of our values are dearer to us than others. But utilitarianism should be able to provide a rational basis for adjudicating such conflicts, and it is not clear what this could be once the common currency of happiness is abandoned.

It is true that we have, in some instances, strong intuitions to guide us in our judgements of the comparative strength of our values. We would not, for example, take value to be very well promoted by someone who folded paper into beautiful flower shapes while ignoring the wants of a desperately sick friend in the next room. But many questions about relative value are much harder to answer if we eschew the appeal to the happiness criterion. There would seem to be nothing to go on when it came to deciding the relative importance of liberty and equality, or of sport and classical music. Must we infer that the kind of Ideal Utilitarianism envisaged above must fail? We must, if we demand that the theory supply us with a non-arbitrary criterion capable of rationally deciding every question about comparative value.

There may, however, be another option. It would be possible to propose a weaker version of Ideal Utilitarianism which acknowledges the partial incommensurability of values and the lack of a determinate answer to many value-dilemmas. A theory of this description would condemn the person who prefers making origami models to nursing his sick friend, but leave it open whether a government with optimific intentions should spend its money on a sports centre or a concert hall. Such a theory might be developed along Humean lines, looking to our natural feelings of approbation and disapprobation to provide the final arbitration on value questions. Incommensurable values would be simply those which we did not feel able to rank on a single scale. (Note that there would be no appeal to a mysterious faculty of intuition to conduct the process of evaluation, for on a Humean picture there is no moral reality to intuit, but only the feelings of approval and disapproval themselves.) This weakened version of Ideal Utilitarianism could still preserve the maximising ideal of classical theories: it could be construed as enjoining us, where comparative judgements are possible, to choose that option productive of the most value, and where they are not, to regard *any* choice as maximising. (The view that utilitarians may have to concede their ignorance of how to answer some value questions is not new. We may be obliged to confess our moral ignorance in the face of many dilemmas. As James Mirlees asks, 'Is there any reason to think that we are in a better position to decide how much to spend on kidney machines, than we are to decide how long this universe will last?' (1982: 80).)

This modified Ideal Utilitarianism may at first sight appear a *pis aller*, a fall-back position to be chosen for want of anything better. Yet it is hardly fair to label the theory as second best if stronger alternatives do violence to our normal conviction that many value-dilemmas are without solution. A moral theorist who produces a solution to an insoluble problem is like the man who finds a non-existent black cat in the coal-cellar. We should not disdain a form of utilitarianism which refrains from promising more than it, or any, theory can pay. There may be no answer to the question whether liberty is a greater intrinsic good than equality, or the ability to sing an operatic aria more valuable than the ability to run a four-minute mile. In any case, incommensurability is rarely absolute. There may be no fact of the matter whether liberty or equality is in essence the greater good, but we may still judge a major loss of liberty to be an unreasonable price to pay for a minor increase in equality. (In cases like this we can make some appeal to a *happiness* criterion to guide our judgement; happiness, after all, is one of the values allowed within the conception, though not the only value.)

Ideal Utilitarianism attempts to take more seriously than other utilitarian theories have done facts about the ways in which we actually think about values. In order to work, it needs to appeal to common, settled beliefs about the ends which are worth advancing, to the degree to which these are available.[5] It need not accept uncritically every popular notion of value (there are fashions and fads in values, as in other things), but it rejects both the neutrality about value questions implicit in the preference-satisfaction approach and the classical idea that only happiness is valuable. Nevertheless it represents a considerable move beyond conventional utilitarian positions (some might accordingly prefer to call it 'Ideal Consequentialism' rather than 'Ideal Utilitarianism'), and it can specify no clear-cut criterion for arriving at moral evaluations. In the end it may seem to amount to little more than the bland instruction: Promote your values.

(B) The second, very different strategy which a utilitarian might adopt in response to the apparent multiplicity of valued ends is to hold that the belief in intrinsically valuable ends besides happiness rests on illusion. On this view, happiness consists in an ordered and satisfying arrangement of pleasures, comforts, securities, freedoms, loving relationships, artistic activity and aesthetic experience, and so on, but in strict independence of any concepts of intrinsic value. As there are no intrinsic goods besides happiness, nothing is worth doing that does not have happiness (the agent's or other people's) as its object. It is misguided to value biodiversity, for instance, as an end in itself. Promoting biodiversity may give a person pleasure, yet on the present view that pleasure is unsoundly based if it rests on the false belief that biodiversity is a worthwhile end in itself; rather, biodiversity is worth promoting only as a brick in the wall of happiness – as an end which, together with other ends, causes us satisfaction.

But is it credible that the only intrinsically valuable end is human happiness? Is a goal like biodiversity quite worthless unless it produces happiness? Promoting the goal of biodiversity appears to make a person happy by providing him with the sense that he is advancing a worthwhile cause; and if this does not prove that what he is doing *is* worthwhile, it at least illustrates our common inclination to ascribe value to ends other than subjective satisfactions. However, a defender of the view at issue might insist that our tendency to glean satisfaction from the pursuit of worthy objects is irrelevant; the real question is whether any objects are worthy which cannot plausibly be regarded either as proper parts of happiness in themselves, or as productive causes of the parts of happiness. Even biodiversity *could* be argued to be an end of this description. Saving rare species of plants and animals evidently pre-serves more natural variety for people to enjoy. And the more species there are, the greater the pool of potential sources of important drugs and other substances which will make future lives go better. (There is also, in the case of rescued animals like rhinos, the ability of the creatures themselves to live whatever kind of satisfying lives are possible for members of their kind.)

Rather similar considerations may be used to persuade us that some other apparently intrinsic goods are real goods only if they contribute to happiness. Great works of art or literature may be held to be valuable only to the extent that they are either enjoyable in themselves, or help us to make more sense of life through the revelations they make about the human condition. Even such states as Mill's 'spiritual perfection' and excellence of character may arguably be identified with a more fully developed (and therefore satisfying) understanding of oneself and the world, and an enhanced ability to make one's own and other existences pleasant. In regard to that supreme example of worthy behaviour, the sacrifice of one's own life in the interests of others, Mill himself argued that such self-sacrifices are pointless unless 'they contribute ... to increase the amount of happiness in the world'. Martyrs die uselessly unless they 'earn for others immunity from similar sacrifices' – that is, enable other lives to be more satisfying (J.S. Mill 1861: 217).

Despite what can be said in favour of theory (B), it too encounters some considerable objections.

(1) If nothing is valuable in itself but happiness, then it should not matter from whence it comes; the only important question about a source of happiness is how fruitful it is. Now people derive deep satisfaction from promoting ends like biodiversity which they believe to be intrinsically valuable, though according to theory (B) such ends are never really valuable in themselves. But if the origin of the satisfaction is unimportant, it should be a good thing, on the theory, for people to believe *falsely* that there are intrinsically valuable ends in order that they can have the pleasure of pursuing them. Indeed, the larger the number of things which people can be persuaded to think are worth pursuing for their own sake, the greater the amount of potential happiness! Hence, believers in theory (B) would do well to treat it as a secret doctrine, one best kept from the ears of the masses; better still, as a view to be publicly pilloried as false. To make people maximally happy they should be taught to think falsely that valueless ends are valuable.

This strategy for creating happiness is clearly disingenuous and manipulative. It involves the deliberate attempt by a knowing élite to instil into an ignorant populace a false view of the world. Concealing from people the valueless nature of their activities smacks of heavy-handed paternalism. If nothing has intrinsic value except happiness, then it is surely wrong to lead someone into the fool's paradise of thinking that it does. However, such a condemnatory judgement presupposes a conception of intrinsic value which is incompatible with the supposition being allowed: for *if* only happiness counts, then it cannot matter that some of those satisfactions depend upon false beliefs. Yet we may think it to be a solid ground for rejecting the supposition that the idea of investing importance in a false cause so strongly repels us. On our normal system of values a life devoted to false causes is futile, and the satisfaction taken in them is worthless.

(2) If theory (B) is true, anything which produces satisfaction in large amounts should be welcome. But consider the following fantasy of Nozick's:

> Suppose there were an experience machine that would give you any experience you desired. Superduper neuropsychologists could

148

stimulate your brain so that you would think and feel you were writing a great novel, or making a friend, or reading an interesting book. All the time you would be floating in a tank, with electrodes attached to your brain. Should you plug into the machine for life, preprogramming your life's experiences? (Nozick 1974: 42).

This is the stuff of nightmares and horror movies. Nozick rightly thinks that few people would opt to be connected up to the machine. Even if we believed that such an existence would provide us with greater subjective satisfaction than we could otherwise expect, the prospect appals us not only because of the systematic deception to which we would be subjecting ourselves but also because of the passive character of a 'life' experiencing only what is fed to us down the wires. (The level of passivity could be reduced by making the machine more interactive, but the scope for interaction is limited by the need to guarantee us a high level of satisfaction; the very bad novel we 'write' must still win the Booker Prize.) A decision to be attached to the machine would be least irrational for someone whose real life was doomed to unhappiness through sickness, oppression or war; but even in this predicament it would not be unreasonable to prefer suicide. People in more normal circumstances would reject the option because they want to *live* their lives, not merely experience a series of mental states, however agreeable. The value of what we do does not reduce to the value of what we feel.

Of course, it could be argued that a life spent wired up to the machine would not really be a *happy* life, no matter how pleasant it felt. On an inclusive-end view of happiness, pleasure is not the only brick in the wall; bricks like autonomy and self-respect are important as well. It might therefore be suggested that a proponent of theory (B) could still reject a 'life' on the machine without conceding that anything mattered ultimately but happiness. But the difficulty is to see how to defend such a line without making a tacit appeal to values which the theory officially rejects. It is true that a person could be fed down the wires a career which filled him with a greater *impression* of autonomy or self-satisfaction than he could have hoped to experience in the real world. But autonomy and self-respect normally matter to us because of their internal connection with concepts of intrinsic value which are independent of the value of happiness. They matter to us because we see the world as divided up into more and less worthwhile things to do and to be; and we both value the freedom to make our own choices from amongst those things and relish the self-satisfaction of fulfilling our chosen courses. Unless, for instance, painting a beautiful picture seemed an end worth accomplishing for its own sake, we should neither care about being at liberty to paint it, nor take any pride in the finished product. Theory (B) is unable to make sense of these perfectly normal and familiar valuational attitudes. Indeed, it is hard to see, in the last analysis, how theory (B) can place value on anything besides simple subjective satisfactions.

(3) Finally, there is an interesting example of something we value which no argument could identify with a state of happiness. Posthumous reputation is at first sight an odd thing to care about, because when we are dead we are no longer able to know what others think about us, or be affected by their opinion. Nevertheless most people do wish for an enduring good reputation, and think of it as a significant evil to be ill spoken of after their death.[6] A concern to have a posthumous good name can motivate a person powerfully during life. The poet Horace was keen to leave behind in his verse a monument 'more durable than bronze, higher than the royal pyramids' (*Odes* III.30); a connoisseur may think twice about forming a secret hoard of stolen art-works which will inevitably be discovered after his death. Caring about our posthumous reputation does, of course, involve caring about mental states, namely those of the people whom we hope will think well of us. But we should not confuse a first-personal concern for our posthumous reputation with a third-personal concern that the people we care about will enjoy pleasant memories of us when we are gone.

It might be suggested that caring what people will think about us when we are dead is irrational – that it rests on a failure, or unwillingness, to recognise the finality of the stop death puts to our interests. *Non omnis moriar* 'I shall not completely die', thought Horace, if people still read my poetry. But such survival through one's works can be understood only in a figurative sense. Aristotle toyed with the parallel question of whether the fortunes of the living can in any way affect the dead. His conclusion was that this would only be possible if the deceased possessed some form of sentient afterlife (Aristotle, *Nicomachean Ethics* 1101a). But Aristotle also gestured towards a model which may throw some light on the value of posthumous reputation. He thought that *eudaimonia* could only be ascribed to a complete life, 'for one swallow does not make a summer, nor does one day; and so too one day, or a short time, does not make a man blessed and happy' (1098a). A life like the Trojan King Priam's which meets with disaster at its close is not *eudaimon*, no matter how contented its earlier phases may have been. Final disaster casts, so to speak, a retrospective shadow over the course of a person's career: that career may have seemed to be going well enough, but it was not destined to be finally successful. In a similar way, the posthumous loss of one's good name may cast a backward shadow over one's previous life: one could not really have been living a satisfactory life when one was (even if unwittingly) sowing the seeds of one's own dishonour. Dispraise, whenever it occurs, damages a life by its negative effect on the significance of what a person has done.

Whatever the merits of this explanatory model, the concern for our posthumous reputation is normally felt with too great a force to be plausibly dismissed as irrational. Yet having an abiding good name cannot be characterised, as theory (B) demands of all valuable things, as a part of happiness or as the causal basis of such a part. It is nevertheless looked on by most people as an intrinsically valuable thing. That being so, we have further reason for doubting the adequacy of theory (B).

The conclusions of this chapter have been largely negative. Utilitarians have conventionally sought an account of utility which represents it as a commodity amenable to quantitative assessment – something about which we can say at least roughly when we have more or less of it. The difficulty is to define a concept of utility which meets this technical condition while doing something like justice to our normal notions of value. Dominant-end views of happiness as consisting primarily in pleasure or enjoyment fulfil the technical condition (in principle, if not so readily in practice), but at the price of ignoring much that we think of as important to human beings. An inclusive-end view of happiness like Mill's does fuller justice to our phenomenology of value, but scarcely specifies a measurable commodity. Ideal Utilitarianism, phenomenologically the most adequate view, fails the technical condition more dismally still. Production of a satisfactory theory of value is probably the hardest, yet at the same time the most vital, task facing utilitarians today.

# CHAPTER VII

# Maximisation, Fairness and Respect for Persons

## 1 Is utilitarian justice just?

One of the most common and potentially most damaging criticisms made of utilitarian moral theories is that they display inadequate concern with fairness in the distribution of benefits and disbenefits. This charge was venerable even by the 1850s. J.S. Mill noted that the view that utility and justice were in basic and irreconcilable conflict had been prevalent 'in all ages of speculation' (J.S. Mill 1861: 240). He also thought that the charge was clichéd and unconvincing. It presupposed that there was a clear and generally accepted idea of justice, whereas in truth 'there is as much difference of opinion, and as much discussion, about what is just, as about what is useful to society'. Not only have different nations and individuals different ideas of the just, but in the mind of a single person justice is not always 'some one rule, principle, or maxim, but many, which do not always coincide in their dictates' (252). However, Mill thought that conceptions of justice typically contained five broad elements. It was usually supposed that people ought not to be deprived of what belongs to them by law; that they should not be deprived of what belongs to them by moral right; that they should receive the goods and evils which they deserve; that they should not break the engagements they make to others; and that they should avoid partiality (that is, showing 'favour or preference to one person over another, in matters to which favour and preference do not properly apply') (241–3). But as Mill showed with shrewdly chosen examples, it was one thing to consent to these schematic principles, another to agree about their interpretation in practice.

Even among utilitarians there is a spectrum of positions on justice. Most radical and uncompromising of all were the views of William Godwin. 'By justice,' he wrote, 'I understand the impartial treatment of every man in matters that relate to his happiness.' Its great principle is to be 'no respecter of persons' (Godwin 1793: 69–70). Like Mill, Godwin thought that everyone should receive his just deserts. But utilitarians of a more moderate stamp have not accepted that people who are capable of 'a more refined and generic happiness' have greater deserts than others; or that 'I may put a man to death for the common good, either because he is infected with a pestilential disease, or because some oracle has declared it essential to the public safety'. Godwinian man has no right to his possessions, or even his life, when his 'duty' (i.e. utility) requires him to give them up (70, 244, 75, 89). Many utilitarians would argue that a world run on Godwinian lines would be less than maximally happy: that it would leave individuals more at risk of falling sacrificial victims to the public utility than is consistent with the preservation of that personal security which Mill considered essential for happiness (J.S. Mill 1861: 251). Nevertheless there is a widespread suspicion that even less extreme forms of utilitarianism fail to draw the protective boundaries tightly enough. Concepts of justice may vary as widely as Mill claimed they do, but most non-utilitarians believe that utilitarian justice is fundamentally flawed.

We have seen in Chapter I why Rawls thinks this is so. Utilitarians are concerned to maximise the net balance of satisfaction of the members of society. Therefore, '[j]ust as an individual balances present and future gains against present and future losses, so a society may balance satisfactions and dissatisfactions between different individuals' (Rawls 1971: 24). This means that some people have to suffer pain or loss in order to increase net social utility: an implication, in the view of the author of *A Theory of Justice*, strongly in conflict with our usual intuitions of fairness. Rawls represents the problem as arising out of the maximising strand in utilitarian thought. We are supposed to produce as much good as we can, not worry about who wins and who loses in the distribution process. It could be argued that the Rawlsian problem would not wholly disappear even on a version of the theory which merely told us to *promote* the good, without worrying about *maximising* it (cf. Slote 1984). Making the most of the good we produce would remain more important than distributing it equitably according to some non-utilitarian idea of equity. Allocation patterns would still be selected for their efficacy at realising the good, rather than for their capacity to provide 'fair shares for all'.

Utilitarians have responded with vigour to accusations like these. They have pointed out that in practice playing fast and loose with individual liberty, holdings or lifestyle, far from enhancing the public utility, is likely to destroy the social fabric and produce a set of discontented and neurotic human beings. Without relations of mutual respect and the sense of belonging to a community which cares for the needs of each constituent member, people might muddle along in some sort of social nexus, but hardly very happily. Admittedly, on rare occasions it may be 'better for one man to die for the good of the people' than for many persons to suffer: as where one hostage is killed to prevent the deaths of many hostages. But such acts are not incompatible with our ordinary intuitions of fairness; they are regrettable deeds rather than wrong ones. By permitting, in extraordinary instances, some relaxation of the usual conventions of behaviour, utilitarianism is really closer to common sense than those rigid deontological outlooks which forbid any exceptions to the rules even *in extremis*.

It is also pointed out that utilitarians are not committed to a policy of mindless multiplication of good things, under the naive impression that where $G$ is a good thing, the more $G$ there is the better. As big is not always beautiful, so most is not always best. One can have too much of some things which, in a reasonable amount, improve the quality of one's life: too much money, or leisure, or sex, or philosophy. Utilitarians should acknowledge, in regard to many goods, a principle of diminishing marginal returns, together with the need for balance and contrast within a life. Maximising the quality of our lives requires an endowment of good things in the right amount – not too little and not too much of them. The extent to which a life is a flourishing one cannot be determined by summing the pleasures and pains and calculating the balance; nor indeed by summing anything else. A life that is happy, or *eudaimon* in the Aristotelian sense, is an organic unity in which the significance of its parts rests on their contribution to the meaning of the whole.

Utilitarians, then, can respond to the charge that they fail to draw sufficiently strong protective barriers around individuals by showing that on a suitably refined view of what makes lives go well, there will rarely be a case for sacrificing the crucial interests of some individuals for the sake of others' benefit. A utilitarian may favour making a millionaire disgorge his surplus wealth in order to help the needy, but that is no more than what most civilised countries do anyway through their tax systems. (The practice can be justified on the ground that while enough is as good as a feast, less than enough means starvation.) Harming people in regard to their essential interests is another matter. Not only does this hardly ever produce a positive balance of utility: it can also subtly damage the seeming beneficiaries, by undermining the basis of their self-respect. How this happens will be explained below.

## 2 *Panem et circenses*

There are some satisfactions which may rationally be rejected for their destructive effects on the complete life. A 20-year-old may derive great enjoyment from smoking tobacco or marijuana, but he would be prudent to stop if he has set his sights on a hale and hearty old age. But there are pleasures which are not obviously imprudent or irrational, yet which are normally condemned as immoral. Some people take pleasure in some rather disturbing things. Take Genghis Khan, for instance. One day, in an interval of looting and pillaging, he explained his view of happiness. 'The greatest joy', he declared, 'is to conquer one's enemies, to pursue them, to seize their property, to see their families in tears, to ride their horses, and to possess their daughters and wives' (Fitzgerald 1961: 432). Genghis got a lot of pleasure out of life: his Mongol hordes were eminently efficient at butchering people. But what is a utilitarian to make of this? Not – apparently – that his pleasures harmed *him*. By Mongol standards, which exalt military conquest, wielding the power of life and death over others, and domination of the weak, Genghis's style of life was an eminently satisfactory one, and hugely enjoyable.

There is a problem for utilitarianism here, not because utilitarians are committed to favouring the Mongol lifestyle – even the fiercest critic of the theory could hardly allege that rape, pillage and massacre were well calculated to increase the general happiness – but because if pleasure is normally a good, then the enjoyment that Genghis and his warriors took in their depredations seems to *offset some of their evil*: it is a positive quantity in the balance sheet which compensates for some of the suffering of the victims. But it conflicts radically with our ordinary moral convictions to assert that the greater the pleasure a murderous maniac derives from abusing his victim, the smaller the net amount of evil produced by his actions. Sadism and *Schadenfreude* have no place in our usual notion of legitimate pleasure sources. To enjoy killing makes the killing worse, not better.[1] This is not because (or not primarily because) we fear that someone with a lust for killing is a danger to society. Our revulsion springs from a deeper level than that, a horror that such things can please people and a sense that whoever feels as he does falls well short of a human ideal. The question for utilitarianism is how it can accommodate this ideal.

What is needed from utilitarianism is a sufficiently subtle theory of human well-being to show why sadistic pursuits are not just other-harming but self-harming too. Crucial to the account, I shall argue, is the idea of self-respect as a paramount human good. Rawls has persuasively

155

ranked self-respect among the primary goods, things that every rational person may be presumed to want (Rawls 1971: 62). Self-respect is plausibly seen both as a necessary condition for happiness, and as a major source of it. For someone to acquire, or retain, self-respect, there are ways of treating others to which he cannot consent. These include not only mistreating people for sadistic ends, but also other types of manipulation or exploitation which, while usually thought of as immoral, are on the face of it justifiable (as critics gleefully point out) in the name of utility.

Consider, to focus ideas, one of the most notorious examples of organised sadism in history. The high point of the Roman games in the Imperial era was always something bloodthirsty – combats to the death between gladiators, wild-beast hunts or the extravagantly cruel execution of criminals. Throughout the *Pax Romana* death was mass entertainment. The Colosseum in Rome could hold 50,000 spectators, but no city, large or small, lacked a venue capable of holding the greater part of its populace. When the emperor or a Roman millionaire paid for a series of games, therefore, he was certainly giving the people what they wanted. How should a utilitarian regard this Roman charity? If giving people pleasure, or satisfying their desires, is praiseworthy on utilitarian grounds, is there any essential moral difference between providing a corn dole and a gladiatorial display? Even if the utilitarian's own preferences run more in favour of listening to string quartets than the cries of the dying, it is what others want that seems to count. He must take people as they are, not as he would like them to be. If crucifixion gives as much pleasure as poetry then it is as good.

Of course, the pleasure of some is bought at the expense of others, and the utilitarian will want to take this into account. But how great is the impact on his calculations? Does ten minutes' agony of a single individual outweigh the ecstatic pleasure of 50,000 spectators who watch him being torn to pieces by wild beasts? But even were the calculations to come out the way the utilitarian would like them to (we may waive at present the question of how they could be carried out), the consequentialist perspective still seems morally skewed in the contingency of its condemnations. Suppose that the suffering of one criminal thrown to the lions outweighed the pleasure of 50,000 spectators. This would make it wrong to throw a man to the lions in the Roman Colosseum. But the moral obstacle could in principle be surmounted by building a larger amphitheatre: what was wrong before 50,000 onlookers could be right in front of 100,000, the numbers being the crucial thing. (And think how the calculations might work out if the Romans had had satellite broadcasting.) Hare, wishing to defend the utilitarian, remarks that when a sadist tortures a victim, 'the suffering of the victim will normally be more intense than the pleasure of the sadist' (1982: 30). But this wholly ignores the situation where there are few victims and many sadists. Deontologists will say: 'Never mind the calculations, consider the side-constraints. Some things should simply not be done, because they are intrinsically wrong. However many people get pleasure from the games, numbers can never justify them.' This rejection of the consequentialist line is attractive for its round condemnation of the games, despite the fact that claims about intrinsic rightness and wrongness are problematical.

Discomfort with the utilitarian position is unlikely to be assuaged by reading J.J.C. Smart's thought-experiment of the deluded sadist:

> [L]et us imagine a universe consisting of one sentient being only, who falsely believes that there are other sentient beings and that they are undergoing exquisite torment. So far from being distressed by the thought, he takes a great delight in these imagined sufferings. Is this better or worse than a universe containing no sentient being at all? Is it worse, again, than a universe containing only one sentient being with the same beliefs as before but who sorrows at the imagined tortures of his fellow creatures? I suggest that the universe containing the deluded sadist is the preferable one (Smart 1973: 25).

This piece of unabashed act-utilitarian reflection is as likely to turn many off utilitarianism as any of the objections levelled by the critics. Smart's disturbing conclusion seems to indicate plainly the bankruptcy of a view which lacks moral values. None of the three possible states of the world he describes is very attractive; but his claim that the world containing the deluded sadist is the best of the bunch is proffered without any acknowledgement that sadism, even of a deluded sort where no one is really suffering, is an evil thing. Taking delight in others' suffering does not become morally neutral, still less a positive good, when it rests on a false existential belief about the sufferers. Smart attempts to explain why we normally think badly of sadism:

> Our repugnance to the sadist arises, naturally enough, because in our universe sadists invariably do harm. If we lived in a universe in which by some extraordinary laws of psychology a sadist was always confounded by his own knavish tricks and invariably did a great deal of good, then we should feel better disposed towards the sadistic mentality (25–6).

But this is a travesty of the truth. Smart describes a situation too counterfactual to evaluate easily, but however we might feel in that

157

hypothetical universe, in our actual one, people condemn the sadistic mentality not merely because sadists do damage but because wanting others to suffer is deplorable in itself. The appeal of a utilitarian theory will remain limited if its conceptual resources are so poor that it can refer only to the likely practical consequences to explain why delighting in human happiness is preferable to delighting in human misery. It is worth enquiring whether a more refined utilitarianism can do better than this.

### 3 'Whoever debases others is debasing himself'

One of the few Romans before the Constantinian age to write against the games was the Stoic philosopher Seneca the Younger. He condemned their brutality and heartlessness, and claimed that they made people more selfish and self-indulgent, crueler and less humane. To the anticipated objection that those who had committed serious crimes deserved to die, Seneca responded: 'Granted that, as a murderer, he deserved this punishment, what crime have you committed, poor fellow, that you should deserve to sit and see this show?' (*Letters* vii; Grant 1967: 118). He evidently believed that the spectator of the games lost more than he gained by his experience. If Seneca was right, he was harming himself, becoming a poorer person than before. Compare Seneca's comment with this by James Baldwin:

> Whoever debases others is debasing himself. That is not a mystical statement but a most realistic one, which is proved by the eyes of any Alabama sheriff (J. Baldwin 1964: 73).

Like Seneca, Baldwin believes that a person who diminishes others diminishes himself too. How does this happen? Treating one's neighbour with contempt, belittling and exploiting him for one's own pleasure or some other selfish end, rebounds on oneself. The point may be put in more Kantian terms. If one fails to respect humanity in other persons, by refusing to treat them as ends in themselves, one loses the basis for respecting one's own humanity and seeing oneself as an end. One cannot disvalue other human beings without implicitly disvaluing oneself, making the growth of self-respect impossible. Without a sense of human worth in general, there can be no sense of *one's own* human worth.

Rawls has proposed that self-respect is the most significant primary good of all (Rawls 1971: 440). There are other goods more immediately essential to keeping life in being, but self-respect is needed to provide a sense that life is worth living. To have self-respect is to have a sense of the value of oneself and one's projects and interests, and a belief that one has at least a modicum of ability to fulfil one's most important intentions. Any cogent form of utilitarianism, I suggest, must likewise take self-respect with the utmost seriousness as essential to the flourishing life. It is hard to see how someone who possessed other primary goods – social and political opportunities, adequate health, strength, intelligence, income, and so on – but who could not respect himself, could be a happy man. His enjoyment of those other goods would be greatly impaired if he did not feel that they belonged to a subject whose life was of value. There is little satisfaction in being healthy, wealthy and wise if you can think of no reason why the world would be worse off if you were dead. Rawls remarks that if we cannot respect ourselves, 'our desire and activity becomes empty and vain, and we sink into apathy and cynicism' (440). Alternatively we may try to avoid facing up to what we are. To avoid looking our worthlessness in the face, we may throw ourselves into a frantic round of distracting activity, or seek refuge in drugs or drink.

To believe oneself worthless is to be wretched. The Old English term *wrecca* meant an outcast, and someone who considers himself a wretch senses that he is in some sort outside the moral community. Wretches are deficient in the qualities that are the entry conditions of that community, basic virtues (*aretai*) and decencies. A person who has done something that he believes is degrading feels that he has lowered his own value and set himself apart from others. This feeling is a painful one, a bar to contentment. 'Whoever debases others is debasing himself.' If this is true, then one has a motive for not debasing others. It impedes one's happiness, by reducing the grounds of self-respect. A victim of the lions in the Roman arena may have been a criminal, but he was a human being as well. If that was insufficient to prevent him being treated as a mere object of sport, slaughtered with as little compunction as a dog or a chicken, then what did the onlookers have to feel so proud about? There, but for the grace of Jupiter, went they! Seneca knew the difference between pleasure and happiness. He saw that the sports of the amphitheatre could not make the spectators truly happy, even in their moments of most frenzied pleasure. Happiness does not, and cannot, lie in pursuits which make it impossible for a person to value himself as a human being. And because it is the same humanity we all share, a person cannot consistently value humanity in himself while disdaining it in other people. As a human being one is worthy of one's own respect because one possesses something worthy of everyone's respect, wherever it is found.

Even Smart's deluded sadist, who lives in a world in which no one is really suffering, is harmed by the self-debasing nature of his tastes. The fact that his beliefs are false does not diminish the self-devaluing effect of his delight in cruelty. Indeed, even if he *knew* that nobody was suffering, but delighted to watch video nasties (as many in our actual universe do) in which only simulated suffering takes place, his tastes are still incompatible with the preservation of his self-respect. It is something, but not enough, to refuse to be cruel, or to permit cruelty, to others. Enjoying fictional cruelty betrays an unsatisfactory attitude to humanity and human values, not merely (as Smart would hold) because it may loosen the grip of one's inhibitions against inflicting cruelty on real people, but because it indicates that one lacks genuine respect for the source of their, and one's own, worth. (Think, as an analogy, of the way in which if you genuinely love someone, you will be pained not just by knowing that the loved one is actually suffering, but by the very *idea* of his suffering.) Smart's deluded sympathiser, who sorrows at the suffering he falsely imagines others are undergoing, does at least keep his self-respect intact. The deluded sympathiser's happiness can be restored by a mere change of belief; the sadist's requires a change of character.

If the foregoing arguments are correct, utilitarians face no difficulty in condemning the blood sports of the amphitheatre. While many people were passionately addicted to them, those entertainments cannot have made them really happy. Throwing people to the lions for fun is incompatible with looking on humanity in your own person as being of value. If you think it proper to turn a human being into a lion's dinner, you must be prepared to universalise your judgement and concede that there would be nothing very wrong with throwing *you* to the lions instead. But you can hardly think this and respect yourself. Yet there is one seemingly powerful objection to this reasoning. Even if self-respect is essential to happiness, some people respect themselves for things apt to be frowned on by the modern liberal conscience. Someone may think very well of himself for being of the male sex, or for having white skin, for being born into the Aryan race or the dominant caste. Those who are not so fortunate he looks on with pity at best, or contempt; and he may consider that as inferior creatures they are ripe for his use and abuse. Thus Baldwin's Alabama sheriff does not think he debases himself when he treats Blacks with disdain – for is he not a white man and a superior being? By mistreating Blacks he may even reinforce his sense of his own specialness, and thereby enhance his self-esteem. Similarly, the Roman citizen in the Colosseum not only enjoys a victim's dying moments but reflects complacently on their difference in social status. There are things you may do to slaves or criminals or members of that new-fangled sect the Christians, which you must not dream of doing to people who matter.

The strategy of the utilitarian argument against sadism was to show that sadistic acts harm not just the victims but the agents and complicit onlookers too. But the objection reminds us of a harsh fact of life: that, for many people, it is not being human that imparts status, but belonging to a particular sex, race, class or religious grouping. The utilitarian contends that a Roman citizen cannot sustain his self-respect while he sees a slave being torn to bits; but the citizen does not see things that way. The worse the ill-usage of the slave, the greater his self-satisfaction at belonging to a category of persons who must not be treated so.

But what does this objection really show? The Alabama sheriff may look in the mirror and like what he sees in his own eyes; but it does not follow that he is looking at a happy man. The chained spectators in Plato's myth of the cave took the shadows they saw for realities because they knew no better. Likewise, someone whose experience of human possibilities has been seriously circumscribed by custom or prejudice may judge a very low-grade state of satisfaction to be happiness. The sheriff, like the citizen-spectator, is a man who has failed to make a certain kind of imaginative leap. Both have failed to grasp what some other lives are like *from the inside*. If they learn to make that leap, they will realise how much they have in common with the people they despise. They will discover that there are richer, more rewarding ways to relate to human beings than by scorning and abusing them. In part those ways are better because of the wider repertoire of satisfying responses – mutual kindness and cooperation, respect, sympathy, affection, love – they bring into play. In addition, they provide the basis for a deeper self-respect, by enhancing the sense that humanity matters.

The early-nineteenth-century campaign to abolish the slave trade in the British Empire published pictures of a manacled slave above the legend: 'Am I not a man and a brother?' This must be one of the most effective rhetorical questions in history. It got many people to make the crucial imaginative leap. Looking on Blacks as brothers was difficult at first for white, middle-class Englishmen. Even seeing them as men was not so easy. But the propaganda struck a chord, and led in time to the banning of the trade. Blacks were not yet regarded as more than younger brothers, but it was an improvement on what had gone before. Fraternity even of a limited kind was better than fratricide.

Those who take pleasure in the pain and degradation of others are deceived about the grounds of happiness. They could get more out of life if they saw other people as men and brothers. They would then be able to see themselves as men and brothers too, valuable beings capable of living valuable lives deserving of their own and others' respect. If they accomplished that mental transformation, they would be well on the road to wisdom. Their blindness to human value closes off a major source of happiness. The loss they suffer is no less grievous because they do not apprehend it as such.

Admittedly, it might be very hard to convince sadists and other exploiters of human beings that their activities harm themselves as well as their victims. A utilitarian transported by time machine to the court of Genghis Khan would have his work cut out to persuade the Khan that his life would be happier if he treated his neighbours with more consideration. Genghis may feel assured that his self-respect is intact even as he watches the impertinent time traveller roasting slowly on a spit. But most utilitarians do not suppose that people are infallible in their judgements about their own utility. One does not need to take a strongly objectivist stance like Brink's to believe that individuals do not always know what is best for them (see Brink 1989: ch. 8). Even a preference-utilitarian like Harsanyi accepts that a person's actual preferences – those determining *his* concept of his utility – may be distorted by 'factual errors, ignorance, careless thinking, rash judgement, or strong emotions hindering rational choice, etc.' (1977: 29). His 'true' preferences, by contrast, are those which he would have under 'ideal conditions' and 'in particular, after careful reflection and in possession of all the relevant information' (29–30). Even if Harsanyi's concept of a person's 'true' preferences is open to question, it is plain at least that what a person would prefer under 'ideal conditions' is not always what he actually prefers. In the language of classical utilitarianism, a person may never realise where his true happiness lies. An upbringing among the Golden Horde is unlikely to generate a frame of mind readily susceptible to the idea that subjects living the most satisfying lives treat other people kindly rather than harshly; but if cruelty and maltreatment of others subvert a person's ability to respect himself for his own most valuable properties – those basic human qualities he shares with the rest of humanity – then they prevent his maximising his own utility.

## 4 But should the consequences count?

Sophisticated versions of utilitarianism, then, need not be embarrassed by the objection that if pleasure is what matters, the satisfactions enjoyed by sadists must mitigate some of the evil done to their victims. A more refined form of the doctrine finds plenty to reprove in the Roman games and kindred amusements: for pleasure is not all that matters.

Critics of utilitarianism, however, may still feel uneasy about the consequentialist nature of this condemnation of sadism. The answer to the question of what makes throwing a man to the lions wrong was compounded out of two elements: the suffering inflicted on the victim and the damage the spectators do to themselves. But is the second element really needed? Why not simply condemn sadistic abuse for what it is, a dastardly practice, and reject the view that it could be made better or worse by its consequences? It is not that the ill effects of sadism on the sadists do not matter; on the contrary, they are part of what makes sadism so utterly repellent. But – the objection runs – we do not need to refer to them when explaining why a man should not be thrown to the lions. The horribleness of the victim's suffering is quite sufficient by itself to justify its unconditional condemnation. Even if throwing people to lions somehow had some good consequences, that would not make it right. The utilitarian account is deeply flawed if it maintains otherwise.

A utilitarian might reply that he, too, finds the suffering of the victim, viewed in itself, utterly repugnant. But this is not, of course, where the disagreement lies. The utilitarian is in principle prepared to allow the moral evaluation of an act initially deemed wrong to alter when its further circumstances and consequences are brought into the picture; theorists of a more deontological stamp characteristically are not. Utilitarians, by taking a broader view of the context in which an act is performed, can sometimes approve of acts which others could not condone. Might there even be instances where throwing people to lions is more regrettable than wrong?

Consider these two cases:

(A) A party of travellers is passing through a desert when they are set upon by a pride of lions. Owing to an oversight on their leader's part, the travellers have left their weapons at home, and, as the lions look hungry, it seems likely that several of them will be killed. While the lions get themselves into hunting order, a resourceful member of the company proposes that they abandon one of their number to the beasts in the hope that they will set on him and give the rest a chance to run away. (There is an oasis, he knows, just beyond the next sand dune.) They quickly bind the feet of their plumpest companion and run . . .

(B) A tribe believes that the end of the world is nigh unless their god is fed with constant blood sacrifices. This deity happens to be of a sporting turn, and particularly enjoys seeing human beings hunted down by lions. Grimly and regretfully the tribespeople organise a weekly spectacle in a special arena. They know it is a cruel thing that they do, but it is better that some people should die to please the god than that all life should become extinct.

(This case is adapted from that of the pre-Columbian civilisations of Mexico.)

If throwing people to lions is wrong, whatever its consequences, then (A) and (B) are examples of crimes. Yet it is at least open to question whether they should be described that way. I admit to having serious qualms about case (A): one would feel far more comfortable with it if one of the travellers had freely volunteered to face the lions. If the plump traveller had protested at his fate, his companions would evoke a somewhat negative response in us: they were very cold-blooded, not at all loyal or brave. They did not consider how insulting it is to prevent a person making his own decisions whether to give his life for others, and if they reached the oasis in safety they may be in for a good deal of soul-searching and remorse. They may conclude that their self-respect has been badly eroded, and wish that they had never listened to the resourceful traveller's advice. (It is a perfectly rational utilitarian choice to prefer the loss of your life to that of your self-respect.) Or they may continue to think that what they did was, on balance, right. But even if one thinks their decision wrong, they do not deserve the unqualified condemnation merited by the supporters of the Roman games. The plump traveller's death was intended to save lives, not produce sadistic thrills for the crowd. Without that death many would have died, including, very likely, the plump traveller himself. The intended consequences *do* count, therefore, in determining that offering a man to the lions in case (A) is less blameworthy than offering them a victim in sport.

The sacrifice in case (B) seems more clearly justifiable still. It is a laudable aim to save the world – more laudable even than saving a few individuals, and infinitely more so than enjoying others' death-agonies. It is not the moral judgement of the tribe that is at fault here, but their empirical beliefs. If they sincerely believe that the end of the world will ensue from a neglect of their weekly sacrifices, branding their actions as criminal is taking the notion of side-constraints to absurd lengths. (This example is structurally similar to the Williams hostages case, but with the numbers increased.) There is a possible argument that self-respect demands that they refuse to play the god's game; maybe it would be better to die, better to let the whole world die, than to go on satisfying his cruel whims. (However one views such an act of Promethean defiance, it is significant that its support still comes from consequentialist reasoning.) But probably most people would vote to continue with the sacrifices. Universal death is a high price to pay, even for self-respect.

These examples help to illustrate the relevant and revealing role which consideration of consequences can play in moral reasoning. So why have so many people found utilitarianism off-putting? Often, perhaps, not so much because they find the idea of counting consequences repugnant in principle, as because they dislike the way (some) utilitarians count them. Many of the counterintuitive 'solutions' to moral dilemmas alleged to flow from utilitarian principles rest, in fact, on overly narrow views of value. More refined versions of the theory can provide quite different and more attractive answers. Where life-and-death decisions are concerned, a utilitarian decision procedure need not reduce to a simple counting of corpses. A flourishing, fulfilled life requires more than just breathing. It calls for a sense of the value of oneself and one's projects, and this lays certain structural limitations on how one relates to other persons. If I could not respect myself and my goals, or if I lost all ability to pursue them, my life would become pointless and empty. But I cannot consistently value myself and my concerns, while seeing others and their concerns as worthless. I am a human being like them: if I matter, so do they. And there are things I cannot do to other people, or consent to be done to them, consistently with respecting them. If I do or allow these things, I undercut the basis of my own self-respect, without which I would be better off dead. But utilitarianism cannot wish on me a fate worse than death.

It might be objected, however, that even refined forms of utilitarianism face difficulty in giving an acceptable account of why we should be sorry for our misdeeds. People who mistreat others in certain ways, the utilitarian says, cannot properly respect themselves as human beings. But by identifying the subversion of self-respect as the cost which a sadist pays for his pleasures, the utilitarian may seem to be laying undue stress on the self-harm, rather than the harm to others, as the main focus of regret. And this, critics will claim, gets things the wrong way round. But the objection is misguided. There is a clear distinction between regretting a sadistic pleasure because of the hurt caused to the victims and regretting it for the harm caused to oneself, but only the former regret makes the latter regret possible. If the sadist did not come to care, genuinely and deeply, about the hurt done to others, he could not grasp how sadism was self-debasing and so doubly regrettable. If he failed to deplore the victims' plight, he must fail to see their suffering as debasing himself. For him to declare, 'I wouldn't have minded degrading them if I could have done so without degrading myself', is to exhibit a confusion which is not only moral but conceptual. For the very wish or readiness to debase is debasing, and the sadist cannot escape debasement unless he is sincerely ready to reject his practices as abhorrent. Far from neglecting the repentant sadist's regret for the price paid by those who supplied his pleasure, the utilitarian can readily acknowledge that without that regret, he can never come to deplore the cost paid by himself.

## 5  Limitations of the self-respect argument

Yet doubts may reasonably remain whether utilitarians can wholly rebut the charge that they must, on occasions, approve of sacrifices of individuals in the name of utility which would ordinarily be rejected as unjust.[2] No matter how refined their philosophical psychology or their account of what makes lives go well, they may still face difficulty in explaining why, *if* the utility sums demand it, there should not be interpersonal trading of welfare which goes beyond the limits normally deemed fair. Discussions of utilitarian justice often focus on cases like these:

(C) Some years after the tragedy of Romeo and Juliet, strife has broken out again in Verona between the noble houses of Montague and Capulet. One day a member of the Montague clan is stabbed in the back by a masked assassin in Capulet livery. Suspicion falls on a bravo of the Capulet household who is known to have uttered threats against the dead man. The suspect is arrested and interrogated by the Prince; the Montagues demand his immediate beheading in the public square. The Prince, however, having put his prisoner to the question, is convinced of his innocence and refuses to sign the death warrant. This enrages the Montagues, who accuse the Prince of being a Capulet stooge and issue an ultimatum. Either the execution will take place within the hour or they will storm the Prince's palace, kill the prisoner and anyone else who opposes them. As such behaviour will clearly inflame the Capulets, it is clear that a terrible riot is in prospect, in which many people, innocent as well as guilty, will die. Should the Prince forestall the riot by executing a man he believes to be guiltless?

(D) Black is a first-rate research scientist, White one of the finest composers of the day. Both men are seriously ill with kidney disease, and the doctors have concluded that their lives can be saved only by transplant surgery. By a further coincidence, both men have blood of an extremely rare type, and replacement kidneys are only acceptable from donors with the same uncommon blood group. Unfortunately only one other member of the population is

166

known to have the right blood, a recidivist criminal called Green who is currently serving a ten-year prison sentence for armed robbery. Would it be right to use Green's kidneys to save the lives of Black and White, thereby preserving two valuable members of society at the cost of a social parasite?

Returning affirmative answers to the questions raised in these cases would offend most people's sense of justice. We do not think it fair to punish the innocent, whatever the benefits it might bring. And few besides Godwin would favour the cannibalisation of social misfits for their useful organs. Yet the problem for utilitarianism is that cost-benefit calculations in (C) and (D) appear to support those affirmative answers. A deontologist might simply declare: 'So much the worse for cost-benefit calculations.' But the utilitarian is unable to take this dismissive line. As a consequentialist theory, utilitarianism rejects the notion of deontological side-constraints and maintains the priority of the good over the right. So it seems that a utilitarian counsellor to the Prince of Verona should advise his master to execute his prisoner; for the death of one innocent man is a lesser tragedy than the deaths of many. Similarly in case (D), if public utility is the paramount consideration, the death of a malefactor seems a small price to pay for saving the lives of two valuable benefactors. Utilitarianism is apparently committed, in both cases, to sanctioning actions which ordinary moral consciousness would disallow.

One might wonder whether rule-utilitarianism could offer a way out of the difficulty. Some rule-utilitarians would say that a utility-promoting rule like 'Thou shalt not kill' should be adhered to even in exceptional cases where killing would produce more benefit than not killing. But we saw grounds in Chapter V for doubting whether a tenable form of rule-utilitarianism would yield moral judgements any different from those of act-utilitarianism. (Only in regard to what Hume called 'artificial' practices like promising, making contracts and owning property is the 'equivalence thesis' plausibly held to fail. These convenient practices are viable only if people consent to abide by their constitutive rules and refrain from calculating the cost of following them in particular cases.) A utilitarian may readily accept 'Thou shalt not kill' as a useful rule of thumb; but it would be against the spirit of utilitarianism to adhere rigidly to it where the result of doing so would be an increased net loss of life. The utilitarian who took this course would expose himself to the charge of 'rule worship'.

One way in which utilitarians sometimes try to resist the complaint that they are insufficiently mindful of the interests of individuals is by drawing attention to the social uneasiness which punishing the innocent, or sacrificing less useful for more useful people, would cause. A society which treated its citizens as expendable in the interest of the greater good would not be a setting for happy lives; it would be a breeding ground for insecure neurotics. Utilitarians reasonably insist that cost-benefit calculations should take into account the predictable long-term effects of our choices. A world in which Black and White survive and Green dies is, superficially, a better world than one in which Green alone survives: but it is not a better world if its inhabitants live in constant fear of meeting Green's fate. Therefore, there is a good utilitarian argument for not cannibalising Green. In the long run it is not a utility-enhancing strategy.

This standard utilitarian defence draws two standard ripostes. The first starts from an obvious point: that people must know about an action in order to worry about it. But what if a potentially disturbing deed is performed in secret? This possibility causes a problem for the utilitarian because he cannot object that an action will cause uneasiness if its disquieting features are never revealed. In case (D), no one, including Black and White, need ever know that Green's death (from a broken neck) was not a matter of accident. This sort of case suggests that utilitarians have less trouble in condemning overt exploitation of individuals than covert, even though the latter involves the additional evil of deception. Most deontologists will find this position bizarre.[3]

The second common objection is that public uneasiness ought not to count as more than a very minor ground for thinking that medical cannibalism or executing the innocent are wrong. Yet in the utilitarian's eccentric moral scheme, it is the most decisive reason to reject them; which only goes to prove that utilitarianism is disgracefully soft on murder! Condemning such practices for their capacity to alarm the public rather than for the harm they do to the victim implies a wholly false sense of priorities. A really strong-minded utilitarian might complain that this objection simply begs the question in favour of the dubious notion of a side-constraint against killing. Yet many more tender-minded utilitarians are scarcely less convinced than deontologists that medical cannibalism and punishing the innocent are wrong; and they too seek an explanation of that wrongness which does not heavily rely on the citation of more remote effects. The question we must consider is whether such an explanation can be given, consistently with utilitarian principles.

It may seem that it can if we appeal again to the idea of self-respect. We have seen that there are some things which a person cannot do, or consent to be done, to others without forfeiting his respect for himself as a human being. So would a truly wise person consent to have his life saved by receiving an organ transplanted from an unwilling donor who is cannibalised so that he and another sick person may live? On first thought, the answer may seem to be a firm no.[4] Killing one human being to save two who could use his organs is deeply insulting to the sacrificial victim whose autonomy is flouted; so the recipients gain their lives but lose something that makes life worth living. They cannot value themselves as self-determining agents if self-determination means nothing to them in their involuntary benefactor's case. Most people would not want to purchase their lives by an act of debasement which recoils upon the debasers. If they agreed to the arrangement, they would have no ground for thinking themselves more valuable than the donor, whom they evidently did not think valuable enough to have his autonomy respected. Considerations of self-respect may have failed in case (A) to prevent the desert travellers from abandoning their plump companion to the lions; but there the plump traveller was a man 'in the same boat' as themselves and his life was already in peril. But in case (D), Green is not in the same predicament as Black and White. He is a man with a future before him, before the transplant operation is mooted. So it would seem particularly difficult for Black and White voluntarily to receive his kidneys and retain their self-respect.

Of course Black and White may never learn that Green was not the genuine victim of an accident; and if so, their self-respect can survive the transplant. But Black and White are not the only people whose self-respect is at issue in this case: there are also the agents who kill Green and transplant his kidneys. Could *they* retain their self-respect after treating a fellow human being so badly? If not, then their loss of self-respect is a considerable negative quantity in the balance sheet. Even if they succeed in fooling everyone else, they cannot fool themselves – they know that they have failed to treat Green as an end in himself. But if they value Green's humanity so lightly, they can hardly set much store by their own.

Unfortunately this argument, which worked well in demonstrating the evil of sadism, is much less persuasive here. Our respect for human beings should certainly make us highly reluctant to kill them. Murdering or mistreating people is normally incompatible with a proper respect for the humanity we all share. However, a respect for humanity should not only dissuade us from killing people: it should also motivate us to keep them alive. But this again raises the question of what is wrong with performing acts of medical cannibalism which *maximise the number of lives saved*. If fulfilled and happy lives are valuable, then the more such lives there are, the better. It is hard to dispute the proposition that the world in which Black and White survive and Green dies is better than

169

the world in which Green alone of the three survives. The puzzle is that ordinary moral reflection refuses to sanction the action necessary to produce the better world rather than the worse. It is likewise hard to see why we should not execute one innocent subject of a valuable life if by doing so we can save many innocent subjects of valuable lives; for if we genuinely value human lives, ought we not to prefer the loss of one to the loss of many? The sadist who delights to see people wantonly killed has no respect for the humanity he shares with them, and debases himself when he debases others. But killing one person to save a larger number could be argued to reflect not a disdain for humanity but, on the contrary, a deep respect. Yet even utilitarians are mostly reluctant to suppose that such sacrifices could be right.

A utilitarian might suggest at this point that something crucial has been omitted from the picture. Moral dilemmas cannot be settled simply by tallying up the quick and the dead. We need to take into account not merely what happens to a person, but who makes the life-and-death decisions concerning him. Any rational individual values his own *autonomy*, his freedom to decide for himself what becomes of him. Autonomy is important not only in enabling us to secure more of the things that we want and to avoid more of the things that we do not want, but also in making us feel better about ourselves: it enhances our self-respect to be self-determining beings, not pawns to be pushed around by other people. Using Green for spare-part surgery not only deprives him of his life but robs him also of his autonomy. Compare his case with that of Oates of the Antarctic, who freely gave his life to save his companions. Oates, unlike Green, died with his autonomy unviolated. If he had not voluntarily walked out of the tent but been forcibly evicted from it, he would have lost more than his life: he would have suffered the greatest possible insult to his status as a self-determining being. The utilitarian who cares not only how many people live or die, but also *how well* they live or die, evaluates cases like (C) and (D) not solely in terms of the net sum of lives lost and gained. He takes into account also the significant cost to the autonomy of the sacrificial victims.

It is hard to disagree that autonomy is a major ingredient of satisfying lives – a primary good, in Rawls's sense. Yet it is doubtful whether this helps the utilitarian much in his present embarrassment. Deprivation of the victim's autonomy is part of the price paid when the Prince's prisoner is punished or Green is cannibalised for his organs. But if the victims' autonomy matters, so too does that of the persons whose lives stand to be saved by their sacrifice. Bringing autonomy into the story seems to make no difference to the essential equations. If the death of one autonomous subject buys the lives of two or fifty autonomous subjects, the purchase price seems a reasonable one. (It is also unclear why the Prince or the surgeons should forfeit their self-respect if they are motivated purely by a desire to maximise the number of autonomous beings.) To be sure, a person who dies of natural causes does not have his autonomy deliberately flouted in the way a victim of human violence does. But the fact remains that he dies, and every death reduces the number of autonomous individuals in the world by one. (Even if we think that there is something especially evil about intentionally depriving someone of his autonomy, the asymmetry between intentional and non-intentional deprivations of autonomy is irrelevant in case (C). The execution of the Capulet prisoner is an intentional deprivation of autonomous existence aimed at averting a larger number of equally intentional deprivations of autonomous existence.)

It would be a mistake to think that cases like (C) and (D) pose a problem only for utilitarians. They raise difficulties too for deontological theorists. As Samuel Scheffler has pointed out in his important book *The Rejection of Consequentialism* (1982), it is one thing to assert that certain actions which enhance utility are wrong, and another to give a rational explanation of that wrongness. Deontologists find it no easier than utilitarians do to provide the required explanation. Scheffler asks what justification there can be for forbidding agents to breach moral constraints where breaching them will avert a greater number of infractions of the same constraints by other agents (Scheffler 1982: ch. 4). Deontologists say that you may not shoot one hostage to prevent twenty hostages being shot by someone else. But why not, given that twenty killings are plainly worse than one? Should not even deontologists actively seek to minimise wrong-doing? Scheffler maintains, against the more rigid forms of consequentialism, that there is an *agent-centred prerogative* to refuse to perform an optimising action, if performing it is deeply incompatible with one's basic values, beliefs or life-plan. (We shall return to this claim in the next chapter.) But the deontological assertion that there is an *agent-centred restriction* against breaching a constraint *C* even where doing so will prevent a larger number of breaches of *C* is, he insists, particularly puzzling. It is, of course, characteristic of deontological theorists to dismiss consideration of the consequences of our choices as a moral irrelevance – this is the force of their claim that the right is prior to the good. But Scheffler contends that it is proper to demand a rationale for this – really rather surprising – position. If one act of killing is wrong, then even an anti-consequentialist can scarcely deny that two acts of killing are worse. So why not kill one person, to save two from being killed?

If agent-centred restrictions are difficult to justify, so much the better, one might think, for utilitarianism. Preventing a greater evil by causing a lesser should raise no moral qualms in those committed to optimisation. (Utilitarians may, of course, feel a keen *compunction* when they have to do something bad to stop something worse taking place, but they should not have a sense of *guilt* about it.) Yet the irony is that most utilitarians are no less convinced than other people that medical cannibalism or punishing the innocent are wrong. It is hard to say, in fact, which theory is in the more unsatisfactory position: utilitarianism, which provides plausible reasons for an answer which even utilitarians disavow; or deontology which cannot defend an answer which most people think right.

## 6 Archangels, proles and the natural man

Is it possible, however, that we are trying too hard to accommodate utilitarian principles to the standards of conventional morality? Perhaps utilitarians should bite the bullet and reject those standards where common views and the theory of utility conflict. There is ample historical precedent for this stance. Utilitarians like Bentham and Godwin wrote their books in a spirit of missionary fervour. They aimed to persuade people that the new morality was more reasonable and more humane than the old. The doctrine they taught was no mere codification or rational-isation of accepted moral views: it was intended to be a superior system, and an eminently practical one. Such writers were ready to follow the logic of the utilitarian argument wherever it led, and encouraged their readers to do the same. It was no reason to doubt the theory that it sometimes led to novel and disturbing conclusions. Utilitarianism as a revisionary morality could not be assayed by the staid and tired principles of conventional morality or the intuitions of conservatives. On the contrary, it provided the touchstone for all pre-existing ideas.

Some utilitarians, however, have been unconvinced of the wisdom of preaching utilitarianism as a morality for the masses. Henry Sidgwick recognised, as the more radical authors had done, that the utilitarian method could yield results at variance with 'Common-Sense' morality. But he also thought that the use of the method was too difficult for men and women of 'untrained intellects'. It was better for them to confront the problems of life with a set of straightforward moral rules than to attempt to solve dilemmas by the delicate calculation of benefits and disbenefits. Fortunately, in Sidgwick's view, the various systems of 'Common-Sense' morality prevailing at different times and places had generally proved adequate to handle the everyday problems of ordinary folk. It was the complex dilemmas of more sophisticated people which they were less well able to cope with.

> (A) contemplation of these divergent codes and their relation to the different circumstances in which men live, suggests that Common-Sense morality is really only adapted for ordinary men in ordinary circumstances – although it may still be expedient that these ordinary persons should regard it as absolutely and universally prescribed, since any other view of it may dangerously weaken its hold over their minds (Sidgwick 1874: 466).

In an ideal world, all men would reason as utilitarians. In the actual world, it could be argued that the rules of conventional morality should at least be revised in the light of utilitarian logic. Yet Sidgwick was doubtful whether 'we can frame with adequate precision a system of rules, constituting the true moral code for human beings as deduced from Utilitarian principles' (467). Such rules would have to be more complic-ated than those of common-sense morality; and it would be hard to frame them to take into account the differences in needs, aspirations and lifestyles of people in different social environments. In Sidgwick's opinion it was best to leave conventional morality alone, and not try to 'construct a morality *de novo* either for man as he is . . . , or for man as he ought to be and will be'. Schemes to remould the morality of the ordinary man were too likely to cause confusion and uncertainty – which were sound utilitarian reasons for rejecting them. Wise utilitarians would not interfere with established mores, nor advocate the general adoption of their own more rational methods of moral reflection (473–4).

Sidgwick thus held that a private utilitarian morality for an intellectual élite could, and should, coexist with a public 'common-sense' morality of a simple rule-based sort. This left the problem of what to do when utilitarianism and conventional morality offered different answers to a moral question. However, Sidgwick believed that such conflicts would, in practice, be rare, for 'the conduct approved by Common Sense has a *general* resemblance to that which Utilitarianism would prescribe' (468). Even when genuine conflicts did arise, a consistent utilitarian might still follow the conventional solution, if doing otherwise would cause scandal and distress.

There are strong echoes of Sidgwick's dual-level account of moral thinking in the writings of the contemporary utilitarian R.M. Hare. Like Sidgwick, Hare agrees that 'critical' moral thinking is, or should be, utilitarian in character; but he does not see 'intuitive' thinking as the preserve of the mentally undistinguished. On Hare's view, intuitive and critical thinking complement one another in the moral lives of all normal human beings. There are both 'practical and psychological' reasons for us to adopt as moral rules of thumb such intuitive 'prima-facie' principles as 'Do not tell lies' and 'Always pay your debts.' Experience testifies that adherence to these rules more often than not promotes utility. They also correspond to 'very firm and deep dispositions and feelings' which are worth reinforcing; and they help to preserve us from cooking our moral thinking to suit our own interests – a perennial hazard at the critical level (Hare 1981: 38–9). By contrast, critical (act-utilitarian) thinking makes no appeal to any moral intuitions. Hare suggests that it 'proceeds in accordance with canons established by philosophical logic and thus based on linguistic intuitions only' (40).[5]

To clarify the relation between the two kinds of moral thinking, Hare asks what sort of beings would operate exclusively on one level or the other. He first describes a creature 'with superhuman powers of thought, superhuman knowledge and no human weaknesses'. This strange being is practically clairvoyant in his capacity for prediction and vastly efficient at scanning the properties of an action, 'including the consequences of alternative actions'. He also lacks the 'weakness' (as Hare sees it) of partiality to self, family and friends. Hare calls this paragon (or monster?) 'the archangel' (44). Archangels will conduct their moral reflection entirely at the critical level because, as super-rational beings, they need no other. He next imagines a quite different sort of creature, a being who has human weaknesses in the highest degree:

> Not only does he, like most of us, have to rely on intuitions and sound prima facie principles and good dispositions for most of the time; he is totally incapable of critical thinking (let alone safe or sound critical thinking) even when there is leisure for it (45).

This limited creature Hare names 'the prole'. Proles, because of their mental dullness, are wholly dependent on intuitive thinking. Most of us are neither archangels nor proles but something in between; hence our thinking is sometimes critical and sometimes intuitive. Hare advises us to accept human nature for what it is, and resist the temptation to wish that we could be more like archangels. It is better occasionally to think like the prole than to end up 'in the wrong Miltonic camp as *fallen archangels*' (45).

Critical reasoning is essential if there is to be a workable *system* of prima-facie principles:

> Critical thinking aims to select the best set of prima facie principles for use in intuitive thinking. It can also be employed when

principles from the set conflict *per accidens*. Such employment may
lead to the improvement of the principles themselves, but it need
not; a principle may be overridden without being altered (49–50).

This last sentence is crucial to Hare's account of conflict resolution.
Prima-facie rules which have proved their worth should not be given up
lightly. Even tried and tested rules can conflict with one another, or with
critical reasoning. To resolve a conflict, a rule need only be suspended,
not abandoned. (Moral principles are thus logically disanalogous to
inductive generalisations, which we reject on the basis of a single counter-
instance.) Hare complains of the serious harm done to 'popular morality'
by people who dismiss traditional rules only because they fail in isolated
instances (48). Such occasional difficulties are no good reason to throw
over principles which generally serve us well.

Hare thinks, like Sidgwick, that serious conflicts between established
rules and critical reasoning will be fairly rare. But conflicts between
prima-facie rules are more common, and require critical reasoning to sort
them out.[6] Consider, for instance, the pair of rules 'Do not tell lies' and
'Do not hurt the feelings of your friends.' It is not always possible to tell
your friends exactly what you think of their talents, goods, children or
hair-dos without hurting them in a tender spot. Resolving such dilemmas
requires ascent to the critical level: you have to consider whether it will
cause more harm than good to reveal your true opinion. Hare points out
that such an act-utilitarian strategy for conflict resolution has the backing
of common sense. Deontologists, on the other hand, must either deny that
apparent conflicts are real ones (an implausible assessment in many
cases), or institute some rule of higher order to adjudicate clashes
between lower-order rules. If they choose the second option, they face
the problem of explaining what grounds *other than utilitarian ones* can
justify the selection of their meta-rules.

Hare allows that clashes between critical reasoning and prima-facie
principles do sometimes arise. But he is impatient with philosophers who
consider this a reason to reject utilitarianism. Their response would only
be justified if conflicts were more common than they really are. In Hare's
view, serious clashes happen only in a few highly unusual circumstances
for which our prima-facie principles were never designed.

> Our common intuitions are sound ones, if they are, just because
> they yield acceptable precepts in common cases. For this reason,
> it is highly desirable that we should all have these intuitions, and
> that our consciences should give us a bad time if we go against
> them (49).

[People's] moral intuitions are the product of their moral upbring-
ings, and, however good these may have been, they were designed
to prepare them to deal with moral situations which are likely to
be encountered; there is no guarantee at all that they will be
appropriate to unusual cases (132).

So, confronted with an out-of-the-way dilemma, we should always be
guided by critical reasoning. Faced with the Williams hostage problem,
for example, we should certainly shoot one hostage to save the rest,
though not without feeling pain at taking a life. (Our inhibition against
breaking the rule against killing has an obvious and important utility
value (49).)[7] But Hare contends that unusual cases like this one, where
utilitarian calculation and prima-facie principles diverge, ought not to
damage our general confidence in either critical or intuitive thinking. In
the majority of everyday situations, the methods of the archangel and of
the prole yield identical advice.

It would be hard to imagine any moral dilemmas more *outré* and
unusual than those in cases (C) and (D). One might suppose that proles
and archangels would have quite different views on how to resolve them.
Proles would be dissuaded by their prima-facie principles (or, perhaps,
their gut reactions) from executing the innocent or engaging in medical
cannibalism, regardless of the utility sums. But archangels, with their
impartial, dispassionate, wholly rational concern for the public good,
would call for the suspension in instances like these of the prima-facie
prohibition against killing. Or so one might suppose. Hare, however,
shows more reluctance than one might have expected, given the trend of
his argument, to allow that archangels would ever consent to 'murder'.
He suggests that critical thinkers in full possession of the facts in such
cases will reach the same conclusions about them as intuitive thinkers.
Thus archangels, more far-seeing than the critics of utilitarianism, would
object to medical cannibalism or the execution of the innocent on the
grounds that, whatever first appearances might suggest, they were not at
all likely to enhance utility.

In the medical-cannibalism case, for instance,[8] Hare complains that
the critic of utilitarianism

has constructed his example with the express purpose of making
the murder the act which will have the best consequences. You
must not allow him simply to *assume* that this is so; he has to
convince the audience, not just that it really could be so in a real-
life situation, but that it could be known to be so by the doctors
with a high degree of probability (133).

The critic, Hare claims, misrepresents the balance of probabilities and utilities. He rightly admits that *if* the truth about the medical sacrifice came out, the anxiety generated in the public mind would outweigh the utility produced by the operation; but he supposes that the truth need not come out. Hare thinks this supposition naive; the critic is demanding too much of the doctors:

> Have they absolute confidence in the discretion and support of all the nurses, porters, mortuarists, etc., who will know what has happened? Add to this the extreme unlikelihood of there being no other way of saving these patients, if they can be saved at all, and it will be evident that your opponent is not going to get much help out of this example, once it is fleshed out and given verisimilitude (134).[9]

Until the opponent of utilitarianism produces some credible real-life examples where murder is justified on utilitarian grounds, we should not, in Hare's view, let ourselves be 'troubled overmuch with fictional ones' (134).

There are, however, two reasons for disquiet about Hare's position. The first is that it is not as difficult as he claims to find cases where utilitarian calculation would sanction what intuitive thinkers would regard as murder. (Note that it does not matter whether these cases are real or fictitious, provided they are possible.) Consider how case (C) might develop. We can imagine the Prince of Verona first trying, and failing, to convince the citizens that the man in custody is innocent of murder. He next attempts to avert the riot by threats of retribution against the ringleaders, but with no better success – the hot-blooded Montagues are impervious to reason. Finally he may be forced to the conclusion that *only* the death of the innocent prisoner will prevent a massacre. Another example is provided by a variant of the story of Captain Oates. Imagine that Oates's exhausted companions, despairing of survival so long as they are encumbered with a man with frost-bitten feet, thrust him out of the tent to die. It is unobvious why an archangelical explorer should not take part in this eviction, if Oates refuses to go willingly. (Admittedly the explorers do not actually kill Oates – the cold does that. But by expelling him from the tent they ensure his death. The desert travellers in case (A) do not seal the fate of their plump companion quite so thoroughly – there is always a chance that the lions will not molest him.) And Hare fails to see that even the hostages dilemma provides a counter-example to his claim that careful utilitarian thinking will never sanction 'murder' where intuitive thinking would condemn it, if 'intuitive thinking' is to be identified with the consultation of prima-facie principles.[10] 'Common-sense' morality, as Hare himself remarks, may not condemn the shooting of one hostage to save others; but it is indisputably ruled out by the prima-facie principle forbidding the taking of human life.

The second ground for uneasiness is that, even if Hare were right to think that there are no plausible examples of dilemmas where the archangel would sanction a killing which the prole would condemn, this would be of limited significance unless both parties based their negative judgements on the same features of the killings they rejected. This brings us back to an important point noted earlier. Critics standardly accuse utilitarians not only of reaching some wrong moral conclusions, but of reaching some right ones by the wrong routes. Hare's chief objections to medical cannibalism are that it would be impossible to keep it secret, and that it is hardly credible that no alternative effective treatment would be available for the patients. But intuitive condemnations (whether based on prima-facie principles or on gut reactions) place the focus in a quite different place: on the wrongness of taking a man's life without his consent. From the prole's perspective, the archangel's objections must appear at best beside the point and at worst indecent. They will also seem to him to be curiously contingent: as if a murder *could* be justified merely by the alteration of a few empirical facts. On the whole, he will thank his stars that he was not born an archangel.

Hare does finally (and grudgingly) admit that circumstances could, in principle, arise in which murder would be justified on utilitarian grounds. But he thinks that if this improbable event occurred, it would still not follow that a rational moral agent should commit murder; he should stay his hand unless he had 'sufficient evidential grounds' for believing his action to be the best of the available alternatives.

> But, giving your opponent everything that he asks for, if he did actually have sufficient evidence (a very unlikely contingency), murder would *in that case* be justified; though even then the agent in question, if he had been well brought up, might not do it, because it would go so much against all his moral feelings, which in a good man are powerful (135).

Having conceded this much, Hare moves on hurriedly to discuss 'some more genuine problems'. But this dismissive attitude is unwarranted. The problem of murder raises deep theoretical questions for the doctrine of utility. In any case, as we have seen above, there *are* circumstances, not so very hard to imagine, in which it seems that Hare's archangelical reasoner should approve of a killing which contravenes a prima-facie rule. Cases of this sort occur, indeed, quite frequently in wartime. The dropping of the atom bombs on Japan in 1945 is sometimes defended on the ground that it effectively brought about a speedy end to the Pacific War, saving a larger number of people than died in the devastated cities.[11] Not everyone would agree that this was a sufficient justification for eliminating tens of thousands of innocent civilians. But it is an interesting fact that people who refuse to countenance the breaching of moral side-constraints in ordinary circumstances are often more tolerant of such breaches in wartime. When a society is fighting for its collective existence, there is a swing of the pendulum of moral concern from the lives of particular human beings to the lives of human beings *en masse*. Desperate times call for desperate measures, including the sacrifice of individuals for the common good. *Dulce et decorum est pro patria mori*: and if one does not go voluntarily to die for one's country, one may have to be sent.

It is probably in war that we come closest to thinking like archangels (ironically so, if war marks the triumph of human unreason). To be sure, the technology of modern warfare has made it psychologically easier to kill one's enemy, by eliminating the need to see the whites of his eyes. (It would have been harder to slaughter 80,000 women and children at Hiroshima by lopping off their heads with cutlasses.) But the *justification* of killing in war has nothing to do with its psychological ease or difficulty. It is striking that both critical and intuitive thinkers concur in the view that the death or suffering of individuals, on one's own side as well as the enemy's, is a legitimate price to pay for success in a war which is vital to the legitimate interests of one's own society.

Utilitarian thinking about killing seems, then, most intuitively accept-able to many people during public emergencies. When society's very survival is in question, the niceties of normal moral thought are found to be dispensable. Even medical cannibalism might be seen as tolerable if no other means were available to save certain individuals who were crucial to a nation's war effort. If Black were designing the weapon which would ensure his country's victory, and White were its most brilliant general, not only *their* survival might depend upon Green losing his kidneys. Cruel necessities may seem no less cruel, but they may seem more necessary, when the chips are down for the whole community. Yet it is a reasonable question whether the onset of a public emergency should really make a difference to our moral perceptions. That difference can be readily enough *explained* by the increased attention we always give to something that is under threat: in war, the survival of the state and the integrity of the social fabric and institutions which we ordinarily take for

179

granted. In these circumstances we think more about the interests of the many than about the interests of the individual. But if we see the interests of the many as morally pre-eminent in desperate times, are we right to think (or assume) that they lose this pre-eminence at other times? Or are we wrong to suppose that community interests dominate individual interests even in emergencies?

The possibility that there is an inconsistency in our attitudes to life-and-death questions, according to whether they arise in socially normal or abnormal situations, is a disturbing one. It does suggest, however, that the question of whether utilitarian justice is just cannot yet be settled. It is clear at least that these matters need to be examined rationally and dispassionately, without reliance on the knee-jerk reactions so unworthily dignified by the title of 'moral intuitions'. It is not that such reactions are a regrettable feature of our nature – on the contrary. An inhibition against taking the life of another human being has obvious utilitarian advantage; it is very probably a psychological trait selected in the course of human evolution and passed down to each of us as part of his genetic inheritance. With such a trait as part of our native endowment, small wonder that 'Thou shalt not kill' is a prima-facie compelling principle. But our capacity for critical thinking enables us to take a step beyond our starting point. We can see that the value which justifies a prima-facie rule is sometimes more to be honoured in its breach than its observance. On such occasions reason may seem to demand that we break the rule.

Breaking conventional moral rules, even for good ends, induces a profound sense of discomfort. That is easy to understand, if we suppose these rules to be backed up by innate (or alternatively socially inculcated) inhibitions. If we aim at evil, even as a means to avert some greater evil or to secure a greater good, our actions seem, in Nagel's phrase, to be 'guided by evil' (Nagel 1986: 181). This (to the good agent) is painful. As Nagel explains, 'the essence of evil is that it should *repel* us'. So, '[i]f something is evil, our actions should be guided, if they are guided by it at all, towards its elimination rather than toward its maintenance'. If we nevertheless choose to do the evil thing, this produces 'an acute sense of moral dislocation'. Yet the rational agent can look beyond the moral colour of his immediate action to that of its consequences. If he brings himself to do the evil thing in order that a better thing will follow, he is entitled to think of his action as 'really being guided not by evil but by overall good, which includes a balance of goods and evils' (182–3).

It is not, then, just our imperfect rationality (a limited ability to calculate) which prevents our becoming utilitarian archangels. Our innate or socially acquired disinclination to do evil, even as an instrument of good, plays a major role as well. In some circumstances, performing the action which utilitarian logic requires may be too hard even for an agent who accepts that logic. But it does not follow from the fact that an action is initially distasteful that it is ultimately wrong; and it can be argued that agents should make an effort to overcome their deep-seated inhibitions against doing instrumental evil where reason plainly warrants it.

But not all philosophers believe that we should strive to become archangels. Some think that however justifiable utilitarian morality may be in the cold light of reason, it is a psychologically unsuitable morality for human beings. This is not only because it sometimes requires people to do things which they feel a strong urge not to do. The broader complaint is that utilitarianism constrains individuals to subordinate their private ideals, projects, interests and tastes – in short, all that makes their lives worth living – to the goal of becoming maximally efficient promoters of the public good. Anyone who follows this course, the objectors say, will end up severely depersonalised (archangels have no character). If this charge is true, utilitarianism faces a serious problem of psychological realism. *Whether* it is true, we shall examine in the next chapter.

# CHAPTER VIII

# Utilitarianism and Personality

## 1 Does utilitarian morality demand too much?

Many moral philosophers think that you can be too good for your own good. Caring too much about others' welfare can lead you to care too little about your own. Even utilitarians often allow that there are limits to the amount of self-sacrifice which can legitimately be expected from individual agents in the name of the general good. Some hold that the public welfare would not be best promoted by agents who cared too little about their own interests. Priestley thought that our beneficence 'should flow the most freely' towards people like our partners and children 'whom we can most conveniently and effectually serve', and that we should normally regulate our conduct 'according to those connexions in life that are of the most importance to our own happiness' (Priestley n.d.(a): vol. 2, 46–7). J.S. Mill accepted that altruism and self-interest frequently coincide; he also believed that it was unrealistic to represent moral demands as boundless: 'There is a standard of altruism to which all should be required to come up, and a degree beyond it which is not obligatory, but meritorious' (J.S. Mill 1865: 337). More recently, Michael Slote has argued for a form of consequentialism which permits 'various sorts of *compromise* between the demands of impersonal morality and personal desires and commitments' (Slote 1984: 158).

Some utilitarians, however, have taken a much more rigorist view of moral obligations. A good example of the harder line is found in Peter Singer's well-known article on famine relief. Singer argued that people in the affluent countries of the world should transfer wealth to those in the poorer countries until the point of economic equality is reached. Giving aid to the Third World, he contended, was not mere charity (as most people complacently believed it was) but a duty of the strictest sort:

> Because giving money is regarded as an act of charity, it is not
> thought that there is anything wrong with not giving. The charitable
> man may be praised, but the man who is not charitable is not
> condemned. People do not feel in any way ashamed or guilty about
> spending money on new clothes or a new car instead of giving it
> to famine relief. (Indeed, the alternative does not occur to them.)
> This way of looking at the matter cannot be justified. . . . On the
> contrary, we ought to give the money away, and it is wrong not to
> do so (Singer 1979: 269–70).

Singer explicitly rejected the traditional concept of 'supererogation', the
notion of a realm of beneficent actions which, while it would be morally
praiseworthy to do, it is not our bounden duty to do.[1] In Singer's view,
if we have the chance to make the world a better place, we are morally
obliged to take it. We are entitled, of course, to consider our own interests
when we do the utility sums, and we should only sacrifice our own good
in order to produce a greater good for others. But Singer pointed out that
our need for new clothes or a new car could never be as great as a hungry
peasant's need for the food required to stay alive; therefore we should
not buy new clothes or new cars while people in the world are starving.

Singer's utilitarianism is of a particularly strenuous sort. It would not
be easy to lead a life in which one accorded no priority to one's own
interests over the interests of others. Moral saints who achieve this
disinterestedness are few and far between. But many philosophers have
questioned whether a fully consistent optimising form of utilitarianism
can really be *less* strenuous than this. T.M. Scanlon puts the case
succinctly:

> If all that counts morally is the well-being of individuals, no one
> of whom is singled out as counting for more than the others, and
> if all that matters in the case of each individual is the degree to
> which his or her well-being is affected, then it would seem to follow
> that the basis of moral appraisal is the goal of maximising the *sum*
> of individual well-being (Scanlon 1982: 110).

Utilitarianism, in other words, seems committed to maximising human
well-being regardless of the identities of individuals. So if you favour
your own interests above those of others (we can extend this formulation
to include your favouring the interests of the people you specially care
about over the interests of strangers), you breach a principle of impartiality which is intrinsic to the doctrine. Utilitarians who fail to recognise
these implications misunderstand their own theory.

This issue is the first-person analogue of the third-person issue we discussed in Chapter VII. We saw there that utilitarianism sometimes seems to prescribe sacrificing some people in the interests of others in ways which conventional morality deems unfair. It now seems that it places no limits, either, on how far I can be expected to sacrifice *myself*, when the public utility requires it. In fact, it enjoins me to become a moral saint, a full-time optimiser of human welfare. A lot of philosophers think that the call to boundless self-sacrifice in the name of utility is unreasonable, and that everyone has a right to hold some non-optimising private interests. They also object that the requirement is psychologically unrealistic, given the limitations of our natural altruism. (So if 'ought' implies 'can', this consideration offers further reason to resist utilitarianism's claims on us.)

That utilitarianism (allegedly) makes excessively heavy demands of the selflessness of individuals is regarded by some critics as a *reductio ad absurdum* of the theory. This criticism has attained extra force in recent years as dissatisfaction has grown with the traditional praise of sainthood. Writers like Bernard Williams (1976, 1985), Susan Wolf (1982), Samuel Scheffler (1982), John Rawls (1971), Thomas Nagel (1986), Dan Brock (1982) and others have challenged the ideal of moral sainthood as intrinsically flawed. Moral saints are people who act as well as possible on every occasion, taking care never to be guided by thoughts of purely selfish advantage. The saint's perspective is a person-neutral one, from which everybody's interests, including his own, count equally with him. As a result his life lacks what Scheffler calls the 'agent-centred prerogative' so jealously guarded in normal lives, and which rests on the thought that he may permissibly accord a special weighting to his own concerns that would not be justified from a purely impartial standpoint (Scheffler 1982: 20–1). The complaint is that to reject the agent-centred prerogative in favour of moral sainthood is radically dehumanising.

Why is this thought to be so? Because, the argument runs, the ideal of sainthood precludes the individual from pursuing his own special projects, interests and relationships, those specific concerns which give shape and direction to his life and enable him to look on himself and be looked on by others as a distinct and distinctive personality. Even *trying* to be a saint is damaging, by progressively stripping away those features which provide individuality. In Susan Wolf's view, 'A moral saint will have to be very, very nice. It is important that he not be offensive. The worry is that, as a result, he will have to be dull-witted or humorless or bland' (Wolf 1982: 422).

Whether saints need be quite as colourless as Wolf portrays them is a moot question; giving away your wealth to the poor is scarcely the action of a bland personality (whatever it may do to your humour), and saints surely do not have to be dull-witted. Yet the saintly disregard of self is undoubtedly unsettling. Even where moral sainthood calls, as it sometimes must, for a heroic self-sacrifice which is anything but bland, the fact that it is a sacrifice of self seems to make it too costly a goal for a rational individual to follow. Saints could be very different from ordinary people, yet fail to be distinctive among themselves. Becoming a saint seems to be less a matter of self-perfection than of self-replacement by an archangelical being of the Hare-type, an efficient do-gooder of the most anonymous kind. But how could it profit a man to aid the whole world, yet suffer the loss of his own soul?

If utilitarianism tells us to maximise human utility without reference to the identity of the persons we affect, then it evidently leaves no room for an agent-centred prerogative. Utilitarian agents will be actual or prospective moral saints, with a colossal capacity for disengagement from their own interests. Williams sees it as a fatal objection to utilitarianism that it presses a demand for people to disregard their own deepest projects and commitments in order to serve the cause of the utility, impersonally considered, of the whole world of moral beings. This is a 'quite absurd requirement', because it robs a person of 'something which is a condition of his having any interest in being around in that world at all' (Williams 1976: 210). If he is not permitted to have a life of his own, he may as well be dead. Indeed, unless people were allowed to have first-order projects, the 'general project of bringing about maximally desirable outcomes' would 'have nothing to work on, and would be vacuous' – because no one would have any personal desires to satisfy (Williams 1973: 110). (Archangels care about their own good as a part of the *general* good.) For utilitarianism to demand what it does

> is to make [the agent] into a channel between the input of everyone's projects, including his own, and an output of optimific decision; but this is to neglect the extent to which *his* actions and *his* decisions have to be seen as the actions and decisions which flow from the projects and attitudes with which he is most closely identified. It is thus, in the most literal sense, an attack on his integrity (116–17).

As Dan Brock writes, 'Our own freely chosen ends and purposes . . . have a special importance to us that the ends and purposes of others do not have' (Brock 1982: 232).[2] This is a baseline truth from which all reasonable moral reflection must start, and no matter for regret, provided that we value distinctiveness and self-concern in people. Saints may do more good in the world than sinners, but at least sinners are human enough to care about themselves; they retain their *personality*.[3]

## 2 The hard line: utilitarians should be saints

Godwin, as usual, took the hardest line of all. 'I should think . . . a man would be the more perfect, in proportion as he endeavoured to elevate philanthropy into a passion.' To the question how much I should do for the common weal, Godwin's uncompromising answer was 'Everything in my power' – even if this means dying for it. There is no agent-centred prerogative. To know how to act, we should imagine ourselves in the role of 'an impartial spectator, of an angelic nature', who makes his evaluations without prejudice or self-interest (Godwin 1793: 324, 374, 373).

Hare, too, believes that we should do our very best to be unselfish, though he acknowledges that sainthood is beyond the powers of most of us. Saintly self-denial is the path chosen by the highest, most heroic moral spirits. 'Each of us . . . has to ask himself what is the level of saintliness of which he is likely to be capable, and strive for that' (Hare 1981: 201). Hare resists the attempt made by Williams to topple saintliness from its pedestal. He dismisses with impatience the objection that as an ideal it runs counter to our moral intuitions. He claims, with some justice, that our intuitions in this area are neither very clear nor very consistent, and that questions such as whether we should give up our surplus goods to feed the world's poor demand 'critical thought, not just an appeal to intuition' (199). Moral theory would be of little value if its conclusions were always rejected whenever they clashed with our pre-reflective notions, or some subset of these; we should expect theorising about morals sometimes to surprise us, and lead to a shake-up of our old opinions and prejudices. Critical thinking is especially important when our intuitions give us no clear lead on an issue. In Hare's view, the intuitions to which Williams and others have drawn attention are only one set we have, alongside and in tension with others in favour of self-disinterested charity. 'Christian humility and *agape* and their humanist counterparts', he suggests, could hardly have attracted so many adherents over the centuries if they really ran as seriously against the native grain as their critics suppose; and from this alternative perspective the 'self-centred pursuit of one's own projects' which Williams defends and labels 'integrity' appears as rank self-indulgence (Hare 1982: 29n.).

Hare believes that most of us could afford to become much less selfish than we are without any danger of losing our character; indeed, the effort to care more for others would be self-improving, making us more resourceful and resilient persons, and increasing our self-respect. Hare would probably approve of Singer's remark that 'What it is possible for a man to do and what he is likely to do are both, I think, very greatly influenced by what people around him are doing and expecting him to do' (Singer 1979: 272). We do not know how saintly we can be, until we try.

### 3 A softer line: utilitarians may be human

No doubt most people would pay lip service to the principle that selfishness is a vice and selflessness a virtue. But not everyone would agree with Hare that we should all strive to be as saintly (or archangelical) as possible. Aspiring to such dizzy moral heights may seem to be more appropriate for disembodied and characterless spirits (if there are any) than for those embodied subjects of personality, human beings. However attractive Christian and humanist ideas of self-sacrifice have been down the ages, very few people have been disposed to surrender their agent-centred prerogative entirely; most have wanted to call a halt to the self-denying process while they still had a self to deny. Hare's utilitarianism permits them to call it only as a concession to human weakness; moral stalwarts will carry on denying themselves far beyond the point at which feebler folk give up. But does utilitarianism have to be as grudging as this in conceding a place for an agent-centred prerogative? Is no softer line possible?

There are two conceivable ways in which a utilitarian might attempt to soften the line, which, following Scheffler, I shall refer to as the 'liberation strategy' and the 'maximisation strategy'. The first involves granting 'moral independence' to the 'natural independence of the personal point of view' – in other words, 'permitting agents to devote energy and attention to their projects and commitments out of proportion to the value from an impersonal standpoint of their doing so' (Scheffler 1982: 62). The liberation strategy frees individuals of the moral obligation always to select the optimising action from among the alternatives available. There are islands of liberty within a life where the subject (provided he does not actually harm other people) may pursue his own interests without regard to the public utility. The second strategy similarly allows individuals some space to pursue their own projects and concerns, but justifies the permission on the ground that not granting it would *impede* the maximisation of the general happiness. The idea here is that, since abandoning one's special concerns is painful, it is reasonable to 'count the cost of such hardships in arriving at our overall assessments of relevant outcomes' (59). To insist that people relinquish these concerns and become full-time optimisers is a self-defeating tactic, for, as Mill explains, 'the notion of a happiness for all, procured by the self-sacrifice of each, if the abnegation is really felt to be a sacrifice, is a contradiction' (J.S. Mill 1865: 338).

Let us look at these strategies in turn. The main problem with the liberation strategy is that it lacks a convincing rationale. It would be a crude variety of naturalistic fallacy to argue that 'moral independence' should be granted to the personal point of view just because it is 'naturally independent'. As Shelly Kagan has remarked, 'personal independence may constitute an implicit appeal for agent-centered prerogatives', but it scarcely provides a reason for *granting* that appeal (Kagan 1984: 253). The fact that people may want to be free from moral pressures does not entail that they are entitled to be. To be sure, the strategy only releases us from doing our best to help other people, not from the prohibition against harming them. But the question remains how it can be defended against philosophers like Singer and Hare who hold that, since all people's interests count equally, the right action is always the one which maximises the satisfaction of everyone's interests. It is far from clear, as defenders of the liberation strategy would have it, that this is a merely question-begging conception of morality; Singer and Hare's position can be defended on the apparently plausible principle that it can never be reasonable to produce a worse outcome where one can produce a better (cf. Pettit 1984). Proponents of the liberation strategy who reject this principle need to explain how sub-optimising behaviour can sometimes be the most rational option.

They also face the task of explaining how to draw a principled line between acceptable and unacceptable self-serving behaviour (assuming that the strategy does not permit a *total* disregard of others' interests). This could conceivably be done by making distinctions among *kinds* of action, holding that some varieties of non-optimising behaviour are more defensible than others; or by proposing that people are free to expend their time and resources however they like, provided that they remain within certain limits of self-indulgence; or by making the limits of people's obligations relative to the level of prevailing need. But it is hard to see how any of these proposals could be articulated in detail without encountering a charge of arbitrariness. For instance, a defender of the strategy might tell us that we should give some, though not all, of our surplus wealth to the starving poor. But he also needs to inform us at least roughly how large the proportion ought to be. A weakness of the liberation strategy is that it lacks the conceptual resources for justifying any specific answer to this sort of question.

In fact, a full recognition of the personal point of view might seem to require nothing less than the rejection of *all* moral demands, including that not to harm other people (cf. Kagan 1984: 253). Even a dedicated anti-utilitarian like Williams does not defend a strategy of total liberation from moral requirements as they have traditionally been conceived. Nevertheless, a leitmotif of Williams's philosophy is that morality, that 'peculiar institution', has loomed too large in Western thought. In his view, moral thinking concentrates attention on some (admittedly important) questions about one sort of social relationship, namely justice, but ignores the significance of other valuable ways in which human beings interact with one another, the variety of affective and emotional modes expressive of personality without which our lives would be vapid and meaningless. Williams's attempt to shift the focus of discourse away from questions about what people owe to others, to questions about what they owe to themselves revives the ancient concern with the shape and content of flourishing lives (a theme which had been unduly neglected in much post-classical moral philosophy – though hardly by utilitarians). Yet the danger with this change of perspective is that it easily leads to viewing the individual's moral relations to other persons through the distorting prism of the subject's requirements for living a life that is (for him) as flourishing as possible. A person who internalises the altered perspective, and whose primary concern becomes his own integrity in Williams's sense, may start to see other people as little more than agents who conduce to, or detract from, the satisfactoriness of his own existence, rather than as Kantian ends whose moral significance is no less than his own. Such a person is in danger of becoming a moral solipsist.

Moral solipsists will only help others when they hope to get something out of it for themselves. They understand the principle of 'I'll scratch your back if you'll scratch mine',[4] but not that of disinterested charity. They may even accept the proposition that everyone's interests matter, but add the significant qualifier *only to themselves*. The more stress that is placed on the subject's prerogative to live a life that maximises the fulfilment of his own special needs, interests and aspirations, the less room there is left for submission to ethical demands relating to other persons. (Although Williams formally admits the validity of ethical requirements of justice, the basis of those requirements is obscure so long as the preservation of one's personal 'integrity' is the prime consideration of practical reason.) However, if our previous arguments have been correct, such moral solipsists would be unable to respect themselves for

189

that humanity which they share with others, and one major source of human satisfaction would thereby be closed to them. Although they would fail to recognise what they are missing, they could actually live more individually fulfilling lives if they concentrated less intently on their private fulfilment.

Still, people are unlikely to live fulfilling lives if they never take the personal point of view. So in a psychologically realistic moral theory some room needs to be made for an agent-centred prerogative. Some utilitarians believe that the *maximisation strategy* is the appropriate way to do this. The basic idea behind this strategy is that a world of people who pay some special attention to their own favoured projects and aspirations is likely to be a happier world than one in which everyone tries to be a moral saint. Allowing people scope to live their own lives and develop individual personalities not only makes them happier themselves, but enables them to become more sensitive and efficient producers of happiness for others. Proponents of this strategy, like other utilitarians, are committed to impartiality in the distribution of benefits, and refuse to permit an agent to count his own interests as objectively more important than anyone else's. But they hold that the cause of general happiness is not best served by the sort of universalistic do-gooding encouraged by forms of the theory which leave no room for an agent-centred prerogative. People will lead richer lives and enrich their communities more by developing their distinctive talents and interests, and by pursuing (within limits) their individual aims and ambitions, than they could ever do as self-denying saints.

The classic defence of the maximisation strategy is Sidgwick's. A long section of *The Methods of Ethics* is devoted to showing that 'the commonly received view of special claims and duties arising out of special relations, though *prima facie* opposed to the impartial universality of the Utilitarian principle, is really maintained by a well-considered application of that principle' (Sidgwick 1874: 439). Williams's point that unless people were permitted to have first-order private projects, there would be nothing for the general project of bringing about maximally desirable outcomes to work on, would not seem to Sidgwick an objection to utilitarianism, but simply a reminder that the theory needs to leave scope for such projects.

Sidgwick argues that a sensible utilitarianism and 'Common Sense' are in substantial agreement about the moral boundaries of egoism and altruism. For instance, conventional morality claims that we have special duties of care towards our families and friends which we do not have towards complete strangers. Utilitarianism for its part approves of 'the

190

cultivation of affection and the performance of affectionate services' for our parents, partners, children and friends, as particularly fruitful means of promoting the general happiness. The mere 'watery kindness' which we feel for people who are not closely connected with us is too feeble a basis for benevolent activity; we are much more likely to create happiness efficiently for people we care about. Sidgwick points out that we are not only prepared to work harder on behalf of persons with whom we have close relations: we usually have a better knowledge of their character and situation and can direct our benevolent efforts to more telling effect. Moreover the naturalness of such affections sets up 'an expectation of the services that are their natural expression; and the disappointment of such expectations is inevitably painful'. In addition we normally derive more personal pleasure from doing good to our near ones than from doing good to strangers. But Sidgwick is on more questionable ground when he suggests that 'specialised affections' of this kind provide a bridgehead to 'a more extended benevolence' to humanity in general. For many people, charity both begins at home and ends there. (433–4, 439).

Sidgwick is at his most Victorian in urging a limit on private charity to the poor on the score that too lavish generosity encourages idleness and improvidence. The 'happiness of all' is best promoted by making people stand on their own two feet; rich people should not distribute too much of their surplus wealth to the poor. We should aim to maintain 'in adults generally' – Sidgwick excepts married women – 'the expectation that each will be thrown on his own resources for the supply of his own wants' (436). One might object to this proposal that while it may be wise for lots of reasons to discourage a culture of dependency, we should recognise that many people are in economically straitened circumstances through no fault of their own. Refusing to help those who can help themselves is morally on a different footing from refusing to help those who cannot. In any case, we can often help people to help themselves, by providing the resources to make them self-sufficient.

But there are other good reasons for 'going easy' in our efforts to help others to live well. (Note that these are reasons both for retaining our own agent-centred prerogative and for encouraging others to develop theirs.) Each of us wants to be the primary actor in his own life, and to assume responsibility for the direction it takes. Being both the star and the script-writer of our own show, we often see even the good-natured attempts of others to promote our welfare as unwarranted interference. It contributes considerably to our self-respect to be the primary satisfiers of our wants; and while we look to other people for comradeship, moral support and occasional practical assistance, we resent the sidelining of our own efforts to achieve our goals. We resent even more strongly other people's attempting to define those goals for us.

Some of these points are amusingly illustrated in a passage in Saki's novel *When William Came*. Cicely Yeovil is a well-to-do woman who 'had long ago planned out for herself a complete philosophy of life':

> Her scheme of life was not a wholly selfish one; no one could understand what she wanted as well as she did herself, therefore she felt that she was the best person to pursue her own ends and cater for her own wants. To have others thinking and acting for one merely meant that one had to be perpetually grateful for a lot of well-meant and usually unsatisfactory services. It was like the case of a rich man giving a community a free library, when probably the community only wanted free fishing or reduced tram-fares (Saki 1982: 692).

On this philosophy, on balance, people make a greater contribution to happiness by pleasing themselves than by trying to please others. They can know themselves far better than they can know their neighbours.

> Cicely studied her own whims and wishes, experimented in the best method of carrying them into effect, compared the accumulated results of her experiments, and gradually arrived at a very clear idea of what she wanted in life, and how best to achieve it (692).

Cicely Yeovil is hardly a proponent of the maximising strategy; she is too self-centred for that. Her occasional good deeds are motivated chiefly by the non-utilitarian thought that one cannot 'live successfully and graciously in a crowded world without taking due notice of the human elements around one' (692). Yet Cicely combines with this drawing-room Hobbesianism a shrewd awareness of when and how to extend a helping hand. Precisely because she is no moral saint but an experimenter in good living, her benevolent interventions are generally judicious and effective: 'She was instinctively far more thoughtful for others than many a person who is genuinely and unseeingly addicted to unselfishness' (692).

Good will is insufficient to make an efficient benefactor; accurate knowledge of people's real needs and wants is required as well.[5] Saints may lack this knowledge, because they do not know well enough what a flourishing life feels like from the inside. They are unlikely to concern themselves much with the domestic, social, artistic, scientific, literary and recreational pursuits of normal lives, or value their associated excellences. (The only excellence which they aspire to have is excellence in charity.) The invigorating diversity of tastes and lifestyles of our non-saintly world would be an early casualty of any general conversion to the kind of saintly ideal favoured by Hare. A world inhabited by saints (or archangels) would be rather dull, much less than maximally happy.

### 4 Maximisation and alienation

Cicely Yeovil's care for others arises wholly out of her care for herself. This is a far remove from the ideal set forth by the maximisation strategy, which encourages us to pursue our own good *as an effective means of promoting the general good*. The great attraction of this strategy is that it permits us to retain an agent-centred prerogative while avoiding the stigma of selfishness. It offers the best of both worlds, allowing us to act in our own interests while claiming to maximise public utility! At the same time, the strategy does not give *carte blanche* to the self-indulgent. It certainly cannot justify, for instance, the pursuit of a lavish lifestyle by the affluent when many in the world scarcely attain subsistence level. And though we might think, with Sidgwick, that 'special claims to services should be commonly recognised as attaching to special relations' (Sidgwick 1874: 434), it is doubtful whether we maximise utility by buying expensive presents for our own children while children in sub-Saharan Africa starve. In short, the maximisation strategy affords no guarantee that we will not have to make some painful sacrifices for utility's sake.

Nevertheless the maximisation strategy does seem to go far towards rebutting the charge that utilitarianism threatens our personal integrity by compelling us always to think of the public welfare. It allows individuals to form private commitments and projects which are not internally directed on the good, impersonally conceived. It permits us to forge Sidgwickian 'special relations' with other people, and to devote more attention to serving the interests of those we love than those of perfect strangers (*more*, but not exclusive attention). It frees us from the obligation, specified by a cruder utilitarianism, of considering only 'the intrinsic circumstances of our neighbour, and acting accordingly' (Godwin 1793: 73). Moreover, leaving a person free to follow his own projects leads, as Brandt has observed, to 'an enormous gain in sense of freedom' which no sensible utilitarian should want to see threatened. All in all, the utilitarian justification for an agent-centred prerogative 'does very well' (Brandt 1989: 96; cf. Harsanyi 1982: 60–1).

However, not all writers have been so sure about this. Utilitarianism permits a measure of agent-centredness only because this conduces to the general good. But this raises the question in what light a utilitarian agent should regard his own special concerns and commitments. Should he pursue an object he cares about only when he sees nothing else to do which would promote utility more effectively? In that case, he will have to ask himself which of his personal concerns are justified from the person-neutral perspective, and be ready to abandon the rest. But a person who seeks to warrant his pursuit of private goals by exclusive reference to the public utility is in danger of losing sight of the special importance they have *for him*: he runs the risk of becoming, in an important sense, *alienated* from his own projects. And someone who is thus alienated from his projects may come, in time, to be alienated from himself. If this reasoning is correct, utilitarianism remains a threat to personal integrity in Williams's sense, even though it incorporates the maximisation strategy.

This problem has been discussed with considerable subtlety in an influential paper by Peter Railton. He asks us to imagine John, a 'model husband', who when praised by a friend for his concern for his wife explains that he knows his wife very well and is better placed than others to ensure that she gets what she wants and needs. 'Besides,' explains John, 'I have such affection for her that it's no great burden. Just think how awful marriage would be, or life itself, if people didn't take special care of the ones they love' (Railton 1984: 135). Railton's comment is that people like John 'show alienation: there would seem to be an estrangement between their affections and their rational, deliberative selves'. They seem, quite simply, to be *too moral*, seeing even their intimate personal relationships primarily as instruments for making the world a better place:

> [A]n abstract and universalizing point of view mediates their responses to others and to their own sentiments. . . . It is as if the world were for them a fabric of obligations and permissions in which personal considerations deserve recognition only to the extent that, and in the way that, such considerations find a place in this fabric (135).

Railton adds that while John's alienation is not itself a psychological affliction, it may be the basis of such afflictions; it could lead him to 'a sense of loneliness or emptiness', or to 'the loss of certain things of value – such as a sense of belonging or the pleasures of spontaneity' (137). In fact, John runs the risk of a triple estrangement: from his projects, from the human objects of his affection, and from himself.

Reflection on cases like John's may prompt us to make a distinction between true and bogus agent-centredness. A truly agent-centred concern is one which is not justified by the agent (even if in principle it is *justifiable*) from a person-neutral standpoint, and which he may well not try to justify at all. To be sure, John's love for his wife may initially stimulate many acts of spontaneous kindness towards her. But true love should never count the cost, *nor* the profit. John runs the risk of alienation from his best emotions when he attempts to rationalise his attentions to his wife. The fact that he may be better placed than other people to help her is not a genuine agent-centred reason to do so. If John loves his wife, he has a motive for acting well by her which other people lack. This motive drops out of sight when he justifies his attentions by an impersonal criterion of benevolent efficiency.[6]

The worry is that utilitarianism is able to accommodate only bogus agent-centredness. Agents who try to justify their individual concerns from the neutral perspective stand to become alienated from those concerns. They feel entitled to take their private interests seriously only in so far as doing so conduces to the public good. If utilitarianism insists on our taking this viewpoint, it may condemn us, as Williams asserts, to alienation from our actions and the source of our actions in our own convictions (Williams 1973: 116). But some authors have remarked on the oddity of supposing that utilitarianism would enjoin us to do anything as self-damaging as this. They point out that if alienation is a species of disutility, then utilitarians would wish us to avoid it. However, if alienation were an inevitable consequence of assuming the person-neutral standpoint, then utilitarians could prevent it only by rejecting that standpoint. And utilitarianism without person-neutrality would be *Hamlet* without the Prince.

Some utilitarians believe that there is a way out of these difficulties if we emphasise the distinction between utilitarianism as a *decision procedure* and as a *theory of rightness*. David Brink has proposed that

> utilitarianism does not require the assumption of the impersonal point of view in normal circumstances. It would require this only if it were a decision procedure. But utilitarianism need provide only a standard or criterion of rightness and not also a decision procedure (Brink 1989: 275).[7]

According to Brink, utility is most effectively maximised (and alienation avoided) if agents in normal circumstances avoid the impersonal perspective and 'adopt a differential concern for their own projects and the welfare of those close to them' (275). Although such agents do not think as utilitarians, they typically realise more utility than agents who do. They not only possess Sidgwickian concerns, but regard those concerns in a non-alienated way, as ends in themselves. Utilitarianism *as a theory of rightness* can readily sanction the formation of such concerns, because they contribute strongly to overall utility. If John, in Railton's story, risks alienation by seeking an impersonal justification of his concern for his wife, he should cease to seek it; it would be better for him, his wife and the world in general if he gave up his profit-and-loss calculations and loved more spontaneously. Writers like Brink and Railton do not consider it paradoxical to suppose that utility is most effectively maximised by agents who are not trying to maximise it. Railton suggests that utility is not unique among goals in this regard. Pleasure, too, is usually best sought indirectly (Railton 1984: 140). The hedonist who single-mindedly pursues pleasure is less likely to find it than someone who takes an interest in many things for their own sake – personal relationships, artistic and literary attainments, recreational pursuits, sport, travel, and so on. Railton and Brink conclude that utilitarianism faces no real difficulty in sanctioning the formation of genuinely agent-centred concerns.

On the other hand, not all genuine agent-centred concerns contribute to the public good. An egoistic disregard for everyone's interests except one's own would certainly not. And even laudable private interests may create disutility if not kept within proper bounds (for example, you would not do much to enhance utility if you cared for your children's success in life by seeking unfair advantages for them). Some recent writers have accordingly favoured Sidgwick's line that utility is most thoroughly promoted by persons who possess a certain fineness of character – people who are guided in their actions by a sense of virtue rather than either by selfish considerations or by strict consequentialist reasoning. Virtuous people frame and temper their agent-centred concerns by reference to a conception of the excellent. Sidgwick thought that the pursuit of 'ideal objects' like 'Virtue, Truth, Freedom, Beauty, etc., *for their own sakes*' was most likely to lead to happiness 'from the universal point of view no less than from that of the individual' (Sidgwick 1874: 405). In a clear echo of Sidgwick, Railton suggests that the most fruitful producers of utility will view a variety of goods as 'intrinsically, non-morally valuable – such as happiness, knowledge, purposeful activity, autonomy, solidarity, respect, and beauty' (Railton 1984: 149). These values will strongly influence their practical decisions, and cause them to act in ways which improve the quality of their own and other people's lives. Similarly, R.M. Adams has argued that utility is better promoted by people who act from certain kinds of worthy motivation than on the basis of consequentialist reasoning (Adams 1976). He suggests that people who act from praise-worthy motives (for example, love, friendliness, spontaneity, a taste for beauty) will sometimes do things which an act-utilitarian would judge to be wrong, or fail to do things which he would judge to be right. But in general, acting from laudable motives produces more utility than acting on act-utilitarian reasoning does, and we should consider people to be acting rightly when they act on such motives. (Adams names his theory of right action 'motive-utilitarianism'.)

All these theories deny that the best way of promoting utility is to pursue it directly. Such 'indirect utilitarianism' has the attraction of leaving room among the springs of action for an agent-centred pre-rogative, virtues and admirable motives, while retaining the maxim-isation of utility as the standard of rightness. It therefore promises to relieve the moral agent of the threat of alienation without compromising the essential person-neutrality of the utility criterion. Yet indirect utilitarianism has failed to silence all the critics. Some accuse it of merely ushering alienation out of the front door while it admits deception (and self-deception) in through the back. Williams has condemned the 'lack of openness' of a system which encourages people to place intrinsic value on certain motivations, yet conceals the truth that their real role is to promote utility. Williams paints a disturbing scene of a manipulative utilitarian élite providing moral disinformation to an unwitting public:

> Thus if those who administer the blame, or some smaller class of knowing utilitarians standing behind those who administer it, do in effect think of the question of fairness as fundamentally the same as the question of efficacy, then there has to be dis-ingenuousness between them and the others, and the institution has to lack openness, in the sense that it will not work as an institution unless there is widespread ignorance about its real nature (Williams 1973: 123–4).

Yet one does not have to envisage a set-up of leaders and led to feel uncomfortable with the idea that the utilitarian standard of rightness, like the head of Medusa, must be kept safely out of the agent's sight. Not many people would want to belong to a knowing élite if the knowledge brought personal alienation from their own projects. If a concern for impersonal utility is alienating, indirect utilitarianism faces a difficult task in mapping out an acceptable personal strategy for the agent who combines a belief in the utilitarian standard of rightness with a disbelief that utility is best promoted by consequentialist decision-making. Some-one who accepted the utilitarian standard would seemingly have to conceal the fact even from himself, and make believe that his private concerns were self-legitimating ends. It is not clear that such self-deception is psychologically possible. But even if it were, it would need to be maintained with a rigorous consistency to prevent the agent falling victim to moral schizophrenia, sometimes thinking as a utilitarian and sometimes not.

However, it might be suggested that this analysis rests on a mis-understanding of what the indirect utilitarian needs to say about the utilitarian agent. On a more charitable construal, indirect utilitarians need not claim that to avoid alienation such agents must believe that they reject a person-neutral criterion of rightness. They simply have to believe that they most effectively enhance utility when, instead of constantly trying to satisfy the utilitarian standard, they focus on promoting their other ends instead. Indirect utilitarians point out that utility is not the only goal best pursued by an indirect route. Just as a sophisticated hedonist refrains from throwing himself into the 'dogged pursuit of happiness' (Railton 1984: 141) and pursues his favourite things as ends in themselves, or the student anxious to pass an important examination puts this daunting objective out of his mind and concentrates only on learning the course material, so too utilitarian agents best promote the ultimate goal when they concentrate on other goals; the effective advancement of utility requires not *self-deception* but merely self-distraction.

Unfortunately, these supposed analogies are open to question. The hedonist and exam candidate realise that directly fixating on their goals is self-defeating; so they pursue them instead by oblique means.[8] They do not need to deny their ultimate objectives, but simply put them from the forefront of their minds. But the case of the agent who believes in the utilitarian standard of rightness is less straightforward. His route to utility involves promoting certain of his agent-centred concerns (most plausibly, those which are informed by virtuous motives) as ends in themselves. But he cannot consistently believe those concerns to be worth pursuing for their own sake and believe that their value is instrumental. Therefore it appears that he must do more than merely relegate the person-neutral standard of rightness to the back of his mind: he needs to tell himself that it is *false*. Unless he can fool himself into disbelieving the criterion, he will not be able to accomplish the transition to seeing his agent-centred concerns as valuable on non-neutral grounds. The utilitarian standard needs, therefore, to be explicitly repudiated in a manner resembling that of any other belief discovered to be untrue. Yet it must not really be discarded, but only stored in a mental buffer from which it can in principle be retrieved. This buffer needs to be secure enough to prevent it re-emerging inopportunely, when agent-centred goals are being pursued.

This is not a very persuasive or attractive story. Indirect utilitarianism not only relies on a doubtful idea of the psychologically possible, but its central recommendation is that agents engage in a form of self-deception which is hardly more appealing than the alienation it is meant to avoid. Of course, a utilitarian may still approve, on consequentialist grounds, of *other* people developing characters that are not consequentialist in nature – even if he rejects, with Williams, the prospect of a utilitarian élite disingenuously encouraging non-consequentialist beliefs in the general public. But the real conceptual strains are those which indirect utilitarians face in determining a course of action for *themselves*. Railton proposes that the motivational structure of such utilitarians (or 'sophisticated consequentialists') needs only to meet the counterfactual condition that they would not depart from strict consequentialist decision-procedures if doing so were not compatible with leading an 'objectively utilitarian' life (that is, one which matched up to the utilitarian standard of right action) (1984: section 6). But this seems to run into trouble on Railton's own terms. As a result of keeping that condition in mind, the husband in his story faces difficulty in regarding his non-consequentialist ends and motives as indirect utilitarians say he should regard them, as worthwhile for purely subjective reasons; he values them rather for their propensity to enhance utility – the very attitude which Railton claims is alienating. Indeed, the counterfactual motivation could never be plausibly ascribed to an agent who permitted his personal concerns (except, perhaps, from weakness of will) to override the requirements of utility, neutrally conceived; if such an agent claimed to be a consequentialist, he must be either lying or confused (cf. Wilcox 1987: 81).

## 5 Non-alienating direct utilitarianism

'Do I care whether value is assigned to projects impersonally, if I am not required to view my own projects impersonally?' (Brink 1989: 276). The answer to Brink's question is that I *should* care, if the subjective value I ascribe to those projects is incompatible with the appropriate valuation of those projects from the impersonal (more properly, person-neutral) point of view. In fact it is not easy to understand how I could be morally permitted to pursue any non-optimising projects of my own, if 'value is assigned to projects impersonally'. On the other hand, if our earlier arguments for the maximising strategy were correct, the most optimising actions I can perform are often strongly agent-centred ones. So maybe instead of Brink's question we should ask: 'Should I care whether value

199

is assigned to projects person-neutrally, if my own projects are valuable from the person-neutral point of view?'

But now we seem to be going round in circles. It was precisely the strategy of valuing one's own projects from the person-neutral point of view that was held by Railton to be alienating. Defending one's personal concerns and commitments for their capacity to contribute to the end of general utility is hard to combine with valuing them for their own sake; yet if we cannot value them for their own sake, we become estranged both from them and (eventually) from ourselves. From the person-neutral point of view, nothing is worthwhile unless it contributes to the public good, and individuals should strive to become efficient servants of utility. Railton's analysis of the consequences for agents of assuming this outlook is persuasive. But is the *instrumental* view of one's projects the only possibility from the neutral perspective? Or is there some other, less personally damaging way in which an agent could vindicate his projects from that standpoint?

Some philosophers speak almost as if utility were an end beyond the ends of individuals. Whatever people do is to be morally evaluated according to its impact on the general utility, neutrally conceived. Should I read a book, take a holiday, marry a wife, study for a degree, give all my money to Oxfam? Answering such questions requires calculating the impact on the world of the actions at issue. On this conception, the public utility transcends my own utility in a very strong sense. It is not merely that my own interests are outweighed by the combined interests of others: it is as if the general utility were an end beyond *everyone's* ends, and 'the public' named a transpersonal subject of utility in its own right. A person who devoted himself to the promotion of the public good understood this way, would see everything he did as of purely instru- mental value, and be a prime candidate for alienation. Yet no real sense can be made of a notion of utility as transcendent as this. There is no entity, 'the public', over and above the individual people who comprise it. And in the absence of a super-personal subject of utility, the general good can be nothing other than the combined good of individuals. It is therefore more realistic to consider utility as a *compound* end, where every individual's utility is a constituent part of the goal, and not a means to the attainment of some further goal. While an agent must still be ready to sacrifice his own interests for the sake of the general utility, he is fully entitled to regard his own good as a proper part of the public good. Serving one's own interests, then, is a quite legitimate way of promoting the general utility – and frequently (given the arguments for the maximisation strategy) – the best way. But there can be no danger of alienation where the agent sees the satisfaction of his own interests as a *part* of the end, and not a *means* to it.

If utility is a compound end in this sense, the apparently stark contrast between personal and neutral points of view needs to be reassessed. Utilitarianism is a moral theory which stipulates a person-neutral criterion of rightness. The problem has always been to explain how this can be a practical philosophy for subjects who (not being archangels) naturally take the personal point of view. The answer we are now considering implies that person-neutral and personal points of view coincide more often than is sometimes assumed. They coincide because the neutral point of view is not the view of a person-neutral (or super-personal) utility, but the view which an individual takes when he considers his own interests alongside those of other people. Taking this view, he looks on his own utility as a constitutive part of the public utility, and thus as an end in itself. So his private interests are part of what he neutrally cares about. Moreover if, as the arguments for the maximisation strategy maintain, permitting him a degree of agent-centredness increases his ability to promote the good, then he can person-neutrally sanction, without alienation or self-deceit, his frequent assumption of the personal viewpoint.

'Do I care whether value is assigned to projects impersonally, if I am not required to view my own projects impersonally?' Brink's question rests on a false opposition between perspectives. Utilitarianism does, in one sense, require us to evaluate our projects from a neutral point of view, but not in the sense of assessing their *instrumental* value for enhancing utility. Utilitarianism allows us to take a personal interest in our projects, because it objectively matters that people should fulfil their personal goals. The fulfilment of each individual's goals is a proper part of the general good. What we must consider from the neutral standpoint is the relation of our personal projects to those of other people. If pursuing our own projects is too costly to others, then we may be morally required to give them up. This may happen less often than some anti-utilitarians claim, if the thinking behind the maximisation strategy is correct.

There is no need, then, to avoid alienation by deceiving oneself into thinking that what one is doing when one pursues one's own projects has nothing to do with utility, neutrally conceived as a good; for there is nothing alienating about promoting one's ends knowing them to be parts of the overall end of utility. The move to indirect utilitarianism is therefore unnecessary. Agents can retain full consciousness of the utilitarian standard of right action without becoming estranged from their projects or from themselves. They can seek to develop fine characters or worthy motivations without having to pretend that they are guided by non-consequentialist ideals. On a utilitarian theory like Mill's, becoming a better person is a good-in-itself, and thus a constituent part of the general good as well as a route to the production of further utility-enhancing acts. Direct utilitarianism has the additional advantage over indirect that it allows an agent's motivational structure to meet the Railtonian counterfactual condition that he would not deviate from consequentialist reasoning were this not consistent with satisfying the utilitarian standard of rightness. The difficulty for indirect utilitarianism was to explain how the 'sophisticated consequentialist' could operate this condition if he trained himself to think of his personal projects as valuable on their own terms and not instrumentally. But the direct utilitarian sees no opposition between an agent's projects being valuable in themselves, and their being valuable from the point of view of general utility; for general utility is composed of the utilities of individuals like himself. A person must be willing to sacrifice his own interests in situations where the overall utility demands it. But the maximisation strategy justifies individuals devoting enough attention to their own projects to enable all but the most ineluctably egocentric to live happy, fulfilled and non-alienated lives.

It is nevertheless hard to decide exactly where to draw the line between legitimate and illegitimate concern for self. The maximisation strategy, unlike the liberation strategy, provides us with a non-arbitrary criterion of right action. Its weakness is that the criterion is far from easy to apply. At what precise point does my promotion of my private interests cease to maximise the public good and pass over into self-indulgence? A credible (and liveable) utilitarianism may not require from us Godwinian self-abnegation or sainthood; most of us probably do more for the happiness of the world by doing what we can to make ourselves and our loved ones happy than by seeking to ameliorate the condition of mankind. But how do I decide, for instance, just how much of my wealth I may keep for myself and how much I should give to the starving poor, in order to maximise utility? Such a question calls for a comparison of interpersonal utilities informed by the thought that we do not always serve utility best by concentrating on our private ends.

Whatever the problems of determining in practice exactly how much self-regard utilitarianism allows us, it is reasonable to consider utilitarianism a more strenuous moral doctrine than some. The theory enjoins us to do more than merely forgo our own advantage in order to avert great harm to others; many positively helpful actions which would be supererogatory on some other systems are plausible moral obligations on the utilitarian. The theory has to grant us sufficient private space to live personally fulfilling lives, or become self-defeating. But this space is liable to be squeezed when general utility levels are low. So long as many persons on the planet starve or lack the basic wherewithal to live a minimally decent life, it is difficult for utilitarianism to justify much spending on luxuries by the affluent. Admittedly, utilitarianism, like any other moral theory, needs to be psychologically realistic. So if the practice of universal love is really as hard as 'carrying Mt T'ai and leaping over the Chi River', it is pointless to make it a utilitarian requirement. ('Ought' always implies 'can'.) But it is tempting to claim a psychological impossibility when we are not really unable, but are merely disinclined, to respond to the moral pull of others. The maximisation strategy cannot justify the Nelsonian eye which many in the affluent West turn to the suffering in the Third World – not to mention the lesser suffering on their own doorsteps. What Mill wrote of his own day is still true in ours:

> [I]n this condition of the world, paradoxical as the assertion may be, the conscious ability to do without happiness gives the best prospect of realising such happiness as is attainable (J.S. Mill 1861: 217–18).

Utilitarianism is not an easy philosophy to live by, but it is not as difficult as the morally lazy would claim. In any case, we should not make the mistake of thinking that a care for the general welfare cannot figure among an individual's most deeply felt concerns. One does not have to be a saint to include among one's *personal* projects a commitment to aiding those worse off than oneself. (The distinction between personal and person-neutral concerns is not identical with that between private and public interests.) Moreover, if one shows little active concern for humanity in the persons of others, one can hardly think very highly of one's own humanity; thus one forfeits a major source of self-respect. To be sure, a concern for suffering humanity tends, in most people, to jostle for space with more agent-centred concerns. But there is nothing to stop the two kinds of concern from converging. Paying to equip a Third-World school with a library, say, could be just as much one's personal project, and as personally satisfying, as climbing the Matterhorn.

Sensible utilitarians take care not to demand the impossible. Their moral advice can be summed up as: 'Always do your best.' This does not mean that we should not take seriously our own agent-centred concerns, but it does imply that we should not take them seriously to the exclusion of all else. More than this, we should look out for opportunities to promote the general utility, of which our personal utility is a proper but only a single part. It is far from clear that these are unreasonable demands, or that bowing to them will cause alienation or the disintegration of character. On the contrary, serving others' needs can be a source of intense satisfaction to an agent with normal human sympathies. We may leave the last word to Francis Hutcheson:

> When we find our whole soul kind and benign, we must have a joyful approbation; and a further and higher joy arises from exerting those affections in wise beneficent offices (1755: vol. 1, 132).

# Notes

## *I  Introduction: The Character of the Theory*

1  Bentham states his indebtedness to Hume in a manuscript edited by Halévy (Halévy 1901: vol. 1, 282). I am indebted for this reference to Mitchell 1974: 180, 185 n.50.

2  Dickens portrayed utilitarianism as 'Gradgrindism', the philosophy of 'facts', whose major feature was to deny the value of 'fancy'. Mill thought Dickens's attack ignorant and misconceived but, owing to the eminence of its author, important to rebut.

3  It is worth noting that Harsanyi has argued that the most reasonable choice for a set of contractors on the Rawlsian model would be a form of average-utilitarianism (1976: 37–63).

4  Mill called these 'intermediate principles' (J.S. Mill 1838: 111).

5  My account is influenced by Kekes 1993: ch. 2, section 5; ch. 7.

6  This principle has recently been disputed. Michael Slote believes that 'less than the best [is] sometimes good enough', and that 'an act might qualify as morally right through having good enough consequences, even though better consequences could have been produced in the circumstances' (Slote 1984: 140). The 'satisficing consequentialism' which Slote defends maintains, unlike 'optimising consequentialism', that we are under no moral obligation to produce as much of the good as possible, but only a sufficient quantity of it. Slote's case rests heavily on examples of the following kind: if we are moved to feed a poor family, it is quite enough to give them a good square meal; we are under no obligation to bring out the caviare and smoked salmon. But Slote's analysis of such examples is questionable. For a family that is hungry, enough is literally *as good as* a feast, and the impact on their marginal utility of being served the culinary delights negligible. (We would do far better, from an optimising point of view, to save the salmon and Château Latour until our gourmet friends come to dinner.) Philip Pettit persuasively contends against Slote that sub-maximisation is an irrational policy to pursue except in very special cases, for example, where the disadvantages involved in computing the best course of action outweigh the advantages to be gained by preferring an optimising to a simpler satisficing policy (though even here choosing the latter policy is justified by an ultimately *maximising* criterion). In Pettit's view, to say that something is 'good enough' is a reason to choose

205

it only so long as one is unaware of a better alternative (Pettit 1984: 172). Moreover, '[t]o evaluate A as better than B is to be disposed to choose A, other things being equal'. Hence '[i]t is not clear what it can mean to rank A above B if when other things are equal one insists on choosing B' (173).

7   These are, in fact, not the only possibilities for a maximising doctrine, though they are the only ones we shall consider. One could in principle evaluate social welfare in terms of the utility of the median person in the utility ranking (cf. Sen 1979: 472), or the utilities of people who fall below a certain threshold level.

8   The ideas of William Godwin represent an exception to this generalisation. See Chapter III.

9   The phrase is John Hill Burton's, in the Introduction to the Bowring edition of Bentham's works. (Bentham 1843: vol. 1, 18). See also Bentham 1834: vol. 1, 328–30; Parekh 1974: 99.

10  Ideal Utilitarianism, as we have seen, incorporates other values as well.

## II  *Four Ancient Moralists*

1   It has also been suggested by recent scholars that the name 'Mo' is not, as used to be thought, the clan name of the founder of the school, but an old Chinese word meaning 'a branded slave', i.e. the humblest of men. The way of Mo Tzŭ is thus the way of the humble man who eschews the pomp and ceremony of the upper and official classes. See Fung Yu-Lan 1952: vol. 1, 79.

2   Whether this is an accurate representation of what *Christ* meant by loving one's neighbour may perhaps be doubted.

3   If Jesus had really valued happiness only in the next life, as Quinton contends, he would still count as a utilitarian of sorts for teaching that our chief business on earth was to procure the reward of heavenly felicity for ourselves and others in the next.

4   'His mother and brothers now arrived and, standing outside, sent in a message asking for him. . . . He replied, "Who are my mother and brothers?" And looking round at those sitting in a circle around him, he said, "Here are my mother and my brothers"' (Mark 3:31–4).

5   The terminology of ethical push and pull is introduced in Nozick 1981: ch. 5.

6   J.S. Mill 1873: 49; 1861: ch. 2.

## III  *Utilitarianism and Enlightenment*

1   St Thomas Aquinas, *Summa theologiae*, 2a 2ae, Quaest. 10, Art. 11; Richard of St Victor, *De officio ecclesiae*, Art. iii, section ii.

2   The earlier phase of the Enlightenment has been argued by Peter Gay to have found its intellectual underpinnings chiefly in the theory of natural law. See P. Gay 1973: vol. 2, 455–61.

3   All translations from Helvétius are my own.

4   This is one of the first appearances in France of the magic formula (1772).

5  Hume appears more prepared in the *Enquiry Concerning the Principles of Morals* (1751) than in the *Treatise* to grant the existence of a generalised spirit of benevolence, speaking frequently of 'principles of humanity and sympathy' (e.g. Hume 1751: 226, 231). It could be argued that this admission is necessary to justify the claim, made in both works, that sympathy gives rise in us to a concern for the utility of *society*; otherwise it is puzzling why we should care about the happiness or misery of people who are unknown to us.

6  These issues will receive much fuller treatment in Chapter VIII.

7  Quinton also ascribes to Paley 'a certain ingenuous openness which often amounts to simple blatancy' (Quinton 1973: 25). The imputation is entirely justified.

8  Alan Ryan has described this conception as 'the epitome of benign illiberalism' (Ryan 1987: 33).

9  Things always present themselves to Bentham's mind, added Stephen, 'as already prepared to fit into pigeon-holes' (1900: vol. 1, 247).

10  For a more detailed discussion of Bentham's felicific calculus and its problems, see Mitchell 1974.

11  Accordingly I disagree with Parekh's opinion that Bentham's 'far more dominant' view of man represents him as capable of a sincerely disinterested benevolence (Parekh 1974: xi and *passim*).

## *IV  John Stuart Mill*

1  David Hume was indeed a greater *philosopher* than Mill, but his contribution to the development of utilitarian doctrine was much less than Mill's.

2  In fairness to James Mill, it should be said that he acknowledges the importance of public opinion in his *Analysis of the Phenomena of the Human Mind* (James Mill 1869: vol. 2, 286, 294f.).

3  '[W]e have associations of pleasure with all the pleasurable feelings of a Fellow-creature. We have associations of pleasure, therefore, with those acts of ours which yield him pleasure' (James Mill 1869: vol. 2, 286).

4  For the origins of *Utilitarianism* see the 'Textual introduction' to Mill 1861: cxxii–cxxv.

5  'There never was such an instrument devised,' Mill comments, 'for consecrating all deep-seated prejudices' (J.S. Mill 1873: 233).

6  It is true that some things appeal to people 'for no reason' – that is, purely as matters of taste. Someone may turn three somersaults before breakfast because he likes turning somersaults. But he would presumably not subscribe to a universalised judgement that turning somersaults was a valuable activity for the world in general.

7  Mill admits that it has not yet made out its claim to be the *only* desirable object (J.S. Mill 1861: 234); the evidence for that further thesis follows later in the work (ch. 4).

8  It might initially be objected to this reading that punishment is not the same thing as the application of socially coercive rules, but rather the penalty for breaking such rules. Lyons might reply, however, that the essential element of Mill's criterion is nevertheless the coercive rule which underlies the

liability to punishment. Some writers have produced slightly different interpretations; for example, John Gray considers Mill to be saying that the necessary and sufficient condition for an act to be wrong is that punishing it has the best consequences (Gray 1983). See also Berger 1984: 105f.

9 Mill's emphasis on the value of security anticipates John Rawls's advocacy of the maximin principle as the most rational principle of decision-making for the contractors in the 'Original Position' (Rawls 1971: section 26 and *passim*).

## V Some Later Developments

1 Though Sidgwick does not say so, it would appear to be Mill's position in *Utilitarianism* that he had in mind.

2 See on Henry More and Samuel Clarke, Sidgwick 1874: 172, 181.

3 He rejected, however, the notion of a hedonistic calculus; evaluation of pleasures and pains could not be reduced to a precise system but depended on the 'empirical reflective' methods with which we are all familiar. He also conceded that people in different social settings have different needs and interests, and that consequently no universal system of conduct could be drawn up (Sidgwick 1874: bk. iv. ch. iv. section 2).

4 Cf. J.S. Mill 1861: ch. 2; J.S. Mill 1838: 111.

5 This anticipates R.M. Hare's distinction between 'archangels' and 'proles' (Hare 1981: ch. 3).

6 Moore seems entirely in ignorance of Mill's more Aristotelian views of the 1830s, and comments only on the ideas expressed in *Utilitarianism*.

7 Moore also singles out as an objective good the possession of material qualities, on the ground that a universe containing physical objects would be a superior universe to a purely mental one (1903: section 123).

8 Some would say that beauty is even more subjective than colour; there is no right answer to the question whether something is beautiful as there is (on the basis of normal intersubjective agreement) to the question whether something is green. And certainly there is more disagreement in aesthetic judgements than in judgements of colour: hence, according to many, 'Beauty is in the eye of the beholder.'

9 For the term 'organic unity' see Moore 1903: 27–8 and *passim*.

10 Note that Moore does not say that pleasure is a great good in itself, but that the pleasure taken in beauty is a great good. Pleasure taken in unworthy objects would be of much less quality; it could even be of negative value.

11 We have seen rule-utilitarianism anticipated by Paley: see Chapter III above.

12 Cf. Harsanyi's recommendation of rule-utilitarianism that it accords better with our 'deepest moral convictions' about the 'demands of elementary justice' and people's 'fundamental rights' (1977: 33, 31).

13 My account of these positions is indebted to Ezorsky 1968, though the labels for positions (B) and (C) are my own.

14 As both of these writers believe that conditional rule-utilitarianism is the only plausible version of the theory, they affirm that rule-utilitarianism collapses into act-utilitarianism.

15 For the notion of a constitutive rule, see Rawls 1955.

16 It is harder to decide whether the wrongness of *lying* is better explained by act-

utilitarian or by rule-utilitarian considerations. It might be argued that lying to someone is wrong only because people have a convention-based expectation that they will be told the truth; the lie is thus an 'artificial' evil, unlike the 'natural' evils of rape or torture. On the other hand, the general practice of telling the truth is put at very little risk even by a substantial amount of lying, because a well-told lie is invisible as a lie in a way in which a broken promise is rarely invisible as a broken promise. It may, therefore, be better to apply act-utilitarian reflection to everyday decisions whether to lie or not; though in certain special contexts, for example during the conduct of international negotiations where trust between the parties is of paramount importance and where false pretensions are likely to be exposed, a switch to rule-utilitarian standards may be appropriate.

## VI  *Happiness and Other Ends*

1  Mill may be presumed to have thought of virtue in the Aristotelian sense, as *arete* or personal excellence, rather than as a disposition to do the right thing according to some deontological conception of right.

2  J.L. Ackrill has argued that Aristotle conceives *eudaimonia* as an *inclusive* end, incorporating 'all activities that are valuable' (Ackrill 1980: 22). But a dominant-end view need not be a monolithic one, and while Aristotle affirms the intrinsic value of other goods besides philosophical wisdom, he holds philosophical wisdom to possess the greatest worth.

3  On the dangers of choosing a life-objective which is beyond our talents, see Somerset Maugham's cautionary tale 'The Alien Corn'.

4  Note that the much-vaunted problem of interpersonal comparisons is not in practice a substantial bar to charitable action. There is not much difficulty about channelling our finite resources for doing good into courses which plainly enhance utility. For instance, it takes no elaborate or taxing calculation to determine that we can produce more benefit by sending £10 to famine relief than by spending it on some luxury for ourselves.

5  A different sort of objection to the theory is that it presupposes a level of agreement in value judgements which does not exist. Are we not constantly told that in modern society values are many and conflicting, and that consensus on morals is irrecoverable? Yet it may be questioned whether there is much disagreement on fundamental values; few people dispute, for instance, that murder, rape, violence, cruelty, injustice, and abuse and oppression of the weak are wrong. There is also much general agreement on such positive values as the development of one's personality and talents, and the service of one's community. In general people disagree less about the fundamental values than they do about their precise field of application, or the best manner of promoting them. There is, for example, much agreement that liberty is a good; but there is room for discussion as to how much freedom should be allowed to *children*. (Should children, as some propose, be allowed to be more self-determining even at the risk that freed from paternalist restraints they will use their freedom to their own hurt?) Again, Samuel Scheffler has talked about the expanding circle of concern which characterises the post-Enlightenment period (1992: 9–11). Most people today

accept the basic proposition that cruelty is evil, but while most believe that cruelty to children is inadmissible, not all yet think that cruelty to animals is also wrong. In the last analysis, a person who wishes to subscribe to an Ideal Utilitarian theory must rely on his own conception of what values there are and how to promote them; but I suggest that the variations in the conceptions of different people are far less considerable than those who speak of a fragmentation (or degeneration) of values in the modern world would have us believe.

6  This is the sentiment underlying the old tag *De mortuis nil nisi bonum*: 'Say nothing but good of the dead'.

## VII  Maximisation, Fairness and Respect for Persons

1  This principle has an application to the long-running debate in the UK over fox-hunting. Some defenders of field 'sports' claim that if the fox population needs to be kept down, people may as well get pleasure out of killing them. One could equally well argue that if active euthanasia were ever to be legalised, its practice should be put into the hands of people with a taste for killing humans.

2  In what follows it should be clear that I am discussing utilitarianism of the act rather than the rule variety.

3  Critics may also point out that the utilitarian reluctance to cause public distress and anxiety is not always available as a ground for desisting from an unjust course. Example (C) is of this kind. As everyone in Verona but the Prince believes the Capulet prisoner to be guilty, executing him will create no disturbing precedent for punishing the innocent. Hence utilitarians cannot object to it on that basis.

4  As I myself once believed: see Scarre 1992: 41–2.

5  Whether this analysis of critical reflection is correct or not need not concern us here.

6  Hare at one point claims that even conflicts between rules will be rare, if the rules have been well chosen (1981: 50); but his own examples of conflicts make this judgement dubious. Clashes between rules can readily arise in the most mundane situations.

7  Hare incidentally questions whether it is right to see this as a 'problem case' for utilitarianism, given that even critics of the doctrine like Williams generally concede that the utilitarian solution is right (1981: 49).

8  Hare is not, strictly, considering case (D), but one like it in essential respects.

9  Hare implies that the critic demands too *little* of the doctors if he supposes that they have no other effective way of saving their patients. Yet it is surely imaginable that all other treatments have been tried and failed.

10  In fact Hare does not always seem to understand 'intuitive thinking' in this manner. (Prima-facie principles are, after all, said to be selected by means of *critical* reasoning.) 'Intuitive responses', for Hare, sometimes means something more spontaneous than this – something more akin to moral gut reactions. It may be granted to him (see n. 7) that many people do not feel intuitively (in the latter sense) that the utilitarian response to the hostages dilemma is wrong.

11 This is not quite the justification offered at the time. President Truman explained the use of the new weapons as a measure to save further loss of *American* lives.

## VIII Utilitarianism and Personality

1 Singer goes further than Jesus, who merely advised the rich young man to give away his goods to the poor if he would attain 'perfection'. Jesus did not suggest that this donation was a moral obligation (Matthew 19:21–2).
2 Compare J.O. Urmson: 'If . . . for most utilitarians, any action is a duty that will produce the greatest possible good in the circumstances, for them the most heroic self-sacrifice or saintly self-forgetfulness will be duties on all fours with truth-telling and promise-keeping' (Urmson 1969: 66).
3 The problem which utilitarians face over the issue of 'integrity' is much sharper in regard to the morality of individual life than to that of social and economic policy. No one supposes that public decision-makers are entitled to shape policies with an eye to advancing their personally significant projects. As Mirlees writes, 'I want government ministers to try to maximise utility, even if their personal sense of achievement is gravely compromised, or their crazy industrial dreams unfulfilled: the ministers' utility deserves no significant weight in our assessments of utility in comparison to the millions who may suffer. To this extent, the morality of economic policy is simpler than that of personal life or culture' (1982: 71n.).
4 This is the principle of contractualist morality (or 'morality', as it ought to be written in scare quotes).
5 Cf. J. S. Mill (1859) for some very similar sentiments, e.g. on pp. 227, 283.
6 Some writers ascribe to utilitarianism an *impersonal* perspective where I ascribe to it a *person-neutral* one. The latter term is preferable to the former because from a strictly *im*personal point of view, nothing that human beings do would seem to matter at all. Utilitarianism cares about personal interests, but in a thoroughly impartial (neutral) way. (Sidgwick's talk of the 'point of view of the universe' is open to a similar objection as talk of the impersonal perspective.)
7 Railton expresses the same distinction in the terminology of 'subjective utilitarianism' and 'objective utilitarianism' (1984: 152). See also Sidgwick 1874: 413, 405–6.
8 The sophisticated hedonist is not in quite the same position as the examinee, because the objects he pursues are not so much instrumental to the attainment of his final goal as constitutive of it; strictly speaking, there is no more 'direct' mode of attaining pleasure than the one he adopts. But less sophisticated hedonists may have the mistaken impression that there is; they follow a will o' the wisp named 'pleasure'.

# Bibliography

This Bibliography lists works cited in the text plus a selection of other writings bearing on the topics discussed in this book. There are many more high-quality books and articles on utilitarianism than there is room to cite below. Readers in search of a more comprehensive list of twentieth-century works are advised to consult the comprehensive bibliography in Miller and Williams 1982.

Ackrill, John (1980) 'Aristotle on *eudaimonia*', in Amelie Rorty (ed.), *Essays on Aristotle's Ethics*, Berkeley: University of California Press.

Adams, Robert M. (1976) 'Motive utilitarianism', *Journal of Philosophy*, 73: 467–81.

Albee, Ernest (1901) 'An examination of Professor Sidgwick's proof of utilitarianism', *Philosophical Review*, 10: 251–60.

Allison, Lincoln (ed.) (1990) *The Utilitarian Response*, London: Sage Publications.

Anderson, Elizabeth S. (1991) 'John Stuart Mill and experiments in living', *Ethics*, 102: 4–26.

Anschutz, R.P. (1953) *The Philosophy of J.S. Mill*, Oxford: Clarendon Press.

Aristotle (1954) *The Nicomachean Ethics*, trans. Sir David Ross (World's Classics edn), London: Oxford University Press.

Arrow, K.J. (1950) 'A difficulty in the concept of social welfare', *Journal of Political Economy*, 58: 328–46.

Atkinson, Ronald F. (1957) 'J.S. Mill's "proof" of the principle of utility', *Philosophy*, 32: 158–67.

Ayer, A.J. (1948) 'The principle of utility', reprinted in his *Philosophical Essays*, London: Macmillan, 1954.

Baker, John M. (1971) 'Utilitarianism and secondary principles', *Philosophical Quarterly*, 21: 69–71.

Baldwin, James (1964) *The Fire Next Time*, Harmondsworth: Penguin.

Baldwin, Thomas (1990) *G.E. Moore*, London: Routledge.

Barnes, Gerald W. (1971) 'Utilitarianisms', *Ethics*, 82: 56–64.

Baumgardt, David (1952) *Bentham and the Ethics of Today*, Princeton: Princeton University Press.

Bayles, Michael (ed.) (1968) *Contemporary Utilitarianism*, Garden City, NY: Anchor Books.

Beccaria, Cesare (1764) *Dei Delitti e Pene*, Milan: Rizzoli, 1981.

# Bibliography

Benditt, Theodore (1974) 'Happiness', *Philosophical Studies*, 25: 1–20.

Bennett, John (1965–6), 'Whatever the consequences', *Analysis*, 26: 83–102.

Bentham, Jeremy (1776) *A Fragment on Government*, reprinted in *The Works*, ed. John Bowring, vol. 1, Edinburgh: William Tate, 1843.

—— (1789) *An Introduction to the Principles of Morals and Legislation*, reprinted in *The Works*, ed. John Bowring, vol. 1, Edinburgh: William Tate, 1843.

—— (1817) *A Table of the Springs of Action*, reprinted in *The Works*, ed. John Bowring, vol. 1, Edinburgh: William Tate, 1843.

—— (1825) *The Rationale of Reward*, reprinted in *The Works*, ed. John Bowring, vol. 2, Edinburgh: William Tate, 1843.

—— (1834) *Deontology*, ed. John Bowring, London: Longman.

—— (1843) *The Works*, ed. John Bowring, Edinburgh: William Tate.

Berger, Fred (1978) 'Mill's concept of happiness', *Interpretation*, 7: 95–117.

—— (1979) 'John Stuart Mill on justice and fairness', in Wesley E. Cooper, Kai Nielsen and Steven Patten (eds), *New Essays on John Stuart Mill and Utilitarianism, Canadian Journal of Philosophy*, Supplementary volume 5.

—— (1984) *Happiness, Justice, and Freedom*, Los Angeles: University of California Press.

Berlin, Sir Isaiah (1969) 'John Stuart Mill and the ends of life', in his *Four Essays on Liberty*, London: Oxford University Press.

Blackstone, William T. (1965) *Francis Hutcheson and Contemporary Ethical Theory*, Athens: Georgia University Press.

Blanshard, Brand (1974) 'Sidgwick the man', *The Monist*, 58: 349–70.

Bradley, F.H. (1927) *Ethical Studies*, 2nd edn. Oxford: Clarendon Press.

Brandt, Richard B. (1959) *Ethical Theory*, Englewood Cliffs, NJ: Prentice-Hall.

—— (1963) 'Towards a credible form of utilitarianism', in H.-N. Castañeda and G. Nakhnikian (eds), *Morality and the Language of Conduct*, Detroit: Wayne State University Press.

—— (1979) *A Theory of the Good and the Right*, Oxford: Oxford University Press.

—— (1982) 'Two concepts of utility', in Harlan B. Miller and H. Williams (eds). *The Limits of Utilitarianism*, Minneapolis: University of Minnesota Press.

—— (1989) 'Morality and its critics', *American Philosophical Quarterly*, 26: 89–100.

Braybooke, David (1967) 'The choice between utilitarianisms', *American Philosophical Quarterly*, 4: 28–38.

Brink, David O. (1989) *Moral Realism and the Foundations of Ethics*, Cambridge: Cambridge University Press.

—— (1992) 'Mill's deliberative utilitarianism', *Philosophy and Public Affairs*, 22: 67–103.

Brittan, Samuel (1990) 'Choice and utility', in Lincoln Allison (ed.) *The Utilitarian Response*, London: Sage.

Brock, Dan (1973) 'Recent work in utilitarianism', *American Philosophical Quarterly*, 10: 241–76.

—— (1982) 'Utilitarianism and helping others', in Harlan B. Miller and H. Williams (eds), *The Limits of Utilitarianism*, Minneapolis: University of Minnesota Press.

Butler, Joseph (1726) *Fifteen Sermons Preached at the Rolls Chapel*, ed. W.R. Matthews, London: G. Bell, 1964.

# Bibliography

Chastellux, Jean François de (1774) *An Essay on Public Happiness*, London: Cadell; facsimile reprint New York: Augustus Kelley, 1969.

Cicero (1931) *De finibus bonorum et malorum*, trans. H. Rackham, London: Heinemann.

Condorcet, Marie Jean Antoine Nicolas de Caritat (1794) *Esquisse d'un tableau historique des progrès de l'esprit humain*, Paris: Agasse.

Conly, S. (1983) 'Utilitarianism and integrity', *The Monist*, 66: 298–311.

Cooper, Wesley E., Nielsen, Kai, and Patten, Steven (eds) (1979) *New Essays on John Stuart Mill and Utilitarianism*, *Canadian Journal of Philosophy* Supplementary volume 5.

Cumberland, Richard (1672) *De legibus naturae disquisitio philosophica*, London: Nathanael Hook.

Dahl, Norman O. (1973) 'Is Mill's hedonism inconsistent?', *American Philosophical Quarterly*, Monograph 7.

Dancy, Jonathan (1993) *Moral Reasons*, Oxford: Blackwell.

Den Uyl, Douglas J. (1992), 'Teleology and agent-centeredness', *The Monist*, 76: 14–33.

DeWitt, N.W. (1954) *Epicurus and his Philosophy*, Minneapolis: University of Minnesota Press.

Dickens, Charles (1854) *Hard Times* (Everyman Library), London: Dent, 1907.

Diggs, B. (1964) 'Rules and utilitarianism', *American Philosophical Quarterly*, 1: 32–44.

—— (1982) 'Utilitarianism and contractarianism', in Harlan B. Miller and H. Williams (eds), *The Limits of Utilitarianism*, Minneapolis: University of Minnesota Press.

Donagan, Alan (1968) 'Is there a credible form of utilitarianism?', in Michael Bayles (ed.), *Contemporary Utilitarianism*, Garden City, NY: Anchor Books.

Edgeworth, F.T. (1881) *Mathematical Psychics*, London: Kegan Paul.

Edwards, Rem B. (1979) *Pleasures and Pains: A Theory of Qualitative Hedonism*, Ithaca, NY: Cornell University Press.

Epicurus (1926) *The Extant Remains*, ed. Cyril Bailey, Oxford: Clarendon Press.

Eyorsky [*recte* Ezorsky], Gertrude (1965), 'Utilitarianism and rules', *Australasian Journal of Philosophy*, 43: 225–9.

Ezorsky, Gertude (1968), 'A defense of rule-utilitarianism against David Lyons', *Journal of Philosophy*, 65: 533–44.

Feagin, Susan L. (1983) 'Mill and Edwards on the higher pleasures', *Philosophy*, 58: 244–52.

Feinberg, Joel (1967) 'The forms and limits of utilitarianism', *Philosophical Review*, 76 368–81.

—— (ed.) (1969) *Moral Concepts*, London: Oxford University Press.

Fitzgerald, C.P. (1961) *China: A Short Cultural History*, 3rd edn, London: The Cresset Press.

Foot, Philippa (1988) 'Utilitarianism and the virtues', in Samuel Scheffler (ed.), *Consequentialism and its Critics*, Oxford: Oxford University Press.

Frankena, William K. (1974) 'Sidgwick and the dualism of practical reason', *The Monist*, 58: 449–67.

Frey, R.G. (1983) *Rights, Killing, and Suffering*, Oxford: Blackwell.

—— (ed.) (1984) *Utility and Rights*, Minneapolis: University of Minnesota Press.

# Bibliography

Fung Yu-Lan (1952) *A History of Chinese Philosophy*, trans. Derk Bodde, Princeton: Princeton University Press.

Gauthier, David (1982) 'On the refutation of utilitarianism', in Harlan B. Miller and H. Williams (eds), *The Limits of Utilitarianism*, Minneapolis: University of Minnesota Press.

Gay, John (1731) *A Dissertation Concerning the Fundamental Principle and Immediate Criterion of Virtue* (prefixed to) Frances King, *An Essay on the Origin of Evil*, London.

Gay, Peter (1973) *The Enlightenment: An Interpretation*, London: Wildwood House.

Glover, Jonathan (ed.), (1990) *Utilitarianism and its Critics*, New York: Macmillan.

Godwin, William (1793) *Enquiry Concerning Political Justice*, ed. K. Codell Carter, Oxford: Clarendon Press, 1971.

Goldsworthy, Jeffrey (1992) 'Well-being and value', *Utilitas*, 4: 1–26.

Goodin, Robert E. (1990) 'Government House utilitarianism', in Lincoln Allison (ed.), *The Utilitarian Response*, London: Sage.

—— (1993) 'Utility and the good', in .Peter Singer (ed.), *A Companion to Ethics*, corrected edn, Oxford: Blackwell

Gorovitz, S. (ed.) (1971) *Mill: Utilitarianism, with Critical Essays*, Indianapolis: Bobbs-Merrill Co.

Grant, Michael (1967) *Gladiators*, London: Weidenfeld and Nicolson.

Gray, John (1983) *Millian Liberty: A Defence*, London: Routledge and Kegan Paul.

Griffin, James (1986) *Well-Being*, Oxford: Clarendon Press.

Grote, J. (1870) *An Examination of the Utilitarian Philosophy*, Cambridge: Deighton Bell.

Halévy, Elie (1901) *La Formation du radicalisme philosophique*, Paris: Alcan.

Hall, Everett W. (1968) 'The "proof" of utility in Bentham and Mill', in J.B. Schneewind (ed.), *Mill: A Collection of Critical Essays*, New York: Doubleday.

Hammond, Peter J. (1982) 'Utilitarianism, uncertainty and information', in Amartya Sen and Bernard Williams (eds), *Utilitarianism and Beyond*, Cambridge: Cambridge University Press.

Hampshire, Stuart (1978) 'Morality and pessimism', in S. Hampshire (ed.), *Public and Private Morality*, Cambridge: Cambridge University Press.

Hare, R.M. (1963) *Freedom and Reason*, London: Oxford University Press.

—— (1981) *Moral Thinking*, Oxford: Clarendon Press.

—— (1982) 'Ethical theory and utilitarianism', in Amartya Sen and Bernard Williams (eds), *Utilitarianism and Beyond*, Cambridge: Cambridge University Press.

Harris, John (1975) 'The survival lottery', *Philosophy*, 50: 81–7.

Harrison, Jonathan (1952-3) 'Utilitarianism, universalization and our duty to be just', *Proceedings of the Aristotelian Society*, 53: 105–34.

Harrod, R.F. (1936) 'Utilitarianism revised', reprinted in S. Gorovitz (ed.). *Mill: Utilitarianism, with Critical Essays*, Indianapolis: Bobbs-Merrill Co, 1971.

Harsanyi, John C. (1976) *Essays on Ethics, Social Behavior, and Scientific Explanation*, Dordrecht: Reidel.

—— (1977) 'Rule utilitarianism and decision theory', *Erkenntnis*, 11: 25–53.

# Bibliography

—— (1980) 'Rule utilitarianism, rights, obligations and the theory of rational behaviour', *Theory and Decision*, 12: 115–33.

—— (1982) 'Morality and the theory of rational behaviour', in Amartya Sen and Bernard Williams (eds), *Utilitarianism and Beyond*, Cambridge: Cambridge University Press.

Hearn, Thomas K., Jr. (ed.) (1971) *Studies in Utilitarianism*, New York: Appleton-Century-Crofts.

Helvétius, Claude (1758) *De l'esprit, or Essays on the Mind, and its Several Faculties*, London: Dodsley *et al.*, 1759.

—— (1771) *De l'homme, de ses facultés intellectuelles, et de son éducation*, London: La Société Typographique, 1774.

Henson, Richard G. (1971) 'Utilitarianism and the wrongness of killing', *Philosophical Review*, 80: 320–37.

Hoag, Robert W. (1986) 'Happiness and freedom: recent work on John Stuart Mill', *Philosophy and Public Affairs*, 15: 188–99.

—— (1987) 'Mill's conception of happiness as an inclusive end', *Journal of the History of Philosophy*, 25: 417–31.

—— (1992) 'J.S. Mill's language of pleasures', *Utilitas*, 4: 247–78.

Horowitz, Irving Louis (1954) *Claude Helvétius: Philosopher of Democracy and Enlightenment*, New York: Paine-Whitman.

Hume, David (1739) *A Treatise of Human Nature*, ed. L.A. Selby-Bigge, Oxford: Clarendon Press, 1888.

—— (1751) *Enquiries Concerning the Human Understanding and Concerning the Principles of Morals*, ed. L.A. Selby-Bigge, Oxford: Clarendon Press, 1902.

Hutcheson, Francis (1755) *A System of Moral Philosophy*, in *Collected Works*, vols 5-6, Hildesheim: Georg Olms, 1969.

Jones, Howard (1989) *The Epicurean Tradition*, London: Routledge.

Kagan, Shelly (1984) 'Does consequentialism demand too much?', *Philosophy and Public Affairs*, 13: 239–54.

—— (1989) *The Limits of Morality*, Oxford: Clarendon Press.

Kant, Immanuel (1785) *Fundamental Principles of the Metaphysic of Morals*, reprinted in Immanuel Kant, *Critique of Practical Reason and Other Works in the Theory of Ethics*, trans. T.K. Abbott, 6th edn, London: Longmans, 1909.

—— (1793) 'Was ist Aufklärung?', in *Kleine Schriften*, Neuwied: J.T. Haupt.

—— (1909a) 'On a supposed right to tell lies from benevolent motives', in Immanuel Kant, *Critique of Practical Reason and Other Works in the Theory of Ethics*, trans. T.K. Abbott, 6th edn, London: Longmans.

—— (1909b) *Critique of Practical Reason and Other Works in the Theory of Ethics*, trans. T.K. Abbott, 6th edn, London: Longmans.

Kekes, John (1993) *The Morality of Pluralism*, Princeton: Princeton University Press.

Kenny, Anthony (1966-7) 'Happiness', *Proceedings of the Aristotelian Society*, 66: 93–102.

Kretzmann, Norman (1971) 'Desire as the proof of desirability', in J.B. Schneewind (ed.), *Mill: A Collection of Critical Essays*, New York: Doubleday.

Kristeller, P.O. (1972) *Renaissance Concepts of Man*, New York: Harper and Row.

Kymlicka, Will (1988) 'Rawls on teleology and deontology', *Philosophy and Public Affairs*, 17: 173–90.

# Bibliography

—— (1990) *Contemporary Political Philosophy*, Oxford: Clarendon Press.

Lively, Jack, and Rees, John (eds) (1978) *Utilitarian Logic and Politics*, Oxford: Oxford University Press.

Long, Douglas G. (1977) *Bentham on Liberty: Jeremy Bentham's Idea of Liberty in Relation to his Utilitarianism*, Toronto: University of Toronto Press.

Lyons, David (1965) *Forms and Limits of Utilitarianism*, Oxford: Clarendon Press.

—— (1976) 'Mill's theory of morality', *Noûs*, 10: 101–20.

—— (1978) 'Mill's theory of justice', in J. Kim and A.I. Goldman (eds), *Essays in Honor of Charles L. Stevenson*, Dordrecht: Reidel.

—— (1982) 'Utility and rights', in J. Waldron (ed.), *Theories of Rights*, New York: Oxford University Press, 1984.

—— (1990) *In the Interests of the Governed: A Study in Bentham's Philosophy of Utility and Law*, revised edn, Oxford: Clarendon Press.

Mabbott, J.D. (1968) 'Interpretations of Mill's Utilitarianism', in J.B. Schneewind (ed.), *Mill: A Collection of Critical Essays*, New York: Doubleday.

Macaulay, T.B. (1829) 'Mill on government', reprinted in James Mill, *The Political Writings*, ed. Terence Ball, Cambridge: Cambridge University Press, 1992.

McCloskey, H.J. (1971) *John Stuart Mill: A Critical Study*, London: Macmillan.

MacIntyre, Alasdair (1967) *A Short History of Ethics*, London: Routledge and Kegan Paul.

—— (1981) *After Virtue: A Study in Moral Theory*, London: Duckworth.

Mackay, Alfred F. (1980) *Arrow's Theorem: The Problem of Social Choice*, New Haven and London: Yale University Press.

Mackie, J.L. (1977) *Ethics*, Harmondsworth: Penguin.

—— (1980) *Hume's Moral Theory*, London: Routledge and Kegan Paul.

—— (1984) 'Rights, utility and maximisation', in R.G. Frey (ed.), *Utility and Rights*, Minneapolis: University of Minnesota Press.

Mandelbaum, Maurice (1968) 'Two moot issues in Mill's *Utilitarianism*', in J.B. Schneewind (ed.), *Mill: A Collection of Critical Essays*, New York: Doubleday.

Marshall, Alfred (1920) *Principles of Economics*, 8th edn, London: Macmillan.

Martin, Rex (1972) 'A defense of Mill's qualitative hedonism', *Philosophy*, 47: 140–51.

Mazlish, Bruce (1975) *James and John Stuart Mill: Father and Son in the Nineteenth Century*, London: Hutchinson.

Mill, James (1819) *Essay on Government*, in James Mill, *The Political Writings*, ed. Terence Ball, Cambridge: Cambridge University Press, 1992.

—— (1869) *Analysis of the Phenomena of the Human Mind*, London: Longmans; facsimile reprint New York: Augustus Kelley, 1967.

Mill, John Stuart (1833) 'Remarks on Bentham's Philosophy', reprinted in *Essays on Ethics, Religion and Society*, ed. J.M. Robson, *Collected Works*, vol. 10, Toronto: Toronto University Press, 1969.

—— (1838) 'Bentham', reprinted in *Essays on Ethics, Religion and Society*, ed. J.M. Robson, *Collected Works*, vol. 10, Toronto: Toronto University Press, 1969.

—— (1843) *A System of Logic*, ed. J.M. Robson, reprinted in *Collected Works*, vols 7, 8, Toronto: Toronto University Press, 1973.

—— (1852) 'Whewell on moral philosophy', reprinted in *Essays on Ethics,*

*Religion and Society*, ed. J.M. Robson, *Collected Works*, vol. 10, Toronto: Toronto University Press, 1969.

—— (1859) *On Liberty*, in *Essays on Economics and Society*, ed. J.M. Robson, *Collected Works*, vols. 4, 5, Toronto: Toronto University Press, 1967.

—— (1861) *Utilitarianism*, reprinted in *Essays on Ethics, Religion and Society*, ed. J.M. Robson, *Collected Works*, vol. 10, Toronto: Toronto University Press, 1969.

—— (1865) 'Auguste Comte and positivism', reprinted in *Essays on Ethics, Religion and Society*, ed. J.M. Robson, *Collected Works*, vol. 10, Toronto: Toronto University Press, 1969.

—— (1873) *Autobiography*, reprinted in *Autobiography and Literary Essays*, ed. J.M. Robson, *Collected Works*, vol. 1, Toronto: Toronto University Press, 1981.

—— (1963) *The Earlier Letters, 1812–1848*, ed. Francis E. Mineka, *Collected Works*, vols. 12, 13, Toronto: Toronto University Press.

—— (1969) *Essays on Ethics, Religion and Society*, ed. J.M. Robson, *Collected Works*, vol. 10, Toronto: Toronto University Press.

—— (1972) *Later Letters, 1849–73*, ed. Francis E. Mineka and Dwight D. Lindley, *Collected Works*, vols 14–17, Toronto: Toronto University Press.

—— (1978) *Essays on Philosophy and the Classics*, ed. J.M. Robson, *Collected Works*, vol. 11, Toronto: Toronto University Press.

Miller, Harlan B. and Williams, H. (eds) (1982) *The Limits of Utilitarianism*, Minneapolis: University of Minnesota Press.

Mirlees, J.A. (1982) 'The economic uses of utilitarianism', in Amartya Sen and Bernard Williams (eds), *Utilitarianism and Beyond*, Cambridge: Cambridge University Press.

Mitchell, Wesley C. (1974) 'Bentham's felicific calculus', in Bikhu Parekh (ed.), *Jeremy Bentham: Ten Critical Essays*, London: Frank Cass.

Monro, D.H. (1953) *Godwin's Moral Philosophy*, London: Oxford University Press.

Moore, G.E. (1903) *Principia Ethica*, Cambridge: Cambridge University Press.

—— (1912) *Ethics*, Oxford: Oxford University Press, 1966.

Motse [i.e. Mo Tzŭ] (1929) *The Ethical and Political Works*, trans. Yi-Pao Mei, London: Arthur Probsthain.

Mulholland, Leslie A. (1986) 'Rights, utilitarianism and the conflation of persons', *Journal of Philosophy*, 83: 323–40.

Nagel, Thomas (1986) *The View from Nowhere*, New York: Oxford University Press.

Narveson, Jan (1967) *Morality and Utility*, Baltimore: Johns Hopkins Press.

—— (1971) 'Utilitarianism and new generations', in S Gorovitz (ed.), *Mill: Utilitarianism, with Critical Essays*, Indianapolis: Bobbs-Merrill Co.

—— (1979) 'Rights and utilitarianism', in Wesley E. Cooper, Kai Nielsen and Steven Patten (eds), *New Essays on John Stuart Mill and Utilitarianism*, *Canadian Journal of Philosophy*, Supplementary volume 5.

Nath, S.K. (1973) *A Perspective of Welfare Economics*, London: Macmillan.

Neumann, Richard von, and Morgenstern, Oskar (1953) *Theory of Games and Economic Behavior*, 3rd edn, Princeton: Princeton University Press.

Norman, Richard (1971) *Reasons for Action: A Critique of Utilitarian Rationality*, New York: Barnes and Noble.

# Bibliography

Nozick, Robert (1974) *Anarchy, State and Utopia*, New York: Basic Books.
—— (1981) *Philosophical Explanations*, Cambridge, Mass.: Harvard University Press.
Nussbaum, Martha and Sen, Amartya (eds) (1993) *The Quality of Life*, Oxford: Clarendon Press.
Paley, William (1819) *Principles of Moral and Political Philosophy*, in *The Works of William Paley, D.D.*, vol. 1, London: Rivington *et al.*
Parekh, Bikhu (ed.) (1974) *Jeremy Bentham: Ten Critical Essays*, London: Frank Cass.
Parfit, Derek (1984) *Reasons and Persons*, Oxford: Oxford University Press.
Pettit, Philip (1984) 'Satisficing consequentialism', *Proceedings of the Aristotelian Society*, Supplementary Volume 58: 165–76.
—— (1993a) 'Consequentialism', in Peter Singer (ed.), *A Companion to Ethics*, corrected edn, Oxford: Blackwell.
—— (1993b) (ed.) *Consequentialism*, Aldershot: Dartmouth.
Plamenatz, John (1966) *The English Utilitarians*, 2nd edn, Oxford: Blackwell.
Popper, Sir Karl (1966) *The Open Society and Its Enemies*, 5th edn. London: Routledge and Kegan Paul.
Prichard, H.A. (1949) *Moral Obligation*, New York: Oxford University Press.
Priestley, Joseph (n.d.(a)) *Institutes of Natural and Revealed Religion*, in *The Theological and Miscellaneous Works of Joseph Priestley, LL.D., F.R.S. &c.*, vol. 2, n.p., n.d.
—— (n.d.(b)) *Essay on the First Principles of Government*, in *The Theological and Miscellaneous Works of Joseph Priestley, LL.D.. F.R.S.&c*, vol. 22.
Quinton, Anthony (1973) *Utilitarian Ethics*, London: Macmillan.
Rachels, James (ed.) *Moral Problems*, 3rd edn, New York: Harper and Row.
Railton, Peter (1984) 'Alienation, consequentialism, and the demands of morality', *Philosophy and Public Affairs*, 13: 134–71.
Rashdall, Hastings (1907) *The Theory of Good and Evil*, Oxford: Clarendon Press.
—— (n.d.) *Ethics*, London: T.C. and E.C. Jack.
Rawls, John (1955) 'Two concepts of rules', *Philosophical Review*, 64: 3–32.
—— (1971) *A Theory of Justice*, London: Oxford University Press.
Regan, Donald (1980) *Utilitarianism and Cooperation*, Oxford: Clarendon Press.
Riley, Jonathan (1988) *Liberal Utilitarianism*, Cambridge: Cambridge University Press.
Rorty, Amelie (ed.) (1976) *The Identities of Persons*, Berkeley: University of California Press.
—— (ed.) (1980) *Essays on Aristotle's Ethics*, Berkeley: University of California Press.
Ross, W.D. (1930) *The Right and the Good*, New York: Oxford University Press.
Ryan, Alan (1974) *J.S. Mill*, London: Routledge and Kegan Paul.
—— (1987) 'Introduction' to J.S. Mill and Jeremy Bentham, *Utilitarianism and Other Essays*, ed. A. Ryan, Harmondsworth: Penguin.
Saki [Munro, H.H.] (1982) *When William Came*, reprinted in *The Complete Saki*, Harmondsworth: Penguin.
Scanlon, T.M. (1975) 'Preference and urgency', *Journal of Philosophy*, 72: 655–69.

219

—— (1982) 'Contractualism and utilitarianism', in Amartya Sen and Bernard Williams (eds), *Utilitarianism and Beyond*, Cambridge: Cambridge University Press.

—— (1993) 'Value, desire, and quality of life', in Martha Nussbaum and Amartya Sen (eds), *The Quality of Life*, Oxford: Clarendon Press.

Scarre, Geoffrey (1991) 'The Second Book of Job', *Cogito*, 5: 92–9.

—— (1992) 'Utilitarianism and self-respect', *Utilitas*, 4: 27–43.

—— (1994) 'Epicurus as a forerunner of utilitarianism', *Utilitas*, 6: 219–31.

Scheffler, Samuel (1982) *The Rejection of Consequentialism*, Oxford: Clarendon Press.

—— (ed.) (1988) *Consequentialism and its Critics*, Oxford: Oxford University Press.

—— (1992) *Human Morality*, New York: Oxford University Press.

Schneewind, J.B. (ed.) (1968) *Mill: A Collection of Critical Essays*, New York: Doubleday.

—— (1977) *Sidgwick's Ethics and Victorian Moral Philosophy*, Oxford: Clarendon Press.

Seanor, Douglas, and Fotion, N. (eds) (1988) *Hare and Critics*, Oxford: Clarendon Press.

Selby-Bigge, L.A. (ed.) (1897) *British Moralists: Being Selections from Writers Principally from the Eighteenth Century*, Oxford: Clarendon Press.

Semmel, Bernard (1984) *John Stuart Mill and the Pursuit of Virtue*, New Haven: Yale University Press.

Sen, Amartya (1970) *Collective Choice and Social Welfare*, San Francisco: Holden-Day, Inc.

—— (1979) 'Utilitarianism and welfarism', *Journal of Philosophy*, 76: 463–89.

Sen, Amartya, and Williams, Bernard (eds) (1982) *Utilitarianism and Beyond*, Cambridge: Cambridge University Press.

Shaftesbury, Anthony Ashley Cooper, 3rd Earl of (1773) *Characteristics of Men, Manners, Opinions, and Times*, 5th edn, Birmingham: John Baskerville.

Sidgwick, Henry (1874) *The Methods of Ethics*, Indianapolis: Hackett (facsimile reprint, with a Foreword by John Rawls, of the 7th edn, London: Macmillan, 1907), 1981.

—— (1886) *Outlines of the History of Ethics*, 6th edn, London: Macmillan, 1967.

Sikora, R.I. (1975) 'Utilitarianism: the classical principle and the average principle', *Canadian Journal of Philosophy*, 5: 409–19.

Singer, Peter (1979) 'Famine, affluence, and morality', in James Rachels (ed.), *Moral Problems*, 3rd edn, New York: Harper and Row.

—— (ed.) (1993) *A Companion to Ethics*, corrected edn, Oxford: Blackwell.

Skorupski, John (1989) *John Stuart Mill*, London: Routledge.

Slote, Michael (1984) 'Satisficing consequentialism', *Proceedings of the Aristotelian Society*, Supplementary volume 58: 139–63.

—— (1985) *Common-Sense Morality and Consequentialism*, London: Routledge and Kegan Paul.

Smart, J.J.C. (1956) 'Extreme and restricted utilitarianism', *Philosophical Quarterly*, 6: 344–54.

—— (1973) 'An outline of a system of utilitarian ethics', in J.J.C. Smart and Bernard Williams, *Utilitarianism For and Against*, Cambridge: Cambridge University Press.

Smart, J.J.C., and Williams, Bernard (1973) *Utilitarianism For and Against*, Cambridge: Cambridge University Press.

Sprigge, T.L.S. (1990a) 'The greatest happiness principle', *Utilitas*, 3: 37–51.

—— (1990b) *The Rational Foundations of Ethics*, London: Routledge.

Stephen, Sir Leslie (1900) *The English Utilitarians*, London: Duckworth.

Stocker, Michael (1969) 'Consequentialism and its complexities', *American Philosophical Quarterly*, 6: 276–89.

Sumner, L.W. (1974) 'More light on the later Mill', *Philosophical Review*, 83: 504–27.

—— (1992) 'Welfare, happiness, and pleasure', *Utilitas*, 4: 199–223.

Taylor, Charles, (1982) 'The diversity of goods', in Amartya Sen and Bernard Williams (eds), *Utilitarianism and Beyond*, Cambridge: Cambridge University Press.

Telfer, Elizabeth (1980) *Happiness*, London: Macmillan.

Ten, C.L. (1985) *Mill on Liberty*, Oxford: Clarendon Press.

Thomas, William (1985) *Mill*, Oxford: Oxford University Press.

Urmson, J.O. (1968) 'The interpretation of the moral philosophy of J.S. Mill', in J.B. Schneewind (ed.), *Mill: A Collection of Critical Essays*, New York: Doubleday.

—— (1969) 'Saints and heroes', in Joel Feinberg (ed.), *Moral Concepts*, London: Oxford University Press.

Vickrey, William (1960) 'Utility, strategy, and social decision rules', *The Quarterly Journal of Economics*, 4: 507–35.

Waley, Arthur (1939) *Three Ways of Thought in Ancient China*, London: Allen and Unwin.

West, Henry R. (1976) 'Mill's qualitative hedonism', *Philosophy*, 51: 97–101.

Wilcox, William H. (1987) 'Egoists, consequentialists, and their friends', *Philosophy and Public Affairs*, 16: 73–84.

Williams, Bernard (1972) *Morality: An Introduction to Ethics*, Cambridge: Cambridge University Press.

—— (1973) 'A critique of utilitarianism', in J.J.C. Smart and Bernard Williams, *Utilitarianism For and Against*, Cambridge: Cambridge University Press.

—— (1976) 'Persons, character and morality', in Amelie Rorty (ed.), *Essays on Aristotle's Ethics*, Berkeley: University of California Press.

—— (1985) *Ethics and the Limits of Philosophy*, London: Fontana.

Wolf, Susan (1982) 'Moral saints', *Journal of Philosophy*, 79: 419–39.

# Index